Cine-Mobility

Harvard East Asian Monographs 449

Cine-Mobility

Twentieth-Century Transformations in Korea's Film and Transportation

Han Sang Kim

Published by the Harvard University Asia Center
Distributed by Harvard University Press
Cambridge (Massachusetts) and London 2022

Printed in the United States of America

The Harvard University Asia Center publishes a monograph series and, in coordination with the Fairbank Center for Chinese Studies, the Korea Institute, the Reischauer Institute of Japanese Studies, and other facilities and institutes, administers research projects designed to further scholarly understanding of China, Japan, Korea, Vietnam, and other Asian countries. The Center also sponsors projects addressing multidisciplinary, transnational, and regional issues in Asia.

Library of Congress Cataloging-in-Publication Data

Names: Kim, Han-sang, 1977– author.
Title: Cine-mobility : twentieth-century transformations in Korea's film and transportation / Han Sang Kim.
Other titles: Harvard East Asian monographs ; 449.
Description: Cambridge, Massachusetts : Harvard University Asia Center, 2022. | Series: Harvard East Asian monographs; 449 | Includes bibliographical references and index.
Identifiers: LCCN 2021056396 | ISBN 9780674267978 (hardcover)
Subjects: LCSH: Motion pictures—Korea—History—20th century. | Transportation in motion pictures—History—20th century. | Postcolonialism and the arts—Korea—History—20th century. | Transportation—Korea—History—20th century. | Motion pictures—Political aspects—Korea—History—20th century.
Classification: LCC PN1993.5.K6 K488 2022 | DDC 791.4309519—dc23/eng/20220204
LC record available at https://lccn.loc.gov/2021056396

Index by Alexander Trotter

♾ Printed on acid-free paper

Last figure below indicates year of this printing
31 30 29 28 27 26 25 24 23 22

For Hee Sook Song and Yeon Kwon Kim

Contents

Part III: Post-Cine-Mobility

Figures and Tables

Figures

Tables

Acknowledgments

Over the course of writing this book, I have been inspired and encouraged by numerous individuals and institutions. Christina Klein and Todd A. Henry have been long-time mentors who have read portions of this manuscript and provided me with great insights. I am grateful to Carter J. Eckert and Sonia Ryang for their steady support during my postdoctoral years. Seungsook Moon's invitation to collaborate for the *Journal of Asian Studies* led me to a paper on automobility (an earlier version of Chapter 3), which marked the beginning of this book project. I am also grateful for the intellectual generosity of the people who shared their insights with me while I was writing this book: Jaeho Kang, Jin-Kyung Lee, Nan Kim, Youngju Ryu, and Steven Chung. Special thanks go to Bob Graham of the Harvard University Asia Center Publication Program, the Faculty Committee, and the anonymous readers for their thoughtful directions and incisive comments.

Parts of this study were developed from my predoctoral research at Seoul National University, where I had the chance to learn from many great teachers, including Keun-sik Jung, Kyung-sup Chang, Jaeyeol Yee, Hong-jung Kim, Ki-soo Eun, Tae Gyun Park, Keong-suk Park, Taekyoon Kim, and Baek Yung Kim. I particularly appreciate the extensive support of my many mentors, including Eunwoo Joo, Il Joon Chung, Sunyoung Yoo, and Jie-hyun Lim, who have stood by me since my doctoral years. I would also like to thank Min Hwan Kim and Eun-hye Kim, inspiring cohorts who provided critical suggestions for my predoctoral studies.

Youngjin Kim and Ungsan Kim have been steadfast friends in and beyond academia. I also thank Chonghwa Chung and Jung Eun Chun for their professional but friendly assistance.

For the most part, this book is the product of my postdoctoral and junior faculty years. I particularly thank those who have encouraged me in various ways during my postdoctoral study: Kyeong-Hee Choi, Ellie Y. Choi, Kelly Y. Jeong, Alexander Zahlten, Younghan Cho, Yoon Sun Yang, John Cho, and Tani Barlow. I was fortunate to be in a postdoctoral cohort with Sandeep Ray and many others, benefiting from the cordial support of Haejin E. Koh, Hae Hun Matos, and Amber Szymczyk. I also have the good fortune to belong to Ajou University's Sociology Department with my colleagues, who together make for an invigorating intellectual environment: Suni Lee, Byoung-kwan Kim, Myungwoo Nho, Jeong-hwa Ho, and Byungho Lee. Discussions with enthusiastic and brilliant scholars in the USIA/S studies network, including Mark J. Williams, Hadi Gharabaghi, Bret Vukoder, Yuka Tsuchiya, Sangjoon Lee, and Jenny Horne, were timely and eye-opening in the final stages of this monograph. I thank the Board Members of the International Visual Sociology Association (IVSA) for their inclusiveness and progressivism, which have inspired me in my work with visual sociological perspectives.

This work was supported by the Ministry of Education of the Republic of Korea and the National Research Foundation of Korea (NRF-2019S1A5A8040231). A Transnational Korean Studies Postdoctoral Fellowship/Lectureship at the University of California, San Diego made it possible for me to expand my research on mobility into a book project. A Transnational Asian Studies Postdoctoral Fellowship at Rice University was crucial for writing the latter part of the monograph. Harvard University's Korea Institute and Boston University's Center for the Study of Asia both generously provided me with the time and space to conduct further research. The Harvard-Yenching Institute also provided me with a superb environment for my predoctoral scholarly endeavors. A Northeast Asia Council of the Association for Asian Studies (NEAC) Korean Studies Grant allowed me to visit Korean libraries and archives while preparing Chapter 4. I would also like to thank Hanae Hayashi of the Toho Stella Nichiei Archive for her generosity in providing a review copy of *Tokyo-Peking: Through Tyosen and Manchoukuo* while I was preparing

Chapter 2. I particularly appreciate Joelle Nazzicone for her meticulous editing and insightful suggestions.

Parts of this manuscript have been previously published in Korean. An earlier version of Chapter 2 appeared in *Yŏnghwa yŏn'gu (Film Studies)*, volume 43, while an earlier version of the second part of Chapter 4 was printed in *Kosoktoro ŭi inmunhak (Humanities on Expressways)*, edited by the Korea Expressway Corporation. Similarly, earlier versions of Chapter 6 have been printed in Korean publications, with the first part of the chapter appearing in *Yŏksa pip'yŏng (Critical Review of History)*, volume 113, and the second part in *Taejung sŏsa yŏn'gu (Journal of Popular Narrative)*, volume 24, issue 3. I thank the editors of these journals and edited volume for the opportunities they granted me, and hope that my book will bridge academic communities across the United States and South Korea.

Finally, this work would not have been possible without the support of my family. I would like to express my deepest gratitude to my parents, Hee Sook Song and Yeon Kwon Kim, for their love and steadfast encouragement. I also greatly appreciate the unwavering belief that my late mother-in-law, Younghee Shim, extended to me. My two feline family members, Tongtongyi and Amie, have consoled and lifted my family when they needed it most. My partner, Yusung Kim, has consistently been the first person I could trust and consult when I was shaping my vague ideas into concrete academic writing. I am grateful to her for being the companion I lean on the most, both in my academic and non-academic life.

Note to the Reader

Korean names in this book are romanized according to the McCune-Reischauer system unless that person has been active or is well-known abroad via a different romanization style (e.g., Park Chung Hee). Authors' names in the journal articles published in Korean with English abstracts are presented as they are in the abstracts, with the McCune-Reischauer romanizations in parentheses in the bibliography.

INTRODUCTION

World-as-Gesture and Learning from Cinematic Experience

This book looks back over a century and examines the scopic regimes of visual mobility that emerged in Korea, a part of the non-Western world then under colonial and postcolonial regimes, with particular attention to cognitive mobility turns under Korean capitalism.[1] This book analyzes those scopic regimes by tracing the link between two modern technologies—cinematographic media and machine-powered transportation. I argue that the encounter with these technologies—primarily through commerce with Western countries, the influx of foreign capital, and colonial/postcolonial occupation—transformed Korean people's protocols of sensing the world, constituting hegemonic modes of movement through visual experiences. Such encounters entailed a procedure whereby the modern world moved toward the viewing subject and, conversely, a procedure whereby that subject was led to recognize movement as an ontological basis for its own understanding of the world: a world the subject did not yet occupy but was expected to join soon thereafter.

To examine the *heteronomous* and *induced* type of spectatorship in such post/colonial, modern scopic regimes, we need to recognize that any shifts the viewer might have experienced were, in turn, likely rooted in the cinematic experiences that introduced new, distant landscapes and unfamiliar cultures. By heteronomous spectatorship, I mean a spectatorship constructed and maintained by force, including the enforced screenings of propaganda by the military, police, and policy authorities, even as the spectator may have still been both active and passive in the course of watching films.[2] Induced spectatorship, in turn, is spectatorship under imperial expansionism and its counterparts in the postimperial Cold War era.[3] When we assume a viewer who encountered unfamiliar landscapes in a heteronomous or induced spectatorship in post/colonial Korea, we might understand this viewer as having very likely experienced a shift in their understanding of the very "world" around them. Viewing strange places and cultures through virtual transportation would have expanded their scope of the world, not only as a physical expansion of the world within immediate reach but also as a cognitive change in reaching out and experiencing the rest of the world. At that point, the world came to the viewer as a picture. Martin Heidegger's concept of "world-as-picture" (*Weltbild*, lit. "world picture") can serve as a useful framework for understanding this change in a colonial/postcolonial territory. By world-as-picture, Heidegger meant "the world itself; the totality of beings taken, as it is for us, as standard-giving and obligating."[4] He stressed that he "does not mean 'picture of the world'" nor "a copy of something" but, "rather, the world grasped as picture."[5] This world does not preexist as an object to re-present but, rather, is present as a picture. What appears to the subject is not a copy of certain substantiality but "the world itself constituted as a picture."[6] The notion of world-as-picture in the post/colonial context of propaganda film exhibitions challenges the prevalent understanding of film as a medium. In particular, Heidegger's concept rejects this belief that the moving pictures on the screen delivered something substantial beyond them, that the pictures themselves were just copies of reality. As Timothy Mitchell lucidly argues, "the significance of this world-as-picture" lies in its revelation of a "double claim" that a representation is only a copy—and, therefore, is not real—and that what the representation replicates is, by contrast, real.[7] When we look into archival documents for propaganda policies, the colonial, postcolonial, and semicolonial authorities on the Korean peninsula shared this understanding that film, as representation, was an effective replica of the real. Accordingly, they believed that they could convey real messages to post/colonial viewers through film. However, if we look at this situation from the framework of world-as-picture, we can recognize that Korean viewers were, in fact, not receiving important messages from the imperial or neoimperial metropoles but rather encountering the reality just constituted as a picture in front of them. In the context of heteronomous and induced spectatorship in the post/colonial world, the world coming as a picture likely generated not one but plural *potentials* for different scopic regimes, even as the distinction between viewer and picture (or, alternately, between subject and object)[8] was almost certainly a default value for mobilized viewers. In this kind of cinematic experience, the audience had a sense of "the whole world" in the illusion being "within reach" and, subsequently, a sense that they were being called upon to respond through action.[9] This aspect of heteronomous spectatorship, which demanded a response, ties in with the issue of subjectivization. According to Karyn Ball, Heidegger's observations lead to the argument that "the emergence of the world as picture coincides with the constitution of man as *subjectum*."[10] Seen in this light, the visual experience of imported images in post/colonial Korea can be understood as a two-part project that, on one hand, was designed by the authorities to constitute the subject, one that would virtually experience the ideal path of modernization suggested in the collected visual fragments of the external world. On the other hand, that visual experience simultaneously presented a world-as-picture that the subject could appropriate in viewing it, generating unintended consequences. It is this latter project that I turn critical attention to throughout this book.

How the world-as-picture has presented itself, or how the picture has come to the subject, in the post/colonial context is intertwined with two modern *technologies* in the Foucauldian sense:[11] modern visuality and mobility. These two technologies have jointly served to establish a sensory infrastructure, on which the subject encounters a world-as-picture. I use the term *cine-mobility* to designate this reciprocal relationship between modern visuality and mobility, particularly in the process of constructing post/colonial modern subjectivity. By cine-mobility, I mean the virtual movement in cinematic media that conveys the viewer's gaze, as well as each individual film's ability to shape the viewer's perception of a world-as-picture. This movement is the very mobility of the cinema—that is, cinema's ability both to move toward the viewing subject and to bring the subject into the flow of the world-as-picture.

To elaborate this concept, I posit a dialectical articulation between Heidegger's notion of world-as-picture and the concept of gesture (*Gestus*) as defined by Bertolt Brecht, Walter Benjamin, and Giorgio Agamben. In Brecht's learning-plays (*Lehrstücke*), actors are encouraged to perform not to present on the stage but to experience the manners and attitudes (*Haltungen*) of the characters they are performing. In doing so, actors can learn from the gestures they perform, and, according to Benjamin, the gestures are subsequently made "quotable"[12]—that is, "learnable" and "imitable."[13] The crucial point here is that the act of imitation, or copying, is an act of changing, an act of criticism—"the acts of copying and criticism are dialectically united . . . in the act of imitation."[14] As is often observed, gesture is fundamentally social (*sozialer Gestus*) and distinct from noncontextual gestures (*Geste*).[15] In learning-plays, actors imitate the tacit gestures of socially positioned characters, more to educate themselves than to inspire and influence the audience. It is a revolutionary vocational training (*Berufsberatung*) technique in theater[16] that recalls Karl Marx's third thesis on Feuerbach: "The materialistic doctrine that men are the products of conditions and education, different men therefore the products of other conditions and changed education, forgets that circumstances may be altered by men and that *the educator has himself to be educated*."[17] Brecht's criticism of the Aristotelian division between the stage and the auditorium stems not just from concerns about empathy and the notion of a passive audience. Rather, his criticism is rooted in the learning-play's prioritization of the actor educating himself or herself and, more importantly, of the way in which the actor learns from acting, from imitating gestures, and not from the plays' messages. In turn, Agamben's thesis that "the element of cinema is gesture and not image"[18] resituates these critical efforts to dismantle the wall between stage and auditorium within a cinematic context. For Agamben, every image in the cinematic experience is a capturing device that obliterates gesture by reifying it.[19] "When they become communication or information" upon being "captured," gestures "cease to be gestures as such"[20] and acquire the potentiality "not to remain merely as a foregone gesture or event but to be summoned into the present to form a dialectical tension with the current situation."[21] At the same time, as Jaeho Kang, citing Benjamin, points out, gestures function to stop the smooth flow of communication or information: "A well-placed citation serves to interrupt the flow of a text, disturbing the reader's absorption."[22] In this way, gestures have considerable overlap with Heidegger's world-as-pictures, as both emphasize the presentness of pictures that have yet to become information and exist as the world itself or, alternatively, as potentiality to be summoned or to disrupt. In the heteronomous spectatorship of a post/colony, pictures were often intended and designed as a medium of direct delivery from the authorities, who believed that they were conveying certain "information" preserved in the images. However, I posit an expanded concept of *world-as-gesture*, stressing the cinematic viewer's capacity to evade capture by the image, communication, or information and, instead, to experience the gestural dimension itself as the world.

In the territory of world-as-gesture, the viewing subject experiences the postures, attitudes, and manners of other humans in certain social situations through the specific medium of cinema.[23] In other words, the dominant form of cinematic experience (especially that of collective and immobile film viewing with a fixed start, end, and duration) defined the early experience of world-as-gesture, specifically in a society of spectatorship as directed by others. Even when they are heteronomous, gestures as the world nevertheless provide potentialities: the semantic meaning of each object in a film's mise-en-scène frequently deviates from the creator's original intention, and human motion that seemingly bears no particular significance may generate unintended or unexpected meanings *from* the body of the viewing subject. According to Vivian Sobchack, the "film experience is meaningful *not to the side of our bodies but because of our bodies*," which have the "capacity not only to see and hear but also to touch, to smell, and always to proprioceptively feel our weight, dimension, gravity, and movement in the world."[24] The encounter with cine-mobility, in this vein, is a phenomenological and ethnomethodological experience that originates in the body of the cinematic viewer.[25] The virtual experience of an unfamiliar mode of mobility through cinema—the movement of newly developed, modern transportation vehicles and their passengers, the moving crowd in a metropolis, or the flow of commodities on shelves and consumers—can disclose "the socially standardized and standardizing 'seen but unnoticed,' expected, background features of everyday scenes" from the foreign world yet new to viewers in the post/colony.[26] Harold Garfinkel described this quality of being "seen but unnoticed" in his seminal book, *Studies in Ethnomethodology*, specifically to designate a set of considerations usually unexamined in sociologists' "accounting for the stable features of everyday activities." While the authorities who screened films for Korean viewers were not conducting academic research or experiments, their intention to *educate* foreign audiences through familiar scenes from the imperial metropole echoes the sociological project of seeking "variables that contribute[d] to their stable features."[27] However, the viewer's experience of what was presented as a "world known in common and taken for granted" yielded gestural, or bodily, potentialities that post/colonial authorities had not expected or recognized.[28] As with the ethnomethodological experiments, viewers were able to encounter gestures, that is, the "attitude of daily life," in new modes of mobility through exposure to cine-mobility.[29]

The crucial point, then, was how heteronomous spectatorship was established. In the post/colonial world, of which Korea is part, cine-mobility has played a significant role in mobilizing post/colonial subjects. This book posits such mobilization as the procedure through which post/colonial subjects became "the central point of reference for all beings within the frame" of the world-as-gesture.[30] Cine-mobility is the politically driven mobility of cinema and modern traffic flow. On a macro level, it connotes the heteronomous nature of cinematic spectatorship's emergence, especially in post/colonial regions, which initially embraced the two technologies of modern visuality and mobility as imperializing and colonizing forces.[31] From another perspective, cine-mobility in a post/colonial context can be understood as the amalgamation of actual military operations and the global proliferation, or the second advent, of the *lanterna magica*,[32] the "magic lantern" that toured with traveling entertainers as a tool for "Counter-Reformation and Jesuit propaganda" in precinematic Europe, the original form of which was exhibited as "by-products or waste products of pure military research."[33] Cine-mobility, in this sense, is cognate with an expansionist mobility that shifts according to its specific historical and political conditions.

Under the regime of cine-mobility, the machine-driven transportation system was a historical-political condition of the lanterna magica's second advent in Korea and led spectators to dream of the future. In 1909, for instance, leading up to the annexation of Korea, the Japanese resident-general and Korea's Emperor Sunjong toured the country by *train*. In September 1945, when the country was liberated from Japanese colonial rule, U.S. Army soldiers paraded as liberators in *Jeeps*. Each of these moving presentations was designed as a unique phantasmagoria for the Korean public, to imply a certain vision of a separate but hegemonic foreign power. These forms of modern transportation introduced mobilities that were not only visually perceptible and spectacular but were also accompanied by an audiovisual medium emblematic of modernity—*film*. The authorities during both periods of occupation organized and dispatched mobile film propaganda units from the seat of power to its far-flung territories. The vehicles that transported those units were well matched to the cinematized movements featured in the films they screened: for example, the railway tourist films were screened by education units that came to rural towns by train, while American films depicting women driving were screened by U.S. Information Service (USIS) units in Jeeps and trucks. Accordingly, these vehicles were able to represent the political structural principles of each occupation regime easily and effectively. This combination of cinematic visuality and its mobility through transportation technology at each turning point of media history constructed virtual stages for world-as-gestures. However, I want to stress here that cine-mobility is not a part of technological determinist historiography. Rather, cine-mobility is an extension of Foucault's concept of subjectivization and, through the dialectics of world-as-gesture, suggests potentialities that can take flight beyond technological reality. Such potentialities partly encompass what Rey Chow, invoking Benjamin's discussion of Brecht's epic theater, calls "reflexivity" that has been "staged/mediated in the form of estranged thought and roughened perception."[34]

We should, of course, also consider equally possible potentialities, such as that of world-as-gestures being highly susceptible to territorialization or control under propaganda authorities or the inducing power. But given the distinctly heteronomous setting of cinematic spectatorship in Korea for many years, there is no doubt that the Korean viewer's subjectivization through the plural potentialities of cine-mobility—specifically at the tensional borderlines between foreign illusions and the improvisatory world-as-gestures staged on-site—was considerably different from that entailed by Europe's model subjectivity. It is this issue of the Korean viewer's particular path to subjectivization that serves as this book's primary concern.

Cine-Mobility as the Macroscopic Regimes of Post/Colonial Modernity

It is imperative to clarify that I frame cine-mobility as a macroscopic concept and simultaneously as a criticism of Western-centered temporality in most theories of vision and visuality. With reference to Martin Jay's categories, I use the term *macroscopic* to designate the mobility-oriented visual culture in Korea. In particular, Jay categorizes the range of ex post applications for his concept, the *scopic regimes of modernity*, into two types: macroscopic and microscopic regimes. Studies in macroscopic regimes lead to "large-scale generalizations about the visual cultures of a period," while those in microscopic regimes focus on "a very narrow and circumscribed set of visual practices."[35] This book, as a study of macroscopic regimes, is an attempt to "characterize epochal configurations, inevitably coarse-grained and bold," and will necessarily "allow many exceptions" and "refinements that will modify original characterizations, which are never to be understood as adequate to the reality they can only approximate."[36] For Jay, the difference between macroscopic and microscopic lies primarily in the former's scale, which periodizes human temporality more broadly, and the latter's temporally limited, geographically "narrow and circumscribed" scale. I, however, find this distinction problematic. Jay is much concerned with the continuity and discontinuity of vision's hegemonic status across different historical eras, comparing the ancient Greeks and the people of the Cartesian era. He subsequently proposes that even "premodern cultures could therefore be understood in part to possess inchoate 'world pictures,' even if they were not yet fully hegemonic," claiming that Heidegger's "The Age of the World Picture" points to a clear-cut distinction between the premodern and modern eras, specifically in terms of "privileging . . . the world picture" or prioritizing vision over other senses.[37] Jay then concludes his macroscopic theorization with the assertion that "it would be wrong to ignore the anticipations and manifestations in premodern cultures, both in the West and elsewhere, of that outcome."[38] In categorizing studies of microscopic regimes, Jay's notion of "elsewhere"—examples for which include Cambodia, Japan, Egypt, Mali, Bolivia, and China—marks a clear departure from the Western-centered examples he provides for macroscopic regimes and, moreover, serves to define a "narrow and circumscribed" spectrum.[39] There is no question that the scopic regimes that emerged in Asia, Africa, and Latin America are inseparable from the modern scopic regimes that had been developed in the Western world, especially in light of post/colonial and American expansionist policies in the nineteenth and twentieth centuries. Nevertheless, it is an overgeneralization to include such non-Western, modern scopic regimes in a spectrum based solely on the

European example and, in the same breath, identify "exceptional" developments in the non-Western world as "microscopic."

Let us look, for example, at a "microscopic" case in colonial Korea. In 1916, a group of farmers and their children gathered to watch a film depicting the enthronement ceremony for the Japanese emperor Taishō.[40] For this screening, a unit from the colonial government's news agency, Maeil sinbo, brought a projector and generator to the rural town of Mokp'o by train. The Mokp'o station had opened in 1913, just three years before this screening. Before any commercial moviegoing cultures had formed among colonial audiences in rural towns like Mokp'o, many films were instead sent to them as propaganda.[41] The colonial authorities at the time, as well as both North and South Korea's postcolonial authorities decades later, saw film as the most effective medium for disseminating their messages. The conditions for such heteronomous spectatorship meant key distinctions between the post/colonial subject's viewing experience and that of the model subject in Western metropoles. As an invention of late nineteenth-century visual culture, cinema was a sphere that encompassed the cultural and technological transformations of modern society. However, in many parts of the post/colonial world, including Korea, cinematic illusions were first and foremost the site of psychological warfare, pushing a campaign to win the hearts and minds of colonial populations. Imported films were not mediums delivering literal rationality but, rather, a shot of multiple images repeatedly fired at audiences unfamiliar with them, developing their own world before the eyes of local audiences. This means that the reception of propaganda films was more of a viewing experience than a rational persuasion. That is, what mattered was not merely the mobility of cinema but also, and simultaneously, the viewing subject's own experience. The force of a propaganda film thus derived primarily not from its message but from the new mobility of the viewing position. The critical issue was the means by which these projectile screens could be effectively delivered to local audiences, so as to offer them visions of a new, desirable mobility. For instance, at the Mokp'o screening, viewers had to gather at a venue to watch the film at a specific time, circumstances that overlap with the gestural practices of riding a train, whereby the passenger enters a confined space, at a specific time, to go to a specific destination. The tour for the Taishō film also exhibited similar types of mobility, including collective gathering, both physically and mentally, and collective directivity, toward both the center of the empire and the future destination of the empire. The vehicle for these mobilities, the train to Mokp'o, exemplified the reciprocity between the cinematic experience and its means of transportation. In other words, the Korean case demonstrates the clear reciprocal relationship between the *delivery* system and the illusions that were being *delivered*, particularly in light of Korea's geopolitical situation in the global context and its local, vernacular practices as a post/colonial territory.

The problem with Jay's macroscopic regime, at this point, comes up in terms of applicability. His criticism of Heidegger's concept of world-as-picture is centered on the "monolithic" argument for a distinct division between premodern and modern cultures in the Western world—an argument that concluded that the modern world was destined to become pictures, whereas in the premodern eras, "world cannot become picture."[42] Jay also criticizes the then prevalent understanding of the modern scopic regime as identical to Cartesian perspectivalism "*tout court*."[43] This understanding ties in with the misinterpretation of Heidegger's philosophy that "everything that exists" was reduced to "objects standing opposed to subjects viewing them from afar" through the "introduction of the modern world picture."[44] In other words, Jay tries to find the plural, sometimes antiocularcentric or even endangered aspects of modern scopic regimes, challenging the monolithic conceptualization of the Heideggerian world-as-picture; in the process, he attempts to bridge modern world-as-pictures and premodern ones. As for the applicability of his macroscopic definition of the modern epoch, however, there is an unavoidable and irreducible difference between the "generic," Western, modern world-as-pictures and the "circumscribed," non-Western, modern world-as-pictures. In the case of Western, modern world-as-pictures, Jay argues that there were prior "anticipations and manifestations" of ocularcentrism from the premodern period that forecasted the modern scopic regime. Such patterns, however, were seldom found in the post/colonial world. In a colony like Korea, which was subjected to imperial expansion as early as the late nineteenth century, the introduction of modern visuality through Western paintings and camera obscura (the result of the forced opening of Chosŏn's ports and the subsequent trade with foreign powers) was a historic event that split the premodern and modern epochs. The forced rupture in the visual culture, the radical shift of vision's status in the hierarchy of senses, and the viewer's embrace of perspectivalist or ocularcentric epistemology as the norm, specifically to learn from the advanced, modern West—these developments were never just "circumscribed" characteristics incidentally occurring outside of the Western world; nor were they easily integrated as extensions of the European macroscopic regimes.

The marked change in the visual field, brought about through intense interaction with the external world, is not necessarily determined by epochal breaks but, occasionally, by the specific, underlying geopolitical circumstances. As a case in point, the Korean Empire's encounter with the newly imported medium of motion pictures might be described as a case of a hermit kingdom nearly at the limits of its closed-door policy, helplessly witnessing the rampant spread of a new visual medium bringing in images of the outside world. It is a description that can also be extended to North Korea's current situation with digital media. The new visual experience enabled by such foreign technology, along with the foreign images it delivers, was and continues to be an outside force designed to win the hearts and minds of Korean people, who, prior to specific points in time, had or have not had sufficient exposure to outside cultures. For example, the first record of a public film screening in Korea attributes it to an American-owned electric company, the Hansŏng Electric Company. In 1903, the company used the screening not only to promote its tram and electricity businesses but also as a means to "subdue the Koreans' escalating hostility against" its owners—namely, for buying out the then Korean emperor's shares in the company.[45] Similarly, the present-day campaign aimed at North Korea's people employs new visual experiences, in this case enabled by digital and drone technologies, in an effort to exert influence over people's minds. These cases clearly show how changes in the visual field have been brought about by the regime's geopolitical circumstances.

In an edited volume on imperial visual cultures, Jay calls the "scopic regime" a "contested territory," where modernity as a "uniform package" competes with "a highly contested range of often incompatible alternatives."[46] He characterizes this contestation as one between modernity and "so-called traditional societies assaulted in the name of modernization."[47] Such a framework exhibits some overlap with the notion of internal colonialism,[48] a process by which colonialism not only expands outside the nation but also points inward to the colonizer's own nation, particularly its traditional or underdeveloped areas. Accordingly, we might say that colonialist expansion and exploitation are fundamentally inscribed in capitalist modernity, such that the difference between external and internal colonialism is only a matter of degree. Can we, however, claim that the contest among the visual cultures of model European society is, allowing for differences by degrees, essentially the same phenomenon as the clash between an Asian society's traditional visual culture and Western scopic regimes of modernity? To answer this question, we will have to account for the fact that the latter case repeatedly involved military or police forces, whereas the former was more often a benign competition that did not need to mobilize such oppressive state apparatuses. By extension, in examining such cases, do we simply have to accept, or even overlook, the violent nature of modernity's introduction to the colonial world, given that modernity is supposedly always violent by nature? What about the visual experiences that forced colonial populations to adjust to a new mode of mobility and to abandon previous ways of life? Are such developments simply a part of modernity's assault against traditional societies across the globe? In an effort to answer these questions, this book turns its primary attention to parallels in the ways that visual knowledge has been delivered from the outside world—namely, through the powerful mobility of the visual experience and the viewing subject.

Methodologically speaking, however, this book is not an attempt to *verify* my hypothesis on the scopic regimes of colonial/postcolonial Korea. Cinema as world-as-gesture is not scientifically decipherable nor numerically quantifiable;[49] therefore, my approach to gestures and their affective effects is essentially interpretive and, admittedly, subjective. In other words, this book is an ethnography of world-as-gestures grasped through cinematic and other visual materials from the past, and this method equates the present-day researcher's ethnographic exploration of gestures in films with the work of ethnographers who collect artifacts and *objets* in field research. This approach shares some similarities with Christina Klein's framework of a "period style," which indicates "a set of formal conventions that are broadly shared at a given historical moment and that express a more or less coherent set of beliefs."[50] According to Klein, Cold War cosmopolitanism as a period style had four dimensions, including as a "political discourse," an "attitude towards modernity," a "material practice of cultural production and dissemination," and a "cultural style."[51] The difference between a period style and a world-as-gesture lies in the latter's emphasis on the bodily and phenomenological nature of gestures, as previously discussed. Because a gesture, by its Agambenian definition, has plural potentialities and once grasped by a meaning ceases to be a gesture, this book does not claim to be a singular reading of cine-mobility in twentieth-century Korea. Rather, much like the anthropologist Sonia Ryang's investigation into North Korean people's life and culture, this book is an attempt to conduct an ethnological study of "culture at a distance," to study the "cultural logic of a society without conducting fieldwork."[52] As such, this book focuses on societies that previously existed on the Korean Peninsula; that have continued to change through adopting, overlapping, and replacing different cultural logics throughout the twentieth century; and that are, as a result, physically inaccessible to contemporary scholars. Similarly, the historian Todd A. Henry adopts this anthropological framework to capture "the nuances of subjects actively engaged with [colonial] assimilation projects," as well as to write about "the past with greater ethnographic sensibilities."[53] The gestural dimension of cinema, including postures, attitudes, and manners, in their appropriate social contexts, constitutes a set of rich resources in the ethnological study of the modern experience in "an unknown land."[54]

While this book does not claim cine-mobility as a universal concept applicable to any post/colonial or non-Western world, I hope this book's attempt to theorize the cognitive mobility turns in film and media history might situate it among and contribute to existing conversations about heteronomous spectatorship in post/colonial or Cold War cinemas.[55]

Overview: Korea's Modernity in Epochal Configurations

The subject's modern experience in colonial and postcolonial Korea has been a central concern for contemporary Korean studies, especially those in film, literature, and cultural studies. For instance, in *Intimate Empire*, Nayoung Aimee Kwon asks, "How then might the modern experience translate differently when refracted through the prism of the perspective of those who had to live through it in colonial subjection?"[56] She calls the disavowed but negotiated "lived experience of the colonial modern subject" a "conundrum of representation" and characterizes it by looking into "an archive of imperial language writings by the colonized."[57] On a similar note, but focusing more on the biopolitics of postcolonial South Korea, Theodore Hughes's *Literature and Film in Cold War South Korea* interrogates the distribution of sensed experiences, which saw "the agreements and disagreements, the visibilities and invisibilities that have organized the postcolonial culture of division, authoritarianism, and developmentalism."[58] In turn, in *Split Screen Korea*, Steven Chung examines images from the two Koreas and asserts that "none of those cinematic elements are avant la lettre democratic or communist or, conversely, purely escapist before their determinations in popular, critical, and institutional practices and discourses," thereby implying an empirical dimension that cannot be definitively articulated.[59] Such concerns are shared with this book, which takes as its focus mobilities stemming from the external world—not, crucially, as completed, delivered, or translated *entelecheia* but as something defined by presentness and motility. That the mobilities are present on-screen does not mean that they are visually represented through preexisting mobilities but that visualization itself is movement unfolding in the present. That is, foreign mobilities as gestures on the screen were experienced at the moment of their creation, precisely through encounter with post/colonial Korean viewers. For scholars, cinema is an archive of such gestural practices. The mobility of the world-as-gesture, together with the gestural potentialities of such experienced mobilities, serves as the primary focus for this book.[60]

This book spans the entire twentieth century, ranging from the era of the train and early films to that of the automobile and commercial features, to the rise of television and aviation mobility, and on to the emergence of automation, computer technologies, and their corresponding popular imaginations—all within the specific geopolitical context of post/colonial Korea. The basic organization of this book is chronological, consisting of three parts, each of which has two chapters and deals with a specific historical period in Korea. To "characterize epochal configurations"[61] of the modern Korean subject's gestural experience macroscopically, I call the first epoch of cine-mobility the "train-cinema interface," referencing Thomas Lamarre's discussion of the association of cinema and trains as "paradigmatic of the modern."[62] The train-cinema interface established a collective mass of spectators and exposed them to the "visible, audible, and kinetic" sense of the regulated movement often associated with trains and railway transportation, both cinematically and corporeally.[63] The train-cinema interface emerged on the Korean Peninsula in the late nineteenth and early twentieth centuries, a time of imperial threats, and persisted under Japanese colonial power until the mid-1940s. The collective film experience of riding a train was "an expression of experience by experience,"[64] in that the virtual movement of audiences distributed itself "according to the way [they] settle[d] [themselves] in the world and the position [their] bodies assume[d] in it."[65] In colonial Korea, under Japan's railway imperialism, cinema provided the virtual train-ride experience as an ideal type of effective, modern mobility and often was delivered to audiences by rail.[66]

To foreground the epoch of the train-cinema interface, chapter 1 examines a number of spectacles and cinema events, such as Elias Burton Holmes's filming of Seoul at the turn of the twentieth century. These events indicate how the advent of the railroad on the Korean Peninsula was a symptom of colonization. Through discourse analysis of the itinerant film exhibition for the Japanese emperor Taishō's enthronement ceremony and detailed analyses of several feature films produced in colonial Korea, this chapter concludes with theorizations of *locomotive modernity* in collective and regulated systems. Chapter 2 is an in-depth study of a tourist culture film sponsored by the Japan Tourist Bureau in 1939, one that presented Japan, Korea, Manchuria, and other parts of mainland China as a unified world with diverse cultures and identities, subsequently declared as the "New Order in East Asia." This railway tourist film displayed the unseen territories of the Japanese Empire, and allowed audiences to experience them before they could actually visit these places. It is possible that the cinematic experience of the gestures in such tourist films served as disciplinary moments for Korean audiences, resulting in a modern, locomotive subjectivity optimized for pseudo-imperialistic expansionism.

Subsequently, there was a profound shift in the regime of cinemobility—alternatively, a cognitive mobility turn in Korean capitalism—that was closely intertwined with the broader transformations in transportation technologies, which came on the heels of Korea's liberation from

Japanese rule in 1945. These shifts, in turn, prompted spatiotemporal transformations of everyday life in Korea. At this juncture, I want to address the question of (dis)continuity between coloniality and postcoloniality. In particular, I do not "assume a colonial/postcolonial historical break"[67]—that is, a rupture that permanently changed the nature of subordination. However, South Korea's transition from Japan's imperial colony to the United States' subordinate ally did not only mean a regime change in a political sense but also entailed a new turn in global capitalism and its local manifestation on the level of the everyday. The cognitive mobility turn brought about by the United States' presence on the peninsula was, without question, an epoch-making manifestation of post-imperialist capitalism. The new epoch of cine-mobility arrived with a "coerced intensive flexibility" associated with automobiles and automobility.[68] As automotive culture spread from the United States to its allies in East Asia, especially to South Korea during and after the Korean War, the "automobile-screen interface" came to link traffic control systems with a private sense of mobility.[69] Chapter 3 focuses its attentions on this rise of automobility under U.S. hegemony, particularly as a visual technology under Cold War government, encapsulated in the late-1960s South Korean neologism *maik'a*, transliterated from the English "my car." While Japanese colonial authorities spread film propaganda units through the nationwide railroad system, the U.S. Army exchanged trains for automobiles, such as Jeeps and trucks, and made them the primary vehicle for their own mobile exhibitions. These automobiles were the embodiment of American state-of-the-art technology, which was also exhibited in the films the automobiles delivered. While the former regime of cine-mobility implied a self-contained arrangement, equipped with regulated systems for collective forward movements, the latter regime meshed with new, liberal technologies of government that were, in turn, connected to the rise of automobile culture and its industry, the establishment of a nationwide expressway system, the nuclearization of the family, and the emergence of post-cine-mobility via small screens for the home. There is no doubt that the individual mobility celebrated in American films was a sensory enticement intended to bring the South Korean population under yet another "dictatorship of movement," specifically by taking them onto the collective circuit of self-disciplined, individual vehicles.[70]

However, the postcolonial context brought the emerging prospects of a new mode of transportation mobility into sharp contrast with the existing, hegemonic mode of the traditional railway system. The construction of the nationwide expressway system in the 1960s and 1970s, therefore, unfolded on the highly discursive battleground between two hegemonic mobilities, the clash between which ultimately resulted in state ownership of the automobile's agency, or, to invoke Seungsook Moon's notion of "militarized modernity," what we might call *militarized automobility.*[71] Chapter 4 traces the nationalizing aspects of automobilization, focusing on the culture surrounding nationwide expressway construction as driven by Park Chung Hee, as well as on the early, popular imageries of the South Korean domestic auto industry and its products. As Carter J. Eckert puts it, Park's regime pursued a vision of "the state and the society in all their parts and manifestations" functioning "in tandem," and the expressway system, on a symbolic level at the very least, was "in harmony with state goal."[72]

At a later point, however, cine-mobility fused with the automobile-screen interface that bore the makings of its own decline. While the culture that fetishized owning a private car did not reach the majority of the postcolonial population until the 1980s, the virtual mobility of automobiles enchanted the entire population as cinematic experiences in the intervening decades. However, the post-cine-mobility regime with the automobile-screen interface eventually arrived at the twilight of cine-mobility, due to the rapid rise of television's small screens in the 1970s and the subsequent increase of noncollective, personalized forms of audiovisual/tactical experience. The phenomenological characteristics of automobility—that is, the individual driver's physical mobility in joining and then leaving the ever-circulating flows of traffic in an irregular, but autonomous manner—better resonated with those of televisual mobility, wherein the individual viewer's sensory mobility in joining and then leaving the ever-circulating electromagnetic flows of television broadcasting was driven by the viewer's own choice. While it rarely provided the same kinds of immersive and phantasmagoric encounters with the world that cinema had offered, television's new experience of the world-as-gesture was accompanied by a sense of immediacy and tactility, delivered through satellite technology and aviation mobility, through which "information traveled faster than physical motility."[73] This twilight of cine-mobility is the focus of chapter 5. It examines the different ways in which television documentaries and talk shows, produced by the U.S. Information Service, represented geographies of the "free world" to South Korean viewers in the 1960s and 1970s—namely, by building on the vision of localism and federalism inherent to American government films, a vision that was subsequently appropriated by a South Korean government film franchise. The imagined geographical hierarchy in many South Korean television shows had their prototype in cinema's transnational visual mobility, which temporarily coexisted with the post-cine-mobility of television media. The similarities between these two media lie in the ways in which the world-as-gesture was delivered and circulated from the outside world. The latter part of the chapter looks at the sense of immediacy and tactility in televisual and aviation mobilities.

In turn, the cognitive mobility turn in the 1980s and 1990s, specifically driven by computerization and the spread of automatic technologies, laid the grounds for the current era of transparent digital mobility. I call this period the epoch of the "immobile-ultramobile interface," downplaying the definition by medium specificities and transportation infrastructures and emphasizing the enduring association between the two technologies in subjectivization.[74] At this historical juncture, both the immersive cinematic screen and the tactile television screen were poised to lose their status as the hegemonic means to encounter world-as-gestures. Then, the personalized and functionalized displays of, first, personal computers and then touch-responsive screens on ATMs and other unmanned machines required immediate gestures from the viewer-user's body. To acquaint oneself with newly adopted, allegedly comfortable, automatic technologies, human mobilities had to be corrected and reorganized to fit with the movement of machines. Under financial automation, the transparent circulation of information amplified the human subject's affect of helplessness before machine-led mobility. In light of these circumstances, chapter 6 interrogates the rosy pictures of flexibility and liberality, which were presented as benefits of the automobilized, visual mobility regime. By investigating the conveyor-belt-like flow of automated mobility, including automated vertical transportation, automatic doors, and automatic teller machines, this final chapter reveals how the

South Korean population was mobilized toward a new biopolitics and a neoliberal mobility.

This book, instead of aiming for a teleological thesis, prompts readers to link this book's observations of twentieth-century Korea with their own time and place, their own past and present, and their future selves. Admittedly, the chronological and epochal survey of scopic regimes of cine-mobility and post-cine-mobilities in this book may seem too dark, pessimistic, or even fatalistic, adding fuel to Doobo Shim's and Kyung Hyun Kim's critical diagnosis of Marxist social critiques' over- and predetermination of "inescapable neoliberalism."[75] However, as an ethnological study of modern human and cognitive mobility, this book's primary concern is not so much capitalism's march to doomsday but, rather, the attitudes and disciplined, physical mobilities of the humans who encounter such mobility turns through cognitive experiences. Accordingly, if this book has any object of critique, it is less the fatalistic mechanization and automatization of capitalist mobility and more the aspects of what Foucault called the *technologies of the self*: "The conclusion would be that the political, ethical, social, philosophical problem of our days is not to try to liberate the individual from the state and from the state's institutions but to liberate us both from the state and from *the type of individualization which is linked to the state.* We have to promote new forms of subjectivity through the refusal of this kind of individuality which has been imposed on us for several centuries."[76]

PART I

Train-Cinema Interface

CHAPTER 1

In a Loop, on the Track

Locomotive Modernity in Colonial Korean Cinema

The train waits for no one. It moves, with its heavy corporeality, toward a destination that will perfect an ontological value—arrival. In *Sweet Dream* (*Mimong*, 1936), the female protagonist Aesun's taxi desperately tries to catch the train, first by taking her to Seoul Station, and then by chasing the train as it departs for Yongsan Station. Aesun, the "Korean version of a Nora Helmer," leaves home dreaming of a modern, free love and runs for her life to shield herself from the gossip surrounding her scandalous extramarital relationship with a swindler.[1] Yet what awaits her is a cruel fate where her taxi collides into her own daughter, Chŏng-hŭi. The train she was chasing vanishes from sight; something that was supposed to take her to freedom becomes the thing she can never reach. The only choices left to her are to punish herself for hurting her own child or to accept censure for being an immoral woman who went against patriarchal mores. Aesun's gestures in the chase scene—her desperate facial expressions in the taxi and her posture when giving orders to the driver to go faster—and the fast movement of the two racing vehicles leave two sharply conflicting impressions of futility and autonomy among many possible potentialities.

The flexible and maximized mobility of an automobile, which is able to move off the track, inevitably goes hand in hand with unpredictability and uncertainty. And in colonial Korean cinema, the uncertain nature of automobility is frequently paired with the tragic destiny of characters who must catch a train.[2] In *Straits of Chosŏn* (*Chosŏn haehyŏp*, 1943),

FIGURE 1.1 Kinshuku's failure to catch the train in *Straits of Chosŏn* (1943).

Kinshuku (Kŭm-suk) wants to arrive at the train station before her lover departs on the military train. Her taxi rushes to get her there in time but eventually fails (see fig. 1.1)—a failure that leads to her long economic and emotional hardship. Yet Kinshuku's hardship is not a type of punishment, as in Aesun's case in *Sweet Dream*. Kinshuku is a woman of noble and pure love, whose steadfastness drives her to wait indefinitely for her lover. She arrives at the station only to realize that the train has already taken him away from her. It takes him to the deadly battleground and physically splits them between the war front and the home front. The train's relentless, mechanical movement, nevertheless, is not presented as something deserving blame or censure but rather as something grand and reliable. Right before the train departs, Kinshuku makes another desperate gesture, similar to Aesun's in *Sweet Dream*, on her way to the train station in a taxi. The couple, along with the intended audience, know and believe that their fates are wrapped up in their devotion to the war.

Eiryu (Yŏng-ryong), the protagonist in *Vow of Love* (*Sarang kwa maengsŏ*, 1945), finds that Eiko (Yŏng-cha), the wife of an officer killed in action, could be his long-lost sister, and he therefore wants to extend his visit to her village, where he is covering the officer's story for a newspaper. He empties the oil out of a bus meant to take passengers from the

THE AVERTED CATASTROPHE

FIGURE 1.2 An averted collision between a streetcar used for cinematography and a bull cart in Burton Holmes's travelogue from his visit to Seoul (1901). From Holmes, *Burton Holmes Travelogues*, 76.

village to the train station. The bus's breakdown delays a volunteer soldier's departure for the military train so that he eventually must run to it on foot. This ethnically Korean volunteer soldier has to run twelve kilometers to catch the train, while villagers cheer the running soldier on, regretting that they cannot have a farewell ceremony at the station. Eiko is deeply disappointed by the incident and warns Eiryu that she might cut ties with him. Regretting his actions, Eiryu finally decides to volunteer for the navy. While the train does not make an appearance in these sequences, the audience can still feel its weighty presence. It is not merely a means to transport soldiers to battlefields but also a medium by which a colonial subject can affirm his or her faith and loyalty to the empire. The train never waits, and the subject-soldier must show his sincerity by arriving at the station on time.

These pivotal moments of family separation recurring in colonial Korean films recall a much earlier scene, roughly a decade before Japan's annexation of Korea, called "the averted catastrophe" (see fig. 1.2).[3] At the time of this event, E. Burton Holmes, the first cinematographer to film Korea, was shooting the scenery in Seoul on a tram, presumably, in 1901.[4] After traveling on the Trans-Siberian Express, he had arrived in Hansŏng (Seoul) with his fellow cinematographer and was filming the city in a cutting-to-continuity style, so as to reenact the mobility of the train, when the accident occurred.[5] The special streetcar that Holmes was on narrowly averted a collision with a bull cart:

> Out through the South Gate we were speeding one day, on a special car provided by the company, to facilitate our cinematographic work, when to our horror we beheld a bull-cart stuck fast in the track, making a collision very imminent; but, continuing to turn the crank of our instrument, we completed the picture to an anxious finish, the car stopping just in time to spare the bull, and incidentally, avoid a shaking up that might have been disastrous. Then, after the balky bull has been led to a place of safety, and the old cart with its sprawling wheels has been backed away, we continue our interrupted trolley party, whizzing out through the suburbs and along the country roads to a pretty village on the banks of the broad, placid river Han.[6]

While images of such "collisions (both literal and metaphoric) between horse-driven carts and electric streetcars that embodied the psychology of chaos and anxiety brought about by this technological era" filled American magazines and newspapers in those days, so much so that such collisions can be called a phenomenon that could happen anywhere, this "averted catastrophe" and its representation in an American travelogue demonstrate a certain power relation, one that was inscribed in the recurring confrontation between Koreans and railroad mobility.[7] To many people in Hansŏng, the tram, the railroads, and their tracks were, in fact, something of a novelty that had been built only recently by foreign capital.

The railroad system itself became a battlefield on which imperialist countries, including Japan, Britain, the United States, France, and Russia, fought for construction and operating licenses. The contract to lay the first line, Kyŏnginsŏn (the Seoul–Inch'ŏn line), had been given initially to an American businessman, James R. Morse, by King Kojong of the Chosŏn dynasty in 1896. However, with Morse facing financial difficulty, it was transferred to Japan, following tense negotiations and without any consent from the Korean government.[8] Kyŏngbusŏn (the Seoul–Pusan line) and Kyŏngŭisŏn (the Seoul–Sinŭiju line) also became the objects of fierce competition among the Great Powers but were ultimately built by Japan.[9] These two lines were considered crucial to military activities, since they crosscut the peninsula, linking northern China, via Manchuria, to Pusan, which had the closest port to Japan. In 1911, construction of a railroad bridge over the Amrok River (Yalu River) was completed, linking Sinŭiju and Dandong in China.[10] The signing of the 1910 Treaty of Annexation served as added incentive to step up use of these railroad lines as a pivotal means for Japan's imperial expansion, as well as a standard by which colonial subjects were directed to adjust themselves to modern temporality and spatiality.

Under these circumstances, the image of a near collision between a foreign moving machine and a Korean bumpkin acquires a specific political significance—that is, a collision between modern Western civilization on the tracks of technological advancement and the newly discovered, alien bodies off the track, those who need discipline to get onto the loop. This loop and its dropouts repeatedly reinforce the relationship between the colonial power and the colonized. The foreign camera-carrying observer's ethnographic gaze on the underdisciplined subject, as manifested in Holmes's travelogue, becomes an iteration of the recurring power relation, exposing the role of the cinema and the railroad in establishing and reaffirming that relation.

By the late 1930s and early 1940s, disciplinary power appears to have successfully permeated everyday life in urban Seoul. In *Keijō* (*Kyŏngsŏng*, 1941), a documentary film sponsored by the Railway Bureau of the Japanese Government-General in Korea, the "mobilized virtual gaze" or the "mobile vision" toward the colonial metropolis inscribes a perfect circle that rarely allows spaces outside of the loop.[11] The film starts with shots of some landmarks in Seoul but makes a distinct rhythmic and stylistic shift after a train arrives at Seoul Station. Subsequently, all scenes of colonial Seoul are presented in a relay of panoramic montages, reminiscent of the view from a tram. After the journey through the city, the film completes the landscape of the city in a loop of a daily routine.

What then can we infer from the frequent off-the-track catastrophes, along with the desperate gestures of the subjects who try to catch the train individually, in colonial Korean films from the 1930s and 1940s? According to Hyun-hee Park, Aesun in *Sweet Dream* is "actually depicted as a non-modern subject who cannot follow the public temporality that is necessary for the order of society and the organic circulation of capital," with the film functioning as a fascist enlightenment project "to urge Koreans to regain consciousness from the delusion of Western modernity."[12] Instead, I would argue that those catastrophes were part of the colonial episteme that endlessly confirmed the gap between the colonial power and the colonized. The sublimity built into the representation of the railroad was perfected, to positive ends, when it was facilitated through the gaze of an auteurist director from the empire, Shimizu Hiroshi, who wanted *Keijō* to be a city symphony film of colonial territory, following Western trends. However, in the colony's self-reflexive gaze in colonial Korean cinema, the railroad's sublime nature could be expressed only through the repeated failure of colonial subjects to get onto the loop.

The National Sublime: Tracks toward Battlefields and the Imperial Center

What happened, as a result, to the minds of the off-the-track colonial subjects? The 1941 film *Volunteer* (*Chiwŏnbyŏng*) is a story of a Korean man, Ch'unho, who agonizes over how he can contribute to the ongoing war as a subject of the Japanese Empire. A great deal of his anxiety stems from the fact that he is not eligible for conscripted service, since he is from the colonies. Accordingly, in a scene where he watches the military train depart the station, left behind where villagers hold farewell ceremonies for soldiers going off to war, Ch'unho is portrayed as experiencing deep, emotional turmoil. Structurally, the film begins with a scene of villagers welcoming the train arriving at the station and ends with a send-off scene for Ch'unho, who eventually boards the train to join the Imperial Army (see fig. 1.3). In this regard, Ch'unho's small village, the film's primary setting, is the space of the colonial subject, while the train is a driving force that brings him to the battlefield, a place of imperial assimilation. The military train is thus a vehicle of the then-emphasized slogan in colonial Korea, "Japan and Korea as One" (J. *naisen ittai*, K. *naesŏn ilch'e*).

FIGURE 1.3 The first (top two) and last scenes of *Volunteer* (1941).

Seen from a different angle, however, the film's viewer neither resides nor remains in the village but rather is already on the train, in the loop. In other words, the entire film can be interpreted as a virtual railroad journey to and from the village. The film starts with an arrival at the small village station and ends with a departure after a stopover. During the visit, the viewer-passenger, who is already en route to the destination, meets the protagonist and learns of his dreams of going on the journey. The protagonist, after overcoming his anxiety, boards the train and travels with other passengers bound for imperial assimilation.

Understanding the film thus helps us see an affinity between cinema and the railroad. A film cinema projector requires wheels, loops, tracks, and a motor. The machine's unidirectional movement produces a new mode of time and space from the reels of multiple framed shots. Spectators need to be punctual for each round and take their seats together in a confined space. Once the machine starts moving, the spectators watch moving images on a framed display, a screen. This machine-related experience resonates with that of the railroad, in terms of the relationship between human subjects and mechanical mobility. *Volunteer*'s opening and ending scenes parallel two mechanical movements—the movement of trains and camera movement—to mobilize the colonial populace for the central imperial force. In the first scene, the materiality of the military train leaves the protagonist with a guilty conscience since he cannot honor his commitments as a loyal subject of the empire. The train first comes toward the screen before the camera cuts to a tracking shot from behind the moving train. The empty track behind the train reminds the spectator of the weight of the moving machine and highlights Ch'unho's feelings of helplessness. In the ending scene, where the villagers give Ch'unho a rousing send-off after he becomes eligible and decides to join the army, the train is seen from the side, moving from left to right. The camera then cuts to a close-up shot of the metal wheels rolling ponderously (see fig. 1.4). The following shot of an empty track now takes on a significance distinct from that in the opening scene. With his fiancée, Punok, looking on, her gaze unseen by the camera at her back, a stretch of the railroad moves toward a far-distant center of the national sublime—that is, to the battlefield for imperial assimilation. Ch'unho has managed to haul himself onto the loop.

What then is suggested in the unexpected close-up of Punok's face (see fig.1.5), which is unusual in the whole film's shooting style—a shot that reverses the gaze toward the national sublime? Throughout the entire film, Punok neither opposes Ch'unho's desire to join the army nor welcomes it. Rather, her first response to his decision is something close to embarrassment:

Ch'unho: Punok, I will go to town to take an exam tomorrow, too.
Punok: An exam?
Ch'unho: It is an enlistment exam.
Punok: Enlistment?
Ch'unho: Koreans can now enlist, too. I will become a professional soldier.
Punok: Will you?

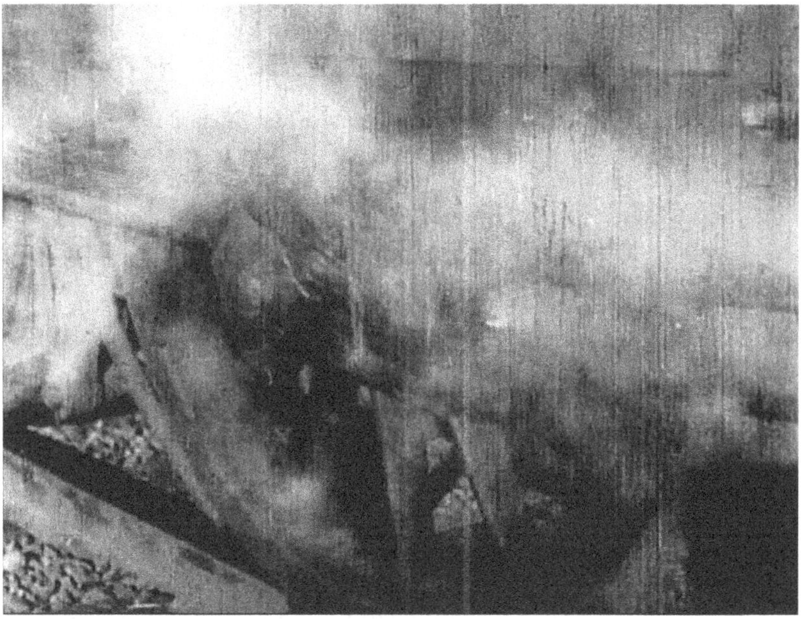

FIGURE 1.4 Moving metal wheel in *Volunteer* (1941).

FIGURE 1.5 Punok's face at the end of *Volunteer* (1941).

Ch'unho: Are you very surprised?
Punok: No . . . Be a soldier. Be a good soldier for the country.

Though she denies it, Punok's face and tone of voice clearly convey her surprise—she did not expect that he would be able to join the army and is confused by his solution to his dilemma, which would lead to a long-distance relationship of unknown duration.

At the end of the film, she is left behind as a remnant, a postscript to the bigger story of a railway journey to the village. In other words, she is a subject who is still, or will permanently be, off the track. Her gaze questions the possibility of being perfectly assimilated into the loop. The male subject who initially lacks a boarding pass for the train just barely acquires one by taking an exam, one that tests his ability to remain in the loop. It is, however, a temporary boarding pass, since he was born out of the loop, which was the fundamental and unresolved reason for his anxiety. Punok, whose identity remains that of Ch'unho's fiancée, is not even eligible to take the exam for enlisting. Her only option is to accept that her union with her fiancé, now a legitimate unit on the track, will be postponed indefinitely, without any promise of resolution. This reflects a certain hierarchy that existed among colonial subjects mobilized through the railroads. As Kelly Jeong points out, "The railroads in colonial Korea—in literature as well as in real life—divided the nation along gender and socio-economic lines, as richer men rode them far more than did the women or the poor."[13] In this way, the one-hour railroad journey to a small Korean town reveals that the two modern technologies of cinema and the railroad worked in conjunction to facilitate colonial mobilization, all the while pointing to the yawning gap between the mobilizer and the mobilized.

Emperor on the Track: He Never Visits the Colony, but His Cinematic Double Does by Train

The parallelism and parallelization of the cinema and the railroad in colonial Korea should be understood as the cultural logic of mobilization. A sense of mobility in a modern society is closely tied to the ways in which the governing power mobilizes the gaze of the governed, as well as how his or her own gaze is directed to them. As Takashi Fujitani has demonstrated, in a modern state, the ruler's visits to the people and how those visits are designed and executed have been "central to the construction of a kind of ocular domination."[14] The cinema was a new medium that mediated the ocular domination of colonial power, intimately tied up with the mobility of the railroad. The colonial authorities' use of cinema as a means of not only making people look up at the ruler but also having them recognize the ruler's gaze, as well as letting them become recognizable to the ruler, was intended to mobilize colonial subjects toward the system of the imperial gaze. It is important to note that the emergence of the railroad system on the Korean Peninsula was meant to organize the colony using cine-mobility as a lens for the imperial gaze.

On January 7, 1909, Korean emperor Sunjong boarded a southbound train at Namdaemun Station in Seoul. It was the first nationwide tour by a sovereign of the Korean Peninsula, intended to give the people a chance to see the emperor in the flesh.[15] The royal tour, however, was actually planned by the Japanese resident-general in hopes of generating a sense of legitimacy for the Japan-Korea Protectorate Treaty.[16] It seemed that because the Japanese emperor Meiji had made a successful nationwide tour in 1872, Japanese officials understood such pageants as an effective means to justify their own rule.[17]

The "roaming ruler" in the great imperial pageants during the Meiji era made "his spectacles visible to all the people of the nation," while, simultaneously, "all the people of the empire" were made "visible to one dominating and all-seeing monarch."[18] Whereas Emperor Meiji's roaming had inspired a sense of shared national identity, Sunjong's royal tour was accompanied by foreign authorities who were threatening national sovereignty. People witnessed the foreign officials attached to the resident-general at the same time they saw their own emperor. Furthermore, Resident-General Itō Hirobumi delivered speeches emphasizing the importance of an alliance with Japan.[19] Ultimately, this was an event that constructed and reinforced a form of ocular domination by the colonial ruler. By accompanying Sunjong on a trip they had organized themselves, Japanese officials expected certain effects on the visibility of the Japanese residency-general, whose resident-general could stand shoulder to shoulder with the Korean emperor, and its modern administration.

The tour *was* truly modern. It was possible precisely because a modern transportation system, the railroad, was an option.[20] On his royal train, Sunjong completed his first tour in seven days and his second in eight days, both of which were extremely short periods to cover the nation, especially when compared to other tours completed via more traditional means of transportation.[21] With this new mode of transport, people could discover and discipline themselves according to new conceptions of time, to a modern temporality informed by the workings of the railroad, all while waiting for the emperor's scheduled arrival.[22] Hirobumi was well aware of the power and significance of such spectacles and had one of the early Japanese film studios, Yokota Shōkai, film events on the royal tour.[23] According to Whan Mo Bok, the primary purpose of filming was to publicize the resident-general's activities overseas to audiences in the home country. The screening records at Kanda's Kinki-kan Theater indicate that the film was indeed shown there in June 1909, but it is possible that the film also made the rounds in Korea.[24]

While Sunjong's royal tour comprised two sets of personal visits to major towns with railroad stations, the emperor of the colonizing power toured the colony virtually in a set of traveling exhibitions. The film shown in this 1916 exhibition tour was called *Enthronement of the Japanese Emperor* (J. *Gotairei*, K. *Ŏdaerye*). According to a news article, it depicted Emperor Taishō's progress from Tokyo to Kyoto, where the enthronement ceremony was held in November 1915 (see fig. 1.6).[25] The film's exhibition tour was jointly sponsored by *Maeil sinbo* and *Kyŏngsŏng ilbo*, the two mouthpieces of the Japanese government-general in Korea, and was shown in major towns, including Suwŏn, Inch'ŏn, Taejŏn, Chŏnju, Kunsan, Kwangju, Mokp'o, Masan, Chinhae, Taegu, Pusan, Kaesŏng, Pyongyang, Sinŭiju, Chinnamp'o, and Wŏnsan.[26]

The tour was an ambitious propaganda project designed by the Japanese government-general during the 1910s. It ran in southern Korea from April 26 to May 16, 1916,[27] and in northern Korea from May 28 to June 13, 1916.[28] An article in *Maeil sinbo* claimed that the purpose of the exhibition was to "allow the general public in Chosŏn a chance to respectfully look up to the Emperor."[29] The film's screening was called *paegwanhoe* (J. *haikan kai*), meaning "a gathering for looking up in worship."[30] In other words, the exhibition was understood as a ritual for colonial subjects to have an audience with the emperor.

FIGURE 1.6 Emperor Taishō departs Tokyo for Kyoto to be enthroned (November 1915). From Nishizawa, *Japan in the Taisho Era*, front matter.

The act of virtual worship through the traveling film exhibition involved a tangle of politics tying back to the imperial gaze. Through the film, the colonial subject-audience could observe the procession of the newly enthroned Japanese emperor moving from Tokyo, the current center of the empire, to Kyoto, the original center of the empire. At the same time, as the language of the news media indicated, each colonial subject-worshiper was understood to be looking up at the emperor himself, even as his body was not physically present. Moreover, given that the emperor's visit entailed a royal inspection, colonial subjects were not only the subject of the gaze during this cinematic event but also the object of an observing gaze. Who, then, was the observer returning the gaze of the colonial subject?

We might surmise that the colonial audience sensed the imperial gaze hidden behind the screen, much like the employees in the Panopticon, who suspected that their director was inspecting them from the empty, central tower.[31] Yet we should also remember that both Emperor Sunjong's royal tour and Emperor Taishō's virtual tour were made possible by a new mode of mobility, the nationwide railroad networks. The organization of time, space, and movement enabled by this mobility set the conditions for the imperial mutual gaze. Most likely, the colonial subject-audience was aware of the reordering power of railroad mobility, of the modern technology that powered the machines' movement, and of the imperial authorities who controlled them. Therefore, the gaze looking back at the colonial audience belonged not merely to the current emperor of Japan but to the constitutive power of modern mobility and visuality in a colonial setting.

The train was vital for the propaganda activities that enabled the exchange of gazes in the colony. Interestingly, the host cities for Taishō's cinematic tour were called the "major port towns" (*yoji hangbu*) of Chosŏn.[32] Considering that many of those cities, including Suwŏn, Taejŏn, Chŏnju, Kwangju, Taegu, Pusan, Kaesŏng, and Pyongyang, were located inland, the term *port* most likely referred to a railroad station. Reporting on the Japanese government-general's nationwide propaganda project in April 1921, a *Tonga ilbo* article noted how the traveling film exhibition clearly depended on the transportation system: "The authorities will put efforts into the traveling exhibition of motion pictures to introduce them to as many audiences as possible. . . . There are provincial areas that are not equipped to project motion pictures due to poor transportation."[33] The venues most frequently used for the traveling exhibition were, unsurprisingly, the towns that had railroad stations.

The Japanese government-general utilized mobile film projection as a tool for propaganda as early as the 1910s, as in the case of the *Enthronement of the Japanese Emperor* screening. A news article from June 1916 reported that the Yongsan Youth Group of the Japanese government-general's Railway Bureau had organized a mobile projection team to tour nationwide for complimentary public screenings.[34] Such touring film exhibitions multiplied prolifically when the Japanese governor-general instituted the Cultural Rule (J. *bunka seiji*) as an appeasement policy after the March First Movement in 1919. A 1923 column pointed out that the increase in propaganda activities had led to the Japanese government-general and provincial governments organizing mobile film projection teams.[35] The specialized groups in charge of mobile film projection were called the Motion Picture Squad (*hwalsadae*; hereafter Squad).

The topics of Squad films varied, covering introductions to modern civilization, lectures on current social issues, moral education, and public health and hygiene.[36] While some of the Squads were set up under government offices,[37] others were affiliated with various half-public, half-private organizations, such as youth associations, educational institutions, and religious bodies.[38] As in the case of the T'ongyŏng Youth Corps (T'ongyŏng ch'ŏngnyŏndan), some of them were organically organized by the local youth, and not necessarily tied to the colonial authorities.[39] Although the objectives of Squad operations varied depending on their sponsoring organizations, there is no question that the majority of them regarded film as the medium of modern enlightenment, one that had the power to attract people.

The reception of the Squad films was highly enthusiastic. In Taejŏn and Mokp'o, there was a huge demand for tickets to *Enthronement* screenings, including a group purchase for 1,000 students, such that the hosts had to schedule extra screenings.[40] In Chŏnju, a total of 2,180 viewers, including students, soldiers, workers, and families, attended six screenings of *Enthronement* over two days.[41] Moreover, the popularity of the Squad movies seems to have maintained momentum over the following years. According to a 1926 news report, a high school in Ch'unch'ŏn indefinitely suspended 28 students for sneaking out of the school to attend Squad film shows.[42] In July 1934, a newsreel covering the flood damage in the southern region was being screened on tour, and over 7,000 viewers attended two shows in Pyongyang, while several thousand could not see the film because the venues were full.[43] Since "not every province secured enough silver screens to show motion pictures," we might attribute this level of popularity to the thrills of the early cinematic experience, of rural audiences' first encounter with a new medium, independent of that medium's content.[44]

It was doubtlessly a magical experience to observe distant worlds, many of which were modern, urban, and sometimes foreign, in lively, moving images, enabled by the delivery system of the railroad. Modern civilization did not fully arrive in every village in Chosŏn, but cinemobility allowed the villager-audience the virtual experience of its affluent lifestyles and manners and promised its arrival in the future. At the same time, cine-mobility situated these subjects in a specific power relation. While neither Taishō nor his successor Shōwa ever visited Korea in person during Japan's colonial rule, colonial audiences could still participate in imperial pageantry and were led to worship the ruler through these experiences of cine-mobility. The emperor never visited the colony, but his cinematic double did by train.

Locomotive Modernity

What, then, was the nature of those gestures of the modern world delivered by train? With the nationwide networks of railroads linking major towns and shrinking the distances between them, a new sense of place, a "panoramic perception," emerged.[45] This new sense of time and space constituted "a new sense of national simultaneity."[46] The panoramic vision enabled by the railroad system resonated with another new mode of seeing—namely, cinema. The panoramic view on the train, for example, has a clear counterpart in film's tracking shot, both of which were entirely new ways of seeing introduced to Korea by the West.

Railway mobility on film was not a new concept but, rather, a feature dating back to the birth of cinema, and not limited to the famous first screening of Lumiere's *The Arrival of a Train* (1895) either. As Lynne Kirby points out, "the train is a mechanical double for the cinema," in that both are "a machine of vision and an instrument for conquering space and time."[47] While the Great Powers were vying for railway construction contracts to further their imperial ambitions in Asia, travelers like Holmes were introducing Western audiences to those far-off, exotic locales by exhibiting photographs and films that employed the ethnographic gaze. Both railway journeys and cinematic experiences taught people a new sense of time and place—compressing, shrinking, and occupying the globe. The "train-cinema interface" is thus not only "paradigmatic of the modern" but also paradigmatic of colonialism.[48]

The Great Powers saw the railroad system as basic infrastructure for colonization, and its objective was to mobilize people for economic, military, and political purposes as well as for cultural and educational reasons.

In turn, colonial authorities used cinema as a tool to make people more cognizant of both the ruler's gaze and the new ways of seeing now available to them—developments indispensable for mobilizing colonial subjects. As a means of imperialist mobility, cinema therefore was coessential with the railroad system, one that enabled the ocular domination of colonial power. The railroad system was a mechanism for the "management of the population," whereby people were induced to accept and internalize discipline under such ocular domination.[49] I call modernity under this type of biopower *locomotive modernity.*

Locomotive modernity presupposes the following features. First, it entails collectivity in motion and vision. The train-cinema interface obliged people to share the same points of departure and arrival with others. "The official timetabling of mobility that accompanied the railways" generated a sense of modern temporality, which compelled everyone to participate in collective discipline under the threat of falling behind.[50] These same conditions applied to every individual who wanted to watch a film, either at the theater or at a traveling exhibition. Spectatorship necessitated the intermingling of groups of people, as well as an uninterrupted stretch of time, since once the movie started, the projector had to run to the end of the final reel without pause. Such collectivity resonated with the politics of cinematic representations in the colonial era. In a spy film in colonial Korea, *Military Train* (*Kunyong yŏlch'a*, 1938), the train is depicted not only as a vehicle of military importance but also as an allegory of the Japanese Empire. Communist spies try to discover the train's schedule, while the protagonist fights to keep it out of enemy hands and preserve national security. In turn, a tourist culture film, *Tokyo-Peking: Through Tyosen and Manchukuo* (1939), adopts the view from a train that departs, ostensibly, from Tokyo and heads for northern China. As discussed in chapter 2, each episode in the film illustrates the train's route on a map, tracing the spatial composition of the empire. In these images of the empire, the future was presented as possible only through collective dreaming, as the cinematic virtual journey was set up as a group tour by train proceeding toward yet-to-be conquered areas.

Collectivity in motion and vision links organically to the second feature of locomotive modernity—namely, centralizing movement. Trains linked each location to one another in a seemingly even network of routes;

however, every movement on the railroads was oriented toward a center. Subsequent distinctions between the central destinations and the rest resulted in a hierarchical rearrangement of living spaces, while a hierarchy was also established among the central destinations. The totality of movement on the system generated both the centripetal force toward Tokyo and the centrifugal force to untapped territories. Furthering this imperializing movement, cinema in turn centralized vision by situating audiences as the imperial subject behind the camera. For example, journeys in tourist culture films, such as *Tokyo-Peking*, feature the train confirming the dominions of the empire and visually hinting at future territories beyond even those borders, letting the audience recognize the centrifugal kinetic energy that comes from the center of the empire to its margins (see chapter 2). Both the centripetal and centrifugal forces constitute a loop of the imperial circulation of people, goods, knowledge, and gaze. Tellingly, in the 1941 commercial Korean film *Spring of the Peninsula* (*Pando ŭi pom*), the protagonist couple boards a train to Tokyo, embarking on the movement toward the center of the empire to bring expertise back to the local Korean film industry. While the Tokyo-bound couple in this film physically moves toward the center, we can figuratively say that the soldier in *Volunteer* heading for the front line also moves to the center, affirming loyalty to the empire.

Scheduling and stability constitute another feature of locomotive modernity. Train journeys and film screenings entailed regularly scheduled events. The forward movement of the train and cinema was tied to the idea of progress, if a rather conservative one, as any altered or derailed courses were seen as unacceptable. In *Military Train*, the train conductor claims that a five-minute delay would be fatal for everyone, underscoring how, in the regulated systems of train and cinema, flexibility was considered unstable and hazardous. In *Sweet Dream*, there is a clear, sharp contrast between the railroad system and automobile traffic. Though the film was sponsored by the *Sŏn-Man (Chosŏn-Manchuria) Traffic Times* (J. *Senman kōtsū taimususha*), specifically to serve as guidance for auto traffic, it nevertheless portrays a taxi car colliding with the heroine's daughter and subsequently foiling the heroine's escape by train.[51] On the other hand, the train is presented as embodying hope for a better future, one that the heroine could not reach because she had deviated from the prescribed route.

Automobile: The Uncontrollable Vehicle of Lust

Although the flexibility of automobiles in *Sweet Dream* raises concerns about unexpected negative developments, such as collision, the contrast between automobiles and trains also leaves room for probing the tensions underlying the popular imagination of modern mobility in colonial Korea. In particular, the taxi's reckless speeding alongside the train highlights its dangerous and uncontrollable qualities, which become irrefutable proof when it collides with Aesun's daughter. However, the automobile's exterior décor and sleek curves not only symbolize the woman's precarious situation by their slippery surface but also, by their agile look, show off her boldness and determination in pursuing her own desires (see fig. 1.7). Effectively, the automobile is another manifestation of her character. While her extramarital relationship and irresponsible behavior toward her daughter are framed in ways that invite criticism and justify her conviction

FIGURE 1.7 The contrast between a train and a car in *Sweet Dream* (1936).

in the last scene, her lifestyle of consumption is presented as a point of attraction in the film. The film uses the extramarital affair scenes to present her views of the department store and the modern theater and simultaneously sets up the viewer to peek at these novelties with ambivalence. As discussed earlier, the flexible mobility of an automobile grants the would-be passenger a slight chance to catch a missed train, even though it would end up in failure in colonial Korean cinema.

It is worth noting that the automobiles populating films in the 1930s served as symbols of the urban elite's consumer lifestyles. In *Crossroads of Youth* (*Ch'ŏngch'un ŭi sipcharo*, 1934), the private car is presented as the vehicle of the leisure classes. Kaech'ŏl, a rich playboy, and his cronies drive Yŏngok, the protagonist's tragic sister, to the riverside in the middle of a weekday. While Yŏngbok, the protagonist, came to the big city from a rural village and works hard as a porter at Seoul Station, these rich men spontaneously leave town in a private car to enjoy nature. The 1939 film *Fisherman's Fire* (*Ŏhwa*) presents a similar scene: when Insun goes to Seoul by train, Ch'ŏlssu, a rich libertine, tricks her into an involuntary sexual relationship. Upon her arrival at Seoul Station, he takes her to suburban tourist attractions in a sleek, open car. His actions strike a sharp contrast with Insun's lover, Ch'ŏnsŏk, who used to recite poetry under a tree in their rural village. Likewise, the rich business owner in *Spring of the Peninsula* also tries to lure the female protagonist, Chŏnghŭi, with his car. In this way, the flexible mobility of an automobile in colonial Korean cinema many times functions as an emblem of urban masculinity, characterized by wealth and power, whereas the regulated mobility of a train is associated with an idealized masculinity, honest, sincere, and firmly rooted in the rural hometown.

However, as mentioned earlier, there is no doubt that such urban mobility was a spectacle intended to attract the audience's attention. As a case in point, the picnic scene in *Fisherman's Fire* takes up a bizarre, lengthy part of the film, where Insun and Ch'ŏlssu hike up a trail in the mountain, enjoy the scenic beauty of the valley, and take a picture in front of a waterfall (see fig. 1.8). With Ch'ŏlssu's hiking outfit, the scene presents itself like something out of a tourist brochure. Likewise, the picnic scene in *Crossroads of Youth* gives the viewer a moment to appreciate natural scenery and take in peaceful images, even though Kaech'ŏl's group

FIGURE 1.8 A picnic scene in *Fisherman's Fire* (1939).

has been marked out as the film's antagonists. The urban mobility attached to the wealthy masculine conjoins here to suggest the ideal urbanite's spectacular leisure trends.

The element of automobile culture in colonial films also points to women's social mobility. In *Crossroads of Youth*, Kyesun, the protagonist's lover, works at a gas station in Seoul. In the exotic Mobil Oil uniform, she strikes a considerably different impression from when she is wearing traditional clothes (see fig. 1.9). In *Fisherman's Fire*, Insun's hometown friend, Okpun, is a bus attendant. She is depicted as a capable woman with confident gestures, one who can afford to live in the strange, new environment of the city. She even rescues Insun from prostitution and rejects Ch'ŏlssu's money. In turn, though she ultimately fails to escape, Aesun's conduct in a car also reveals her ability to navigate the busy urban spaces in *Sweet Dream*, while her chase scene serves as thrilling entertainment.

FIGURE 1.9 Kyesun in a Mobil Oil uniform in *Crossroads of Youth* (1934).

The question, then, is how these potentialities posed by automobility lead to the deadlock of locomotive modernity. The frequent contrasts between train and automobile underscore their respective roles in colonial Korean cinema, with the former signifying sublime destiny, and the latter individual endeavor that cannot overcome that destiny. Even so, it is important to note that all these failures with respect to automobiles encapsulate unrealized desires.

There is a distinct difference in how women's mobility, its functions and potential, are conceived in the colony and in the space of the colonizing power. This difference might be best observed in two consecutive films by the Japanese director Fushimizu Osamu (also known as Fushimizu Shu): *Woman in Tokyo* (J. *Tōkyō no josei*, 1939) and *China Nights* (J. *Shina no yoru*, 1940). The first film tells the story of a car saleswoman in Tokyo, who forges her own career path. Originally a typist at a car company, she sets out to enter the male-dominated world of car sales and is a great success. When her fellow salesman, to whom she is attracted, chooses her sister as his bride, the director presents his viewers with an impressive chase scene, one that visualizes the main thrust of the film: the female protagonist drives her sleek, open car to pass the train carrying the newlyweds, and once the car reaches an overpass before the train, she directs a proud smile at the camera.

The same director's subsequent film, *China Nights*, stars Li Xianglan, an ethnically Japanese actress who pretended to be Chinese. Born Yamaguchi Yoshiko in Manchuria, she rose to fame as an actress for the Manchukuo Film Association (J. Manshū eiga kyōkai, hereafter Man'ei). Man'ei was a propaganda film studio sponsored by the State of Manchuria (C. Mǎnzhōuguó, hereafter Manchukuo) and co-owned by the South Manchuria Railway (J. Minami manshū kabushiki kaisha, hereafter Mantetsu).[52] As a propaganda machine, Man'ei was cultivated by Mantetsu and its film infrastructures, such as "the exhibition of films along the railway lines."[53] Fushimizu's decision to cast Li Xianglan as the heroine of *China Nights* was, no doubt, motivated by a desire to capitalize on her fame, which had grown on Mantetsu's railway lines. Li's on-screen image, however, was obviously the antithesis of *Woman in Tokyo*'s protagonist. Though Li's character appears, at first, like a wild animal who rejects social mores, as is typical of such a story in the style of *Taming of the Shrew*, the rebellious, young Chinese woman gradually becomes a docile and sweet companion for a Japanese marine officer. She does not own a vehicle that she can fully control; rather, as she sits on the banks of the Suzhou, a famous tourist attraction near Shanghai, she is presented like an object in a tourist postcard, one that might have attracted passengers for the Sen–Man–Shi tourist train (see chapter 2). When juxtaposed with *Woman in Tokyo*, *China Nights* clearly glamorizes a woman fully dependent on her male partner, on an unseen flow of railroad mobility—an end shared, notably, with the female *antagonist* in the first film.

For women both in the empire's metropole and in the colony, the promised freedom of automobility likely remained a prolonged aspiration, since it was never entirely realized under the actual conditions of everyday life or even in the popular imagination. In fact, the idea of women's freedom of automobility in the cinematic imagination was nearly postponed indefinitely until the end of World War II. Therefore, we might understand the desire for individual mobility by car as primed to undermine the locomotive modernity of the Japanese Empire such that when the U.S. Army paraded in Jeeps among the newly liberated people, they were able to win the hearts and minds of the majority, developments I discuss further in chapter 3. After colonial rule, it seems that people had instead chosen to get off the track of railroad mobility, even as that meant entering into another power relation that generated new sets of loops and hierarchies.

CHAPTER 2

Cinematic Railway Tourism in the "New Order in East Asia"

As the Japanese Empire entered a state of war in the 1930s, particularly with the invasion of Manchuria in 1931 and the Second Sino-Japanese War in 1937, culture film (K. *munhwa yŏnghwa*, J. *bunka eiga*) came into its golden days and flourished in the empire's film markets. "Culture film" was a term imported and translated from the German *Kulturfilm*, broadly conceived as a category of film that included documentary, newsreel, and educational films. The shift to wartime attitudes extended the scope of culture film production, including news from the battlefields, scenery and customs of newly occupied territories, and educational pictures to enlighten wartime audiences. Moreover, conditions favoring culture filmmaking in the empire fostered the industry's growth. Major Japanese film production companies, such as Toho and Shochiku, established independent units for culture filmmaking,[1] and colonial authorities, including the Japanese government-general of Korea, supported the distribution of culture films with legal and structural mandates, such as tax favors and mandatory showings in movie theaters.[2]

In colonial Korea, a vast array of screening events was organized in the name of "social reform films," "propaganda films," "military films," or "hygiene films."[3] The government-general's Regulation for Censorship of Motion Picture Films, enacted in July 1926, was revised in 1933 to include a clause that exempted "films with contents for the social good," "films that were used by public offices, schools, and public bodies for the public interest," and "films that were released at no charge by newspapers or news agencies for the common good" from censorship fees, while the Regulation for the Control of Motion Picture Films, enacted in August 1934, included a clause for "compulsory screenings when acknowledged as necessary for social reforms" of culture films in Korean movie theaters.[4]

In this heyday of culture films, it is worth noting that their major themes were not limited to education, social reform, or the military but also included tourism. Records show that most tourism-oriented culture films from the late 1930s were sponsored by railway authorities, such as the Railway Bureau of the government-general of Korea and Mantetsu, and produced by private film production companies, such as Nikkatsu and Shochiku. No doubt these films were meant to encourage railway tourism. Nikkatsu, for instance, chose Ch'oe Sŭng-hŭi, a famous dancer, to star in *Tae kŭmgangsan po* (*The Great Mt. Kŭmgang Saga*, 1938), a film commissioned by the Railway Bureau when it weighed its potential box-office value and distributed through "each tourist information office for visitors to Chosŏn and Manchuria."[5] It enjoyed "extensive" publicity,[6] and it reportedly "achieved great success in promoting journeys to Chosŏn and Manchuria."[7] A number of strategies were deployed in producing the film, such as having the popular novelist Hamamoto Hiroshi contribute an original script, filming directly on the mountain to obtain magnificent views, and sending Japanese writers to Chosŏn to gather sources for scripts.[8] A similar trend runs through several other films commissioned by the Railway Bureau, including the Shochiku-produced *Kyŏul ŭi chosŏn* (*Chosŏn in Winter*), *Yaktong hanŭn chosŏn* (*Vibrant Chosŏn*), *Tae kyŏngsŏng* (*Great Keijō*), *Kyŏngsŏng* (*Keijō*), and *Tongmudŭl* (*Friends*) and Nikkatsu's *Chosŏn ŭi yŏhaeng* (*Journey to Chosŏn*), *Tae kŭmgangsan po* (*The Great Mt. Kŭmgang Saga*), and *Taeryuk eŭi kil* (*Road to the Continent*). This is also true of films commissioned by Mantetsu, which include *Hikyō nekka* (*Untraveled Regions in Jehol*), *Sōgen Baruga* (*Barga Grasslands*), *Mantetsu sanju-nen* (*Thirty Years of Mantetsu*), and *Manshū daizu* (*Manchurian Soybean*) (all directed by Akutagawa Kozo).[9]

Barak Kushner points out that, at the time, propaganda publicized Japan's modernity by taking up the theme of *tourism*.[10] Since they promoted an image of the Japanese Empire as "bringing" modernity and technology "to Asia," tourist guides, travel brochures, and blueprints for train-related projects were seen as "indicative of its imperial prestige."[11]

The railroad authorities promoted tourist attractions, ranging from colonial Korea to northern China via Manchukuo, that were entirely new to the majority of audiences. Likewise, most audiences had yet to experience things like modern lifestyles and modern cities connected by trains. Accordingly, tourism-oriented culture films served as a means of acquiring that experience, allowing many audiences to virtually visit these previously unseen, imperial territories as the modernized world.

This chapter looks at culture films, particularly those with tourist narratives, to identify what experiences propaganda authorities intended for colonial audiences through such virtual tourism. However, this chapter does not approach virtual/cinematic tourism as structured by a binary propaganda sender-receiver relation but, rather, traces the success or failure of its intended shared world-as-gesture and the negotiation of its consumption.

Tourist Culture Films and Ocularcentrism

We might speculate that, through tourist culture film production and distribution, propaganda authorities sought to show the as-yet-unseen imperial territories and as-yet-unknown modern world to audiences largely unfamiliar with both. It is important to note that these authorities saw the visual (particularly cinematic) experience of unfamiliar objects as an effective propaganda tool. This view is inextricably linked with the belief that new experiences, particularly as presented by visual media, could influence viewers and mobilize them in specific ways. What, then, were the epistemological grounds for such a belief?

Clearly, for the authorities in production, propaganda filmmaking was a way of exercising photographic indexicality. Newsreels were seen as advancing the empire's efforts by visualizing the "true picture" of government projects and conditions of war. Documentary films were thought to be instructive, since the "true images" of these strange, distant places were seen as furthering people's understanding of the world. This perception of film as a recording tool, one that proves the reality of existing objects, resonates with the West's long-standing preoccupation with the hegemony of vision. As Heidegger observed, ocularcentrism has dominated

Greek and Western philosophy, in which vision is distinctly prioritized over the other senses.[12] Vision is understood as enabling the subject to perceive the world objectively, while photography and film were the media of the ocular objectivity rooted in science and technology. Jonathan Crary argues that in the nineteenth century, photography became a "form of social power" "homologous" with money, given that "they are equally totalizing systems for binding and unifying all subjects within a single global network of valuation and desire."[13] Photographic indexicality was regarded as a scientific tool, as calculable and exchangeable as the value of money. Therefore, propaganda film, misunderstood as a successive construct of photographic images, should instead be understood as a medium embodying the empire's presence—its power to direct the scientific gaze over the governed and its wealth to exercise such power—through its indexing function.

Vision as a tool of the empire equated to imperial expansion. Anne Friedberg cites Comolli in observing, "The second half of the nineteenth century lives in a sort of *frenzy of the visible*," the effect of "something of a geographical extension of the *field of the visible* . . . by journies [sic], explorations, colonizations."[14] While this statement describes the colonial world's inclusion in the field of the visible, visibility here remains the property of Westerners or, more precisely, the expansionists. If the second half of the nineteenth century was "the frenzy of the visible" under the European scopic regime, for the non-European scopic regime, it was the frenzy of the imperial gaze penetrating everyday life, which, up until that point, had been invisible to Europe. Friedberg's historiographical question, whether "the invention of photography produced a crisis that led to continued optical research, or the nineteenth-century obsession with optical research produced a crisis that led to photography," is not so relevant to these new territories of the visible, where the invasion of photography produced a crisis that necessitated optical research.[15] As Paul Virilio has theorized, optical modernity in the West led to the "logistics of military perception" under its own scopic regime;[16] however, the process of "extending the field of visible" through such logistics is necessarily different from the experience of being targeted under such an extension, of being deceived by visions from extending foreign forces, as was the case for optical modernity in the post/colonial world.[17] The Western scopic regimes have maintained expansionist or imperialist mobility as a core component of their interactions with the rest of the world. Similarly, the historian Jie-hyun Lim asserts that "Western modernity had colonialist genocidal violence as a built-in part" and that "Nazism was not exceptional or unmodern, but it just overstepped the line by slaughtering White people [Ashkenazi Jews] in the heart of Europe instead of colored people,"[18] the latter a reference to W. E. B. Du Bois's memoir of his third trip to the Warsaw ghetto.[19] If one examines the features of scopic regimes in the non-Western post/colonial world, or its modernity in general, the key distinction from their Western counterparts will be the lack of expansionist or imperialist mobility as a built-in feature. It is therefore important to identify what post/colonial modernity has had as built-in parts, which will lead to a better understanding of the heteronomous spectatorship under the imperial/colonial authority—more so than focusing on the imperial colonizer's violent expansionist habitus or what kinds of scopic regimes emerged among those subjected to the expanding vision.

In the imperial expansionist projects, photographic images captured new and unfamiliar objects in the framed world, and the viewer could enjoy the sense of possessing the world through the act of viewing. Tom Gunning points out that using postcards as "evidence of travel" was an act of "appropriating the world through images."[20] We can understand the boom in tourist culture films within the Japanese Empire as tied to this sense of possession through ocularcentrism. When Chosŏn and Manchuria appeared in tourist culture films, they became objects of possession for the imperial viewer. Through those films, Chosŏn and Manchuria were appropriated as new territories of the empire, and their images became part of the cine-mobility as imperial visual practices. Furthermore, the cinematic practice of moving images, paralleling the virtual movement of trains in films, likely assured audiences of the empire's expansion. In this sense, tourist culture filmmaking in colonial Korea can be understood as a project to constitute the modern subject, one that could experience and realize industrial modernization and imperial expansion.

However, Gunning defines the early tourist film audience as "not a detached contemplative spectator" nor a Cartesian subject but, rather, as "a physiologically stimulated observer."[21] This is in line with Crary's definition of the modern observer as "one effect of the construction of a new kind of subject or individual in the nineteenth century," one that marked a departure from Cartesian vision "to found human knowledge on a purely objective view of the world."[22] It was the subject that spontaneously and productively found arbitrary meanings in a vast array of subjective experiences. As Gunning's theorization has been drawn from Western audiences' experiences in the late nineteenth and early twentieth centuries, a time when burgeoning transportation industries were promoting mass tourism, his conclusions cannot simply be superimposed upon the processes of subject formation in the imperial Japanese colonies. However, he argues that "the viewer of travel films is not simply a surrogate of the tourist" but someone who "can have her thrill" of illusory travel safe in the cinema seat that "the tourist never enjoys."[23] Gunning's characterization thus allows us to link the modern observer and the colonial audience in Korea. Much like the modern observer, the viewer of tourist culture films in colonial Korea did not simply accept a single, monolithic worldview promoted by propaganda authorities but more likely faced a world-as-gesture constructed in response to viewers' desires and needs.

In the following section, I investigate the "pictures" that tourist culture films sought to present and explore the possibility of "escape and flight" in those world-as-gestures, whereby the viewer might resist the ruling authorities' attempts at persuasion.[24]

The Tourists in Nai-Sen-Man Tourism

Bruno Lasker, a researcher who studied the relationship between the East Asian region and the West, produced a report for the Institute of Pacific Relations, where he examined printed propaganda materials distributed by Japan and China in the United States, specifically from July to December 1937. His conclusion was that the United States, then a potential opponent of the Japanese Empire, had sensed Japan's efforts to promote tourism for propagandistic reasons.[25] "Promotion of tourist travel and the staging of special events to bring foreign visitors" highlighted "a country's hospitality, exhibitions, 'embassies of good-will,' the dispatch of cultural emissaries—musicians, lecturers on non-political subjects, touring dramatic companies—participation in scientific congresses and athletic meets, gifts to nations and communities, usually of characteristic art products, publications picturing the finer sides of the national social life," all of which were "reliable messengers."[26] Starting in 1913, the Railway Bureau of Japan (J. Tetsudō-in) began introducing mainland Japan, "Chōsen &

Manchuria," and northern China as tourist destinations by publishing an English guide called *An Official Guide to Eastern Asia: Trans-Continental Connections between Europe and Asia*.[27] Similar tourist information projects were underway even amid wartime conditions in the 1930s.[28] For instance, the Japan Tourist Bureau (J. Kokusai kankō kyoku) invited twenty American female elementary schoolteachers and athletes to tour Japan in order to spread propaganda.[29]

Tourism as propaganda, however, was not aimed just at those outside the Japanese Empire. The rapid industrial success of tourism since the early twentieth century accelerated with changes in technological and spatial conditions, such as the development of the railroad industry and the expansion of the empire. The extended radius of the Japanese transportation system stimulated people's interests in traveling outward. The Japan Travel Association (J. Nippon ryokō bunka kyōkai) was established in February 1924, representing the heads of organizations like the Ministry of Railways of Japan, Mantetsu, the Japan Mail Shipping Company (J. Nippon yūsen kabushiki kaisha), the Osaka Commercial Shipping Company (J. Ōsaka shōsen kabushiki kaisha), and the Taiwan Railway Company (J. Taiwan tetsudō kabushiki kaisha), and its magazine, *Travel* (J. *Tabi*), which was first published in April the same year.[30] Beginning roughly around 1937, the Ministry of Foreign Affairs of Japan supervised the Eastern Cultural Affairs project (J. Tōhō bunka jigyō), which organized student tours of the Man-Sen-Shi (Manchuria-Chosŏn-China, J. Manshū-Chōsen-Shina) regions for cultural exchange, vocational training, and language study.[31] The 1937 *Manshū no tabi* (*Journey to Manchuria*), commissioned by Mantetsu and the Railway Bureau of the Japanese Government-General in Korea to promote tourism, had a "Naichi-hen" (Mainland episode) that suggested Japan as a starting point, largely by introducing the Sen-Man tourist information centers in Tokyo, Osaka, Shimonoseki, and Moji. Tourism in Chosŏn and Manchuria, referred to as Sen-Man or Man-Sen tourism, catered to the demand for outbound travel, while simultaneously educating Japanese people about the dynamism of imperial expansion, letting them see the borders and territories of their empire expanding toward northern China via Chosŏn and Manchuria. This kind of outbound travel was occasionally referred to as Nai-Sen-Man (Mainland-Chosŏn-Manchuria) tourism, as evidenced by the 1937 film *Nai-Sen-Man shūyū no tabi* (*Journey from Mainland to Chosŏn and Manchuria*).

Tourism as propaganda also affected colonized Koreans. "Group sightseeing trips to the mainland" (*naeji kwan'gwangdan*), popular in the 1900s and early 1910s, were intended to persuade Korean participants of the necessity of Japanese colonial rule, mainly by exhibiting modernized sceneries of Japan.[32] On the other hand, the promotion of tourism in Manchuria, which took off in the 1920s and 1930s, aimed to characterize Chosŏn as the empire's subordinate partner, largely by depicting Koreans as imperial subjects who could travel and witness, firsthand, the underdevelopment of newly subjugated imperial territories and yet-to-be conquered areas. As it had done in Japan, the Japan Tourist Bureau opened information offices in Kyŏngsŏng (J. Keijō, Seoul) in 1930 and later in Pyongyang.[33] The Information Office for Korean Students' Educational Tours (Chosŏn haksaeng kyŏnhaktan annaeso) also opened in 1930 and promoted school trips to Manchuria.[34]

Lasker identifies the participants in these tours as "involuntary propagandists," a view that sets the tourists apart from voluntary propagandists, or the propaganda authorities.[35] By contrast, Min-ju Han argues that those tourists were "quasi-imperialists," mobilized to "search for their romantic self in the power of systemical construction of the Japanese Empire."[36] These two contrasting views have their own limits that curtail a fuller inquiry into the tourists' visual experiences. In particular, the former ignores the possibility of subjectivization even in the involuntary mediation of propagandistic ideas, while the latter assumes only one relation between the tourist experience and the participant's reaction. These limits are theoretically related to the heteronomous or induced spectatorship of tourist culture films, which I discuss later in this chapter.

Imagined Geographies of the "New Order in East Asia"

The tourist films sponsored or produced by the Japan Tourist Bureau, Mantetsu, or the Railway Bureau of the Japanese government-general appear to have followed a similar format. Both *Manshū no tabi* and *Sen-Man shūyū no tabi* (*Journey to Chosŏn and Manchuria*), the 1937 films sponsored by the Osaka Commercial Shipping Company, have the

"Naichi-hen" (Mainland episodes) that introduce the ways tourists could acquire information and make reservations in Japan, which would subsequently serve as their point of departure. These opening episodes were followed by other films on Chosŏn and Manchuria in an omnibus format, as evidenced by the "Manshū-hen" (Manchuria episode) in *Nai-Sen-Man shūyū no tabi.*

Tokyo-Peking: Through Tyosen and Manchoukuo (*Tokyo-Beijing: Through Chosŏn and Manchukuo*, 1939; hereafter *Tokyo-Peking*) also uses the omnibus format. Sponsored by the Japan Tourist Bureau and produced by the Tōhō Film Company (hereafter Toho), *Tokyo-Peking* seems to make its first appearance in the media in 1938, when a Korean newspaper reports on the start of its filming.[37] According to the article, filming was initially intended to take place in several locations, including Tokyo, Kyoto, Nara, Osaka, Miyajima, Kyŏngsŏng, Mt. Kŭmgang, the Amnok River (Yalu River), Mukden (Shenyang), Hsinking (Changchun), Harbin, Dairen (Dalian), Jehol (Chengde), Shanhaiguan, Peking (Beijing), and Datong.[38] However, there are no confirmed records of the entire range of filming locations.[39] Currently, the longest version of the film is in Toho's Nichiei Archive in Tokyo, and it shows how tourist attractions in colonial Korea (the "Tyosen" episode), planned cities in Manchukuo ("Manchoukuo"), and some northern cities of China ("North China") could be reached by train.[40] While the Toho version is dubbed in English, likely to better attract foreign tourists, there was also a Japanese version that could have been shown throughout the empire. *Chosŏn Sketch* (J. *Chōsen sobyō*), a tourist culture film in Japanese, has the same images and editing as the "Tyosen" episode of *Tokyo-Peking*.[41] Most likely, *Chosŏn Sketch* shared key elements of its visual and narrative structures with other tourist culture films produced and distributed in the Japanese Empire.

The "Tyosen" episode consists of three major parts. The first part depicts beautiful natural and cultural heritage sites in Chosŏn, such as Mt. Kŭmgang, the Pulguksa Temple, and the Sŏkkuram Grotto. The second part introduces Kyŏngsŏng as a modernized city, while the third shows a boat excursion on the Taedong River and a train departing for Manchukuo. The "Tyosen" episode presents a comprehensive and accomplished picture of the colony, including the images of everyday life therein, particularly when juxtaposed with the "Manchoukuo" episode, which involves disjointed images of different ethnic cultures, and with the "North China" episode, which focuses on exploring China's famous tourist destinations, such as cultural and historic heritage sites. The differences in portrayal show that Chosŏn was recognized as a stable colony, in light of its relatively longer status under colonial rule.

The "Tyosen" episode also predominantly features images of femininity. Most scenes with human figures in this episode depict Chosŏn women in white *hanbok* (Korean traditional clothes; see fig. 2.1), taking up roles that range from domestic labor, such as washing and ironing clothes, to traditional cultural activities, such as *nŏlttwigi* (a seesaw-like jumping game), archery, and Buddhist dance, to partaking in imported foreign customs, such as Shinto ceremonies and modern college education. Likewise, Chosŏn as a whole is represented as feminine. This representation is in keeping with "a trope in colonial thoughts," specifically the "feminising of colonised territories."[42] For example, the episode's male narrator jokes about a woman at a washing place—"Watch out, my fair one, or you'll thwack your little fingers!"—pretending that he is hitting on her, perhaps bearing in mind male audiences. Both this flirting scene and the exotic portrayal of a boat excursion on the Taedong River with *kisaeng* (female artists providing entertainment and sexual services) in the latter part of the episode position the viewer as a colonizer that can consume or possess feminine images of the colony.

In the same vein, a train bound for Manchuria through Chosŏn conveys a masculine image that contrasts with the "feminine penetrability" of the colonial territory.[43] The steam locomotive traversing the peaceful plains of Chosŏn (see fig. 2.2) is a rapid, steel machine that contrasts sharply with the low speed and malleable texture of colonial lands. White women and men, together with Japanese tourists who are dressed smartly, occupy the train, which has a Western-style interior design. The train demonstrates the dynamism of embarking on the path toward Manchuria, with the sound effect of the train puffing, as soon as the trip to Chosŏn ends and the "Tyosen" episode wraps up. In this universe, the locomotive thus functions as a phallic signifier that organizes the modernity of the Japanese Empire.

Compared with the other two episodes, the "Manchoukuo" episode noticeably emphasizes the presence of the train. It repeatedly stresses that each region representing Manchukuo, such as Mukden, Hsinking, Dairen,

FIGURE 2.1 Women in the "Tyosen" episode of *Tokyo-Peking: Through Tyosen and Manchoukuo* (1939). Courtesy of Toho Stella Nichiei Archive.

FIGURE 2.2 A train traversing the plains in *Tokyo-Peking* (1939). Courtesy of Toho Stella Nichiei Archive.

Harbin, and Jehol, is linked with the others through the railroad system. While the train is shown only at the beginning and end of each trip in Chosŏn and northern China, it takes on a major role throughout the whole trip in Manchukuo. This distinction is due to the fact that the state of Manchukuo worked closely with Mantetsu to manage the territories.[44] Since Mantetsu commenced operations in northeastern China in 1907, the company had grown not only to provide transportation for the region but also to administer the "semi-colonial territories."[45] In these territories, the company functioned as a "quasi-governmental" body until 1945.[46] The "Manchoukuo" episode shows that the organizing principle of Manchukuo was still based on the railroad system in the late 1930s, even though management of the territories had been seized by the Kwantung Army after its invasion of Manchuria in 1931.[47] The next section of this chapter provides a deeper analysis of this episode.

The final episode of *Tokyo-Peking*, "North China," provides an exploratory look at the Orient. Right after showing the train's arrival at Peking Station, the camera makes its way through the crowd in a busy marketplace in downtown Peking. This one-minute dolly shot consists of dynamic movements filmed from the viewpoint on a rickshaw, reminding the viewer that the view is from the eyes of a tourist curiously observing the new scenery. The following scenes of historic sites in Peking also demonstrate the conventional style of encountering exotic tourist attractions on film. A series of door-opening scenes cuts through the frames to disclose the magnificent palaces of the Forbidden City or the authentic pavilions of Jingshan Park, while a shot evoking the composition of a tourist postcard showcases a woman in a traditional Chinese outfit next to the Temple of Heaven, and a sequence with a guardian lion in the Forbidden City uses increasingly closer shots—sequentially, a full shot, a close-up, and an extreme close-up—to examine the exotic stone statue (see fig. 2.3). All of these moments exemplify the ethnographic gaze, aesthetically seeking knowledge of an Oriental location—in this case, China—and stirring desires to possess yet-to-be-colonized territories in China. At the same time, such depictions constituted a cinematic apparatus that demonstrated Japan's geopolitical understanding of this region when Japan maintained a "radical anti-Western policy," as manifested by its withdrawal from the League of Nations in 1933 and its entering the Second Sino-Japanese War in 1937.[48] The episode therefore represents the

FIGURE 2.3 Temple of Heaven (top), Jingshan Park (center), and a guardian lion in the Forbidden City (bottom) in the "North China" episode of *Tokyo-Peking* (1939). Courtesy of Toho Stella Nichiei Archive.

space of Asia as anti-Western, in an effort to achieve the goal of "transcending modernity" (J. *kindai no chōkoku*).[49] The cryptic and mystical gaze on old palaces and sculptures in China can be understood in terms of this geopolitical context—that is, as an expression of awe at old Asian tradition comparable to that of the West.

The omnibus format of *Tokyo-Peking*, as discussed in this section, is composed of local imagery from each region in the sphere of the Japanese Empire's influence. But these three regions are interconnected by the railroad system and, therefore, are shown as integrated into a single, seamless tourist route. The same narrator and soundtrack bridge the three episodes and paint a comprehensive picture of the route. In this omnibus format, the stories of three regions are combined into a single travelogue, connecting Tokyo to Peking in a cinematized map of the imagined geographies of *tonga* (J. *tōa*, East Asia). The "new order in East Asia" (K. *tonga sinjilssŏ*, J. *tōa shin chitsujo*), conceptualizing Nai-Sen-Man-Shi (mainland Japan, Chosŏn, Manchuria, and China) as a bloc after the outbreak of the Sino-Japanese War, was cinematically implemented in this imagined geography.[50]

Visual Discipline: Becoming a Tourist Traveling within Imperial Territories

The virtual experience of traveling the world in *Tokyo-Peking* demonstrates the (un)intended visual discipline imposed on colonial audiences by Japanese propaganda authorities—a discipline that implies subsequent forms of subjectivization.

One notable feature in this film is the way it visualizes its geographic worldview. The film opens with an animated sequence that puts "Tyosen," "Manchoukuo," and "North China" together as a whole. When a semicircular line from "Tokyo" reaches "Peking" in "North China," passing through "Tyosen" and "Manchoukuo," a dotted line is drawn from "Peking" to "Tokyo" (see fig. 2.4). This movement, much like the film title, traces a path between the capital of the Japanese Empire and the capital of the former empire yet to be fully conquered.

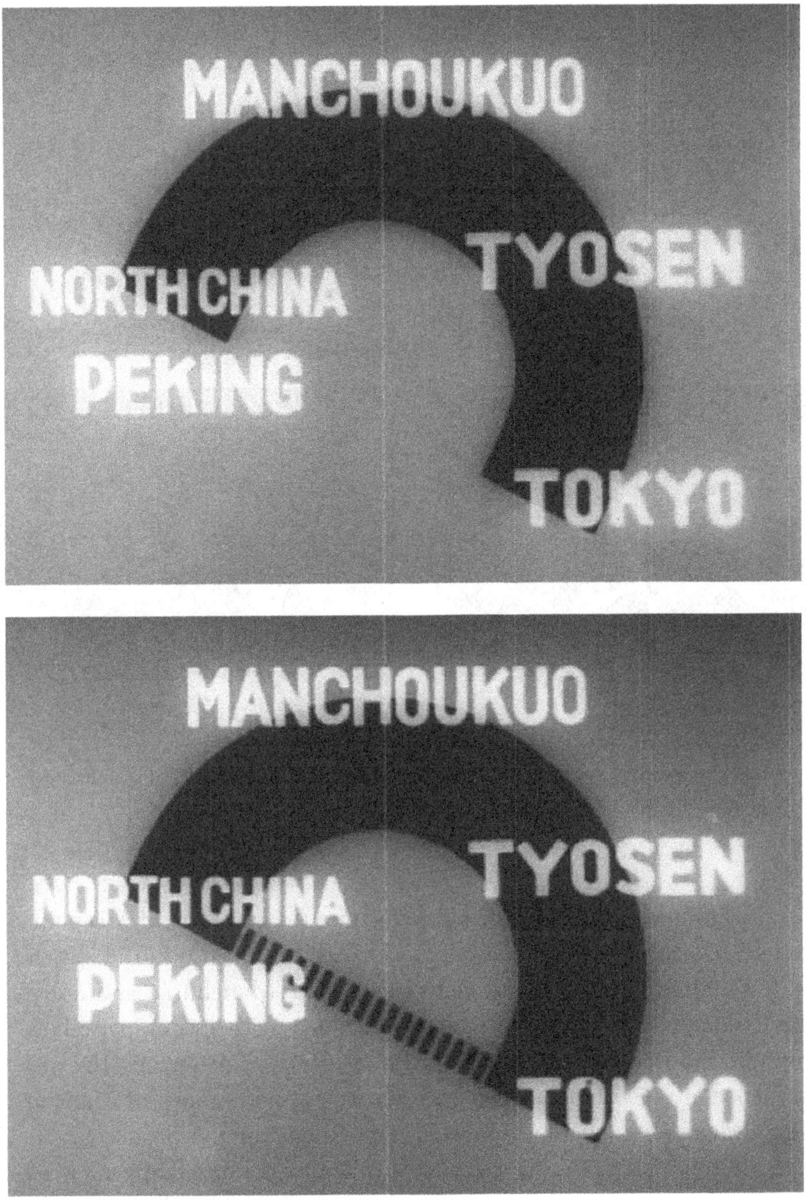

FIGURE 2.4 The opening sequence of *Tokyo-Peking* (1939). Courtesy of Toho Stella Nichiei Archive.

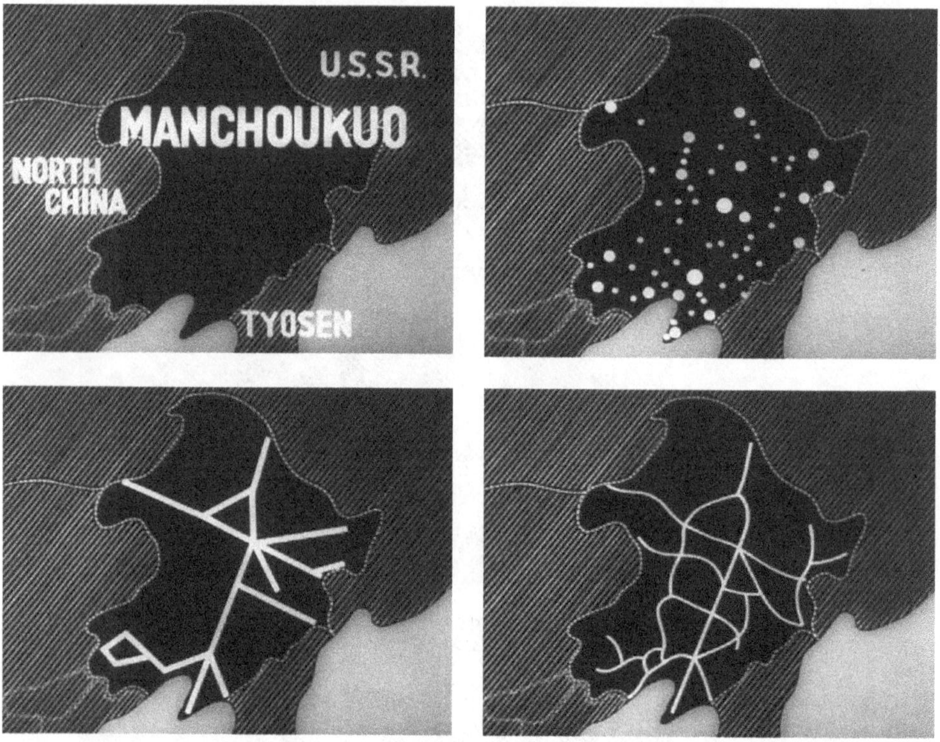

FIGURE 2.5 The map sequence of "Manchoukuo" in *Tokyo-Peking* (1939). Courtesy of Toho Stella Nichiei Archive.

The following depiction of advancing into the continent of Asia points to its purportedly scientific, measurable basis, specifically, in the way the film visualizes the railroad systems in Chosŏn, Manchuria, and northern China. As a case in point, each episode opens with a set of maps showing railroad networks and major cities in the relevant region. The map sequence of the "Manchoukuo" episode begins with a map of Manchukuo drawn to show its geographical position, on the borders of the U.S.S.R. and China (see fig. 2.5). As the names of nations disappear, Manchukuo's major cities are shown on the map with dots. Then, railroad lines and road networks appear, linking these dots. The tracing of railroad lines on the animated map mirrors the railroad journeys in the following sequences, each of which is composed of a departure, in-between movements, and an arrival at the next location. It is a mode of visualization that marks each location as a point of departure and arrival, outlining the development of a traffic network between two points in a linear flow. Through this mode of visualization, space becomes measurable, a development that David Harvey has also identified in Renaissance maps, which, as he argues, generate "a 'coldly geometrical' and 'systematic' sense of space" or "an ability to see the globe as a knowable totality."[51] This sense of space supports the development of a totalizing gaze, one that seeks to measure and comprehend the world. Furthermore, the geometric representation of the empire's current and future territories visually expresses a sense of ownership of those spaces. It presents space as "something usable, malleable, and therefore capable of domination through human action," open to "conquest and control."[52] Tonga, a geography that had mostly existed in the imagination, was given shape through this mode of visualization.

As mentioned above, *Tokyo-Peking*'s "Manchoukuo" episode features sets of departure, movement, and arrival scenes. This episode reconfirms the railroad networks from the map sequence through a montage of destination signs, designating major cities in Manchukuo and northern China (see figs. 2.6–2.11). Images of crowds in and around Mukden Station are juxtaposed with images of moving trains and vehicles so that the resulting montage effectively connects human bodies with transportation mobility. The train whistle in the last shot of the Mukden Station scene smoothly links to the sound of church bells at a cathedral in downtown Mukden, viewed from the front. This is followed by scenes of major tourist attractions, such as the Yamato Hotel, the Manchuria Medical University, the old walls of Mukden, busy commercial streets, a memorial to Japanese soldiers, and the East Mausoleum, where the founding emperor of the Qing dynasty is buried. In the subsequent scene, where the narrator says, "Now our express runs to Hsinking," the episode's setting switches from Mukden to Hsinking. The interstitial shot, depicting the rapid movement of the express, underlines a sense of immediate transition (see fig. 2.12).

The "Manchoukuo" episode connects several locations with one another through this structure of the railroad journey. It presents and encourages viewers to recognize space as a sequence of consecutive images, segmented in shots, recalling what Wolfgang Schivelbusch identifies as

FIGURE 2.6 An establishing shot: daybreak, a view of the street in front of Mukden Station, and the train's arrival in *Tokyo-Peking* (1939). Courtesy of Toho Stella Nichiei Archive.

FIGURE 2.7 Scene from a montage of busy people, vehicles, and streets, accelerated by the speed of the incoming train in *Tokyo-Peking* (1939). Courtesy of Toho Stella Nichiei Archive.

FIGURE 2.8 Scene of people inside the station, waiting for the train in line on the platform in *Tokyo-Peking* (1939). Courtesy of Toho Stella Nichiei Archive.

FIGURE 2.9 A close-up of an incoming train in *Tokyo-Peking* (1939). Courtesy of Toho Stella Nichiei Archive.

FIGURE 2.10 Scene from a montage of destination signs on the sides of trains for Tsitsihar (Qiqihar), Peking, Hsinking, Fushun, and Dairen in *Tokyo-Peking* (1939). Courtesy of Toho Stella Nichiei Archive.

FIGURE 2.11 Scene from a montage that connects the sound of the train's whistle with the front view of a cathedral ringing its bell in *Tokyo-Peking* (1939). Courtesy of Toho Stella Nichiei Archive.

FIGURE 2.12 A train to Hsinking in *Tokyo-Peking* (1939). Courtesy of Toho Stella Nichiei Archive.

"panoramic perception."[53] That is, the world becomes a panoramic view that a viewer takes in by moving from a point of departure to a destination. Through the movement of the mechanical body, the places between the points of departure and arrival—or, the disappearing landscapes that the passenger passes by—become "foreclosed."[54] This panoramic view, along with the in-between "foreclosures," connotes an understanding of space under the model of the modern nation-state, as pursued by the producers Manchukuo and Mantetsu.

Notable among tourist culture films, *Tokyo-Peking* highlights each region's traditions, customs, and cultural heritage, even as the main settings are modern cities. The express running from Mukden to Hsinking arrives in Harbin via Dairen. The narrator calls Harbin "little Russia," and the camera pans along a Russian-style church. The next scene shows local Mantetsu employees dancing and performing traditional music. Soon after, another scene depicts the express rapidly departing for Jehol from Harbin. As that train arrives in Jehol, a former Chinese territory that bordered Inner Mongolia, the viewer is presented with various elements of Tibetan Buddhist culture, including the Lama Temples (Xumi Fushou Temple and Puyou Temple), the Mongol style of architecture, the 500 Arhat statues at Puyou Temple, and the Cham Dance that the narrator calls the Lama Devil Dance (see fig. 2.13).

While these Russian and lama cultures are portrayed as existing within the cultural diversity of Manchukuo as a modern state, the film portrays the railroad—specifically, as a modern transportation system—as that which serves as the link between such diverse cultures and customs. These putatively authentic images are juxtaposed with modern, urban everyday life in Mukden and Hsinking to compose a picture of the state as a whole. The local and ethnic images presented panoramically in the film are tourist attractions in themselves and, at the same time, are also the sine qua non for the imagined geography of Manchukuo and the Japanese Empire. However, such diversity cannot be seen as an apparatus compensating for the foreclosure of in-between spaces; rather, it is a kind of reductionism that attaches each region's characteristics to certain stereotyped images. The select number of pictures taken from local reality, then presented as an unbroken continuum, generates a vision of local spaces as a string of separate, postcard pictures, leaving out in-between spaces and building a map of the nation-state as a totality.

The spectacles of modern living, which repeatedly appear in juxtaposition with these traditional Asian images, further the construction of this imagined map of the nation-state. For instance, the Hsinking sequence demonstrates an interesting mix of modern and traditional imagery (see fig. 2.14). This sequence consists of several shots of what look like a planned city, Hsinking, as the capital of Manchukuo. While the narrator introduces the "Hsinking Second 5-Year Construction Plan" and its effects, the viewer is presented with a series of dynamic scenes, depicting construction sites and well-organized city blocks. Obviously, these images of impressive buildings under construction and stretches of newly built streets were intended to make a spectacle out of the construction itself. The appearance of land surveyors and their instruments, in turn, symbolizes the scientific and rational reason that has pushed the construction of the modern city forward. Then, the camera moves along with a

FIGURE 2.13 Jehol Province in the "Manchoukuo" episode in *Tokyo-Peking* (1939). Courtesy of Toho Stella Nichiei Archive.

FIGURE 2.14 The Hsinking sequence in *Tokyo-Peking* (1939). Courtesy of Toho Stella Nichiei Archive.

van that traces the layout of the streets. After a short scene of children picking flowers, the setting shifts to a film production scene at Man'ei, breaking this documentary's fourth wall by revealing that the scene itself has been performed by an actress. The closing scenes of the Hsinking sequence are a montage of dynamic images of magnificent factories and scenes of harvesting apples and soybeans at a farm. The factory scene consists of several close-up shots of a blast furnace and molten metal, a low-angle shot of the factory with rising steam, and a high-angle shot showing its immense size. The montage parallels these tokens of industrial modernization with traditional Asian customs and natural scenery. The background music of wind instruments lends to the grandeur of this chain of images. This assemblage of diverse images and sounds generates a spectacle for virtually experiencing modernization, depicting Hsinking as the epitome of mechanically driven industrialization.

The Hsinking sequence demonstrates how the world reified in this film is intimately tied up with the "tourist gaze," which consumes the territories of Manchukuo, or of the Japanese Empire.[55] The industrial sites are depicted as tourist attractions or even as amusement parks, something the audience is supposed to experience as a spectacle in the virtual tour. This new entertainment—the tourist gaze over industrial landscapes—acts as an inevitable liaison among the different ethnic traditions that are paraded as images of "Asian" authenticity. Altogether, these attractions become destinations in the virtual tour for experiencing the prosperous near future promised by the nation-state of Manchukuo.

It is important to remember that the tourist culture film's aims extend beyond the promotion of tourism and the railroad system. That is, it follows the mechanism of image production that suggests that the glimpse of modernization's fruits, as yet unknown to audiences, that it offers is an image of the future. The new way of life enabled by the railroad and urbanization, new commodities and services, new modes of mobility, and new places to visit—these were just features of the discourse around modern living, which most audiences had not yet encountered, since such features were from the future. In contrast, the world presented by the tourist culture film could allow audiences to *experience* the future virtually. Each travel destination in Manchukuo, reachable by cinema-train, not only provided the viewer with information about imperial territory but also realigned the viewer's perceptions within a new sense of space. These developments led to the embrace of a homogeneous and exclusive circulation of experiences in modern urban everyday life, whereby the embrace entailed not merely an understanding of this circulation but also, and more importantly, a way of disciplining to fit in that circulation.

Out of the Frame: The Extrasensory World-as-Gestures and the Remnants

Did the tourist culture film then function solely as a disciplining mechanism? Or did it generate other effects aside from that of disciplining audiences? It has been more than eight decades since the film was made, and the audiences who shared the experience of viewing it have since disappeared, so it is almost impossible to answer these questions with any certainty. Gunning, who grapples with a similar concern, borrows Giuliana Bruno's notion of *transito* to capture the "utopian power of cinema" that Benjamin considered "destructive," as well as "liberating."[56] *Transito*, in Italian, means "a wide-ranging and multifaceted notion of circulation, which includes passages, traversals, transitions, transitory states—erotic circulations."[57] It is a "methodological in-between" that travels "in and out of the home, inside and outside space," eroding "binary oppositions,"[58] as well as "a neglected source of cinematic pleasure, one which escapes from the strategies of containment and ideology."[59] Using this framework, Gunning examines a scene of African American children in Nassau from an early travel film. He points out that the moment a group of children "flees, dashing out of the frame, away from the camera's view," is also the moment when the subject refuses and undermines the camera's intention to capture the spectacle of primitive life.[60] This moment does not merely encapsulate the relationship between the camera and the subject, but it is also the point in time when *the world* that is perceivable and capturable overlaps the other side of perception, or a far-off side of desire. In this moment, the audience enters negotiations between the presented gesture and desire.

There are similar moments of transito in *Tokyo-Peking*. Early in the "Tyosen" episode, the narrator introduces Korean women, who "can be found anywhere in Chosŏn, washing clothes" while wearing white hanbok. After a high-angle shot of the washing place, the camera moves closer toward the women, showing a number of them in twos or threes, beating clothes with bats. Soon afterward, the camera settles on a woman, and she smiles at one of her peers outside the frame, seemingly conscious of the camera. First, the narrator speaks to the audience: "Uhm-hmm, isn't she pretty?" Then, he addresses the woman herself: "Watch out, my fair one, or you'll thwack your little fingers!" In this series of asides, the narrator invites the audience to collectively consume the charm and beauty of the young woman in the colony. In that instant, the woman, who seems to be conscious of the camera but has avoided its gaze, looks straight into it, wiping the smile off her face (see fig. 2.15). The woman has been situated as the camera's object, but in the moment, she takes up the role of subject by gazing directly at the camera and at the audience behind the lens.

This is a bizarre, jarring moment, given the consistency of the entire film's representational style, whereby the subjects rarely call the viewer's attention to the existence of the camera. The intrusiveness of this reverse gaze is able to trigger the audience's discomfort. In an anthropological study of how Western tourists reacted when faced with the reverse gaze of Ladakhis, Alex Gillespie points out that the tourists felt discomfort and embarrassment, since they thought they were no different from the typical tourist, whom they believed had shown disrespect "by taking a photograph of a local," so as to consume the romantic or Orientalist representation of "traditional" cultures.[61] We can observe this psychological process at work in the case of *Tokyo-Peking* as well. The exhibition of the tourist culture film throughout the Japanese imperial territories could subjectivize colonial audiences as quasi-imperialists, but, at the same time, the reverse gaze could also arouse a more critical process of subjectivization. Simply put, the reverse gaze opens the way to a moment where the owner and the object of the gaze switch positions, where ownership of the gaze shifts and subsequently disturbs the otherwise solidified identities of colonizer and colonized.

Additionally, this is the moment when the so-called authenticity, allegedly raw footage captured from the tourist site, reveals its true nature. The "authentic" features of Chosŏn women emphasized their pure, white clothing, their submissiveness and preoccupation with domestic labor,

FIGURE 2.15 The filmed subject returns a gaze in the "Tyosen" episode of *Tokyo-Peking* (1939). Courtesy of Toho Stella Nichiei Archive.

FIGURE 2.16 An old man talking in the "Tyosen" episode of *Tokyo-Peking* (1939). Courtesy of Toho Stella Nichiei Archive.

their docile yet sensual nature. However, the reverse gaze strongly suggests that this kind of authenticity can be "staged."[62] The unexpected "return of the gaze" or a "visual riposte" by this filmed female subject undercuts the myth of authenticity in cinematic tourism.[63]

Another key moment is the scene of an interview with an old Chosŏn man. The scene opens with a shot of a straw rope hung on the main door of the man's house, decorated with bunches of charcoal and chili peppers (signifying that there was a recent birth of a son in the household), which is followed by a full shot of the man seated in a doorway (see fig. 2.16). The narrator introduces him to the audience: "This grand old man says he has only one dozen boys at his happy home." It is difficult to decipher what the old man is actually saying beneath the narration. His voice is indistinct from beginning to end and does not seem to have been recorded for audience intelligibility; his voice functions merely as a sound effect that gives proof of the narrator's alleged translation of the interview.

However, even after the three-second narration is over, the old man keeps talking for roughly eight more seconds and gives the impression that he is trying to explain or persuade someone of something, sporting a confident smile and moving his shoulders in shrugging gestures. The viewer has no way of verifying the accuracy of the narrator's short interpretation of the old man's words.

This scene, with its unintelligible dialogue, is another moment of transito, in which the audience—the colonial subject who had been constituted as a quasi-imperialist—might fail to understand the conduct and language of other colonial subjects exhibited in the cinema of colonial tourism. The inarticulate and meaningless sound scatters in the air, becoming a secret language that cannot be parsed or consumed by the audience. This scene's utterance of nonlanguage recalls a moment in Primo Levi's memories of Auschwitz, as identified by Agamben. It was a moment when a dying child in the camp uttered "an inarticulate babble" with purely undecipherable letters, such as "m-a-s-s-k-l-o" and "m-a-t-i-s-k-l-o."[64] Due to the paradox that a witness must survive to bear testimony to a fatal event, a victim of that event cannot ever become the witness. As this paradox reveals an inevitable lacuna in the "language of the testimony," Agamben suggests that "language, in order to bear witness, must give way to a non-language in order to show the impossibility of bearing witness."[65] Much like the inarticulate babble of a victim at Auschwitz, the mumble of an old Chosŏn man becomes a nontestimony, a testimony given in a nonlanguage. It testifies to the impossibility of testimony in the colony—that is, of the victim's knowledge, which the colonial audience turned quasi-imperialist (or a quasi-assailant) could neither capture nor appropriate. The nonlanguage that was not comprehended but, instead, scattered as remnants in the air could yet generate refraction on the smooth surface of the tourist culture film.

There is no way of knowing whether these scenes represented "escape" or "liberation" for the colonial audiences who viewed this tourist culture film. However, we can certainly understand these two scenes as moments of transito, whereby the cinematic experience, designed by the ruling power to mobilize and discipline the audience, did not necessarily yield a solitary teleological track. Rather, the fact of these moments raises the possibility of plural exit points to the cinematic experience as a forum for complex negotiations.

Conclusion

Tourist film was a popular genre in other parts of the world, including Europe and North America, particularly as mass tourism grew in the first half of the twentieth century. However, tourist culture film in the Japanese Empire's colonies was the product of a specific historical context, including imperial expansion into Korea and northeastern China, particularly as facilitated by the railroad industry and the implementation of the "new order in East Asia" as an anti-Western bloc. *Tokyo-Peking* demonstrates the ways in which the railroad (as a modern transportation system) and the cinema (as modern visual experience) jointly contributed to the construction of the imperial order. They were not only the means of such construction but also the principles of that order's operation.

However, as the scenes from the "Tyosen" episode show, locomotive modernity also included certain spheres of negotiation. The moments of transito in tourist culture films testify to the possibility of negotiations and deviations through "distraction" in cinemas, much like how Siegfried Kracauer saw the "political significance of distraction" in its ability to reveal the "*disorder* of society."[66] Such hermeneutic possibilities can dialectically sublate the pessimistic fatalism of scopic regimes and subvert them in the utopian power of cinema.

PART II

Automobile-Screen Interface

CHAPTER 3

My Car *Modernity*

U.S. Army Jeeps and Private Car Ownership

Sŏng-il: Ten years from now, our eldest here will be ten years old, the second will be eight, the youngest will be five, and . . .
Chŏng-hŭi: Gee, dunno. Think birth control!
Sŏng-il: Ha-ha, but we should have at least two boys and one girl. Then we will build our own nice house with a large yard.
Chŏng-hŭi: In our own car, we'll enjoy weekends touring all parts of our country on the completely paved expressways. It's like a dream!
Sŏng-il: It's not a dream. When we understand each other and work together, tomorrow will come with happiness.
Chŏng-hŭi: All right. I will work hard. For you and me, and for our baby!
Sŏng-il: Thanks. Let's hang in there until that day comes!

—*P'aldogangsan of Our Own* (1972)

In the 1972 South Korean government propaganda film *P'aldogangsan of Our Own* (K. *Uri-ŭi p'aldogangsan*), a young couple makes a promise to one another about their future upon learning that the wife, Chŏng-hŭi, is pregnant. The husband, Sŏng-il, dreams of owning their own house, while Chŏng-hŭi dreams of traveling the country in their private car. Interestingly, the film ends with a montage of various scenes, depicting, in succession, a speech made by their grandfather encouraging diligence, handwriting on a wall by South Korean president Park Chung Hee emphasizing the spirit of Saemaŭl undong (New Village Movement), and an express bus cruising an expressway.[1] The young couple's hope for a bright future is embodied by the house and car they desire. The young bride's wish to travel the country in their own car is visually linked to a scene of an open stretch on the expressway. Situated between the scene of the bride's wish and that of the expressway, Park Chung Hee's writing appears to emphasize the message that his leadership can realize these wishes.

In this way, the goals of nuclear family units were promised by a specific type of modernity, which, in turn, was organized around the automobile and automobile traffic. In a way, it would be appropriate to call this *automobility*, "a system that coerces people into an intense flexibility" or a system of "fluid interconnections."[2] Automobility is not just a system; it also signifies a specific "principal socio-technical institution through which modernity is organized," an "ideological or discursive formation," and a "way of experiencing the world."[3] However, Chŏng-hŭi's dream of a private family car, of being able to drive wherever she wants, corresponds to something beyond those dimensions defining automobility in general. In particular, her dream reflects that which drove the population toward certain slogans in postcolonial Korea. As narrated in the government propaganda film, that dream could become reality once multiple transformations in South Korea were completed—transformations such as the nuclearization of the family, the rise of the automobile industry, and the completion of expressway construction. The long-term presence of the U.S. military, in turn, might be understood as one of the factors facilitating these transformations.

In this chapter, I contend that the shift in mobility and its perception was not merely a reflection of social transformation but also one of the (un)intended cultural consequences of American military and nonmilitary presence in Korea, and especially of the influence of its film propaganda activities. The U.S. Army and the U.S. Information Service in Korea (hereafter USIS-Korea) used film as a tool for propaganda, one that showcased a sense of mobility different from that of the colonial period. The way they delivered such cinematic illusions to Koreans, coupled with the gestures of modernized civilization as represented in those films, helped change the cultural logic of mobilization in postcolonial Korea, specifically by promoting automobile-related dreams of the future. This new paradigm, which I call "*my car* modernity," aroused a fixation with ownership and a desire for privately owned, self-regulated units. In the late 1960s, many Koreans began to use *maik'a*, the Korean transliteration of "my car," to refer to a privately owned car, and this new development strongly suggests that the automobile-related utopia was rooted in American influence.

Into Capillaries: Organizing the Gaze through Flexibility in Motion

Let us return to the discussion in chapter 1 on the cultural logic of mobilization that constructs the colonial power's ocular domination. Whereas the railroad mobilized the public with centripetal and centrifugal kinetic energy by simultaneously extending the colonial power's gaze and organizing the gaze of the governed in a regulated system, under the automobile utopia of my-car modernity, the new ruler's gaze seems to float, penetrating into territories and confronting people face-to-face.

The film *P'aldogangsan* (also known as *Six Daughters*, 1967), which was the first in a series that ended with *P'aldogangsan of Our Own* (also known as *Our Land of Korea*) in 1972, and its sequels show how the imagination of an automobile utopia was propelled by cinematic representation. It was the first commercial, full-length feature film sponsored by the ROK Ministry of Public Information and its affiliate, the National Film Production Center (NFPC). The film was publicly promoted in tandem with the sixth presidential election, which preceded the film's release by about two months, and its success led the ministry to make sequels.[4]

One remarkable fact was that the star of the film, Kim Hŭi-kap, placed great importance on his experiences with the director Pae Sŏk-in in an exchange program in the United States, specifically as the inspiration for the film project.[5] From 1955 to 1958, Pae was affiliated with USIS and made its newsreel series, *Liberty News*, and such documentaries as *Korean Editor* (*Chibang sinmun p'yŏnjipcha*, 1958). Kim also had gained experience from collaborating with USIS-Korea's Liberty Productions, appearing in an educational feature, *Birds of a Feather* (*Ŏkchi pongjabi*).[6] The history between USIS-Korea and these two film-industry professionals points to an interesting angle for interpretation—that is, the idea that this film bears the influence of twenty years of film propaganda activities, as conducted by the U.S. Army and USIS-Korea.

Both men were invited to participate in the film specialist exchange program offered by the U.S. State Department and visited American cities from September 1964 to January 1965. According to Kim, the idea in *P'aldogangsan* concerning going sightseeing throughout South Korea first came about when they were staying in New York, notably, after a nationwide tour of the United States.[7] After visiting nineteen representative cities in the United States, Kim appeared on a USIS television show, *Korea-America Today* (1965), and spoke of his experiences with the help of a slide show. Its panoramic visual composition of American local attractions, which Kim and Pae had accessed mostly by car, constructed an overall view of that nation. For Kim, Los Angeles was a tremendous sight with its over five million cars (see fig. 3.1).

As Kim Hŭi-kap wrote about the film *P'aldogangsan*, the narrative of traveling around the country bears considerable structural similarities to Kim and Pae's visit to the United States. The film's main story is about an old couple, Hŭi-kap and Chŏng-sun,[8] who travel around the country to visit their daughters and sons-in-law. Much like *Korea-America Today*, Hŭi-kap and Chŏng-sun's tour in *P'aldogangsan* collects typical images of local attractions and key industries, as if they were mosaic tiles that they subsequently arrange to create a bigger picture. Indeed, after the long trip, the map of the nation is finally completed. The local color and dialect of each province appear as convention when the parents visit each daughter's family. After the parents' long, winding trip, the whole family gathers in Seoul to celebrate the father's sixtieth birthday.

Tourism intended to ignite the national imaginary, however, was not entirely new, especially when considering Emperor Sunjong's tour at the beginning of colonization, as described in chapter 1. What differentiates the tour in the *P'aldogangsan* series from the royal tour is the flexibility of the "roaming ruler."[9] While it is obvious that Kim Hŭi-kap's father figure was set up to metaphorically link the Park Chung Hee regime to the model of a harmonious family, the father-ruler does not have his children positioned at centralized points on the transportation system, as Sunjong did on the railway system, but reaches their homes personally.[10] Moreover, as the sequels develop, the father's flexibility increases. While Hŭi-kap and Chŏng-sun travel on a train in the first film in 1967, the second (1971), third (1971), and fourth (1972) sequels showcase their

FIGURE 3.1 A bird's-eye view of Los Angeles (top) and Kim Hŭi-kap getting out of a car (bottom) in *Korea-America Today* (ca. 1964) (RG306-586). Courtesy of National Archives and Records Administration (NARA).

motor tours on the expressways. In these films, Hŭi-kap is a gentle, humorous, and rational character with the economic means to move freely.

Between the transition from Sunjong's centralization of the gaze to the allegorical father's flexible, mobile gaze, one can locate the role of American film propaganda practices and their use of Jeeps. While the Japanese colonial government had used mobile projection to spread propaganda in the 1910s, the U.S. Army used a different primary vehicle for mobile exhibition, foregoing trains for automobiles, such as Jeeps and trucks. In the early days of the occupation, Jeeps were used primarily for transporting U.S. authorities, but they seem to have gradually become tools for civic purposes. One such purpose was mobile film propaganda. Early in 1946, the U.S. Army Military Government in Korea (USAMGIK) lifted the Japanese colonial administration's restrictions on Hollywood films and began importing U.S. Army propaganda films. However, the U.S. film propaganda agencies did not eliminate colonial policies. Instead, they swiftly adopted colonial practices whenever they saw them as useful. Mobile film propaganda was one such practice that was repurposed under American occupation.

In the early days, U.S. mobile film propaganda activities also depended on the railway system, but eventually Jeeps became more important for their circulation. In 1946, the USAMGIK Department of Public Information planned a nationwide tour of mobile propaganda by railway, called the Mobile Education Train.[11] However, in a report dated November 10, 1947, written by James L. Stewart, director of the Office of Civil Information (OCI), after the public information function was transferred to the U.S. Army, it appears that Jeeps and trucks had to be transported on railway flatcars, specifically for mobile propaganda activities in July 1947. For these activities, greater emphasis was placed on the provinces, which were inaccessible by rail, over urban areas. The report stated that OCI considered "decentralization in operation" as an essential aim and that it endeavored to "operate into the countryside" from "a smooth, impressive headquarters" in Seoul.[12]

While the traveling exhibition of propaganda films continued throughout both the Japanese and the U.S. occupations, the use of Jeeps gave projection units an unprecedented degree of flexibility under USAMGIK. Unlike urban areas, which had been actively absorbing new culture and information from the outside world, the provinces suffered from a persistent information gap. The ruling powers therefore concluded that in these locations, messages would be more easily received through verbal propagation, performances, and moving image exhibitions than through the more conventional distribution of printed media. Under these circumstances, mobile film screening served as a form of maneuver warfare. With Jeeps and trucks, film units flowed into the provinces that trains could not reach. While city cinemas were important bases for luring urban audiences, traveling film exhibitions were primarily intended to directly affect the everyday lives of people in the countryside and, in so doing, mobilize rural audiences.[13]

In the course of such propaganda activities, the Jeep itself was the embodiment of American state-of-the-art technology, exhibited in the films it delivered. It was a vehicle of high maneuverability, a self-contained unit that was not bound to any preassigned timetables. General Douglas MacArthur's statement encouraging the Japanese to develop and industrialize—"These people will soon make their own Jeep"—makes clear that the Jeep was a symbol of both advanced technology and self-reliance.[14] In a February 1949 news article, it was reported that hundreds of Jeeps had been stolen since the liberation, demonstrating how much the newly imported vehicle appealed to Koreans.[15] The outbreak of the Korean War had a considerable role in showcasing the effectiveness of American motor vehicles to Korea. While as many as 80 percent of existing automobiles had been destroyed during the war, the Korean War opened a new chapter in the South Korean auto industry with the importation of over six thousand Jeeps for the U.S. Army.[16] The war also provided opportunities for the Japanese auto industry, with the U.S. Army ordering such companies as Toyota to build war transports for the Korean peninsula.[17] These Jeeps and trucks were recycled and served as models for early South Korean cars after the war.

Regarding film propaganda, weapons carrier trucks became an essential component for the wartime mobile units that replaced trains. In October 1950, the U.S. Department of the Army initiated procedures for procuring film equipment and resources for psychological warfare.[18] Ten mobile film units—equipped with 16 mm sound and 35 mm slide projection equipment, public address systems, recording and record-playing equipment, and related supplies—were shipped from Japan, along with three hundred sets of 16 mm projectors with screens and twenty-five prints of 16 mm films in the Korean language.[19] Each mobile unit and its equipment necessitated a vehicle for transport. Weapons carrier trucks with "a locally built aluminum body" were regarded as the most viable solution under wartime conditions.[20] Due to the high value of these vehicles and their equipment, mobile screening units were sometimes vulnerable to guerrilla attacks. In November 1951, one vehicle was reportedly ambushed and lost to Communist guerrillas. The guerrillas let the crew flee and took the vehicle.[21]

Wartime audiences' reaction to the propaganda films was "enthusiastic."[22] U.S. ambassador John Muccio sent a telegram to the State Department, reporting that the wartime USIS newsreel series *Segye nyusŭ* was received with fervent enthusiasm from Korean audiences. According to the operations report on Taegu in September 1950, the USIS film *President Truman's Speech* and five *Segye nyusŭ* issues were shown in the Taegu USIS center with a total of 75,960 people in attendance and in mobile screenings at rural villages around Taegu to 37,870 people.[23]

The increasing use of Jeeps and trucks in U.S. film propaganda activities, which became standardized during the occupation and the war, signifies that the gaze of power, in Michel Foucault's sense of surveillance and governmentality, gained more tactical agility and coverage.[24] The automobile replaced the train because it was a compact, self-directed unit, ideal for maneuvering in as-yet-inaccessible areas. Its flexible mobility allowed better visibility, visualizing as-yet-unseen rural areas for the foreign propaganda authorities. People in the rural areas could feel and see the presence of the ruling power and its state-of-the-art technology embodied in these maneuvering vehicles, without themselves being mobilized to welcome the monarch at the train station in bigger towns. They not only were observing the delivered spectacle but also were observed by the delivery personnel who were the agents of a U.S. information agency.

Off the Track: Individual Flexibility for High Mobility

The arrival of flexible mobility also began to change how people were gathered, organized, and mobilized. Unlike the railway system, the new vision enabled by automobile traffic and privately owned cars lit people's imaginations of a self-regulating and unrestricted unit, one that allowed them to choose their own destination, speed, and companions. In transitioning to this new breed of mobility, the idealized type of individually flexible, self-regulated units came to be embodied by the nuclear family. Just as Chŏng-hŭi in *P'aldogangsan of Our Own* dreamed of "our own car," the ideal of a privately owned car was widely understood as a family-owned car driven by a young father. This vision of the nuclear family as the normative model is also well represented in other *P'aldogangsan* sequels. The films in the series were, in fact, visual textbooks on the Korean version of the nuclear family. Despite the appearance of a large family, the old couple and their married daughters did not live together, and each household was economically independent of one other. Under the construct likening the family to the nation-state, the nuclear family is itself the basic labor unit that completes the internal reproduction procedure, including both biological reproduction and all other domestic labor that reproduces labor power, based on the gendered division of labor.[25] In *P'aldogangsan of Our Own*, the last of the film series, the future of the nuclear family is promised in the forward movement on the expressway, which symbolized not only rapid economic growth through government-led mobilization but also a reified system of the free movement of goods and capital.

Modern, everyday American life as depicted in the USIS films was also rooted in nuclear family units. One such film, *American Working Women* (n.d.), was shown in the mid-1950s with Korean footage added as an introduction and was made available in the USIS film library for rentals.[26] In this film, which was intended to educate audiences on the ideal role of women in contemporary American society, one of the female protagonists commutes to work in her own car (see fig. 3.2). On her way home from work, she picks up her husband from the factory, along with their children from the babysitter's house next door. They are the very picture of a harmonious family, preparing a meal together. The woman's car embodies the family as a self-contained unit of four people. Similar depictions of American automobiles and nuclear families pervade the USIS films shown in Korea, such as *The American Road* (1953) and *Country Editor* (1954).

Another important symbol of flexibility and individual mobility was the expressway. Construction of the Kyŏngbu Expressway began in 1968 and was completed in 1970. It was the beginning of a series of large-scale

FIGURE 3.2 A nuclear family in *American Working Women* (n.d.) (RG306-21). Courtesy of NARA.

construction projects in South Korea, which aimed to complete five major expressways in five years. As I discuss in chapter 4, the Park Chung Hee government used the construction of expressways as a presidential election pledge for Park's reelection in 1967. Construction was presented as transforming South Korean industry from railway- to automobile-based. It is also important to note that the ideals of an automobile utopia stemmed mainly from existing images of Western consumer culture, as portrayed primarily in Hollywood and American propaganda films, while the construction of expressways and the auto industry were understood to be national projects. Park's argument against the railway system made use of anticolonial sentiment in South Korea, while simultaneously expressing admiration for a specific form of Western civilization.

In 1956, the Eisenhower administration completed the national expressway system by establishing the Dwight D. Eisenhower National System of Interstate and Defense Highways.[27] As earlier studies have demonstrated, this interstate highway system became the solid foundation on which American national identity was reconceptualized, specifically by combining Fordism and consumer culture.[28] The Korean War, in turn, contributed to the rapid growth of the American automobile industry. During the war, railway system defense had shortcomings that were made evident when railways proved "vulnerable to disruption through strategic bombing."[29] This established the case for motor transport lobbyists, who persuaded the Eisenhower administration to construct "a toll-free interstate highway system."[30] The American highway experience had been shaped by global historical events, such as the Great Depression and the two World Wars, so it was proposed as a universally applicable development for newly independent nations like South Korea, in spite of the historical particularity of that experience. As early as 1947, when the U.S. Army's OCI started to distribute and screen imported American propaganda films in South Korea, for the express purpose of fighting indigenous, left-wing, nationalist groups for hegemony, films depicting American automobile culture were a frequent exhibit for Korean audiences. While the Jeep was an embodiment of cutting-edge technology delivering American images to the newly liberated people, the private cars depicted in those U.S. Army films were a refined version of that embodiment, optimized for everyday life. *The Story of Lincoln Tunnel* (ca. 1943), which was first shown in Korea in January 1948, begins with a scene of

FIGURE 3.3 Scene from the opening sequence of *The Story of Lincoln Tunnel* (ca. 1943) (RG306-3086). Courtesy of NARA.

Manhattan, showing its skyscrapers as attractions.[31] In the following scene, a line of automobiles is seen entering the Lincoln Tunnel (see fig. 3.3). Then, the film presents a brief history of the tunnel's construction, with some animated scenes illustrating the technological principles behind the process. In the final scene, several private cars are seen exiting the tunnel quickly, completing the picture of modern urban spaces.

A privately owned car in a picture of the American way of life was also a signifier of American democracy. The paradigm of individual mobility gradually came to be seen as a principle of modern democracy, specifically, the American vision of democracy. In late 1947, the OCI started a nationwide project to educate Koreans on establishing a separate government in South Korea and distributed films about elections and democracy. *Tuesday in November* (1945) was the American film shown most frequently during the course of this project.[32] In this film, privately owned cars are depicted as an embodiment of voters' free will. The film was produced by the Overseas Branch of the U.S. Army Office of War Information (OWI) to visualize the American election system and government structure. The film's main narrative links a small local constituency (Riverton, California) to a federal event—namely, the 1944 presidential election—and, in so doing, visualizes the basic principle of American federalism. Riverton therefore is not only an example of American local constituencies but also a miniature representation of the American constitutional structure.

The first sequence shows a woman, the principal of Riverton Public School and the chair of the election board for the presidential election, arriving at the polling station in her own car. After she gets out of the car, she opens the station, sets up the board table, and checks the voting booth and the ballot box. The first voter in Riverton arrives in the next scene, also in his car (see fig. 3.4). While these two figures embody the electoral system and its constituents, their cars represent constituents' autonomy and free will to elect their own delegates. Voters driving to the polling station in their own cars, along with the female chair of the election board, were, for Korean audiences, likely as new and curious as the idea of universal suffrage.

Clearly, the political structure imagined and represented as individual mobility in American propaganda films marked a sharp divide from the tactics of Japanese colonial propaganda films, as discussed in chapters 1 and 2. Locomotive modernity in the colonial era implied a self-contained regime equipped with regulated systems for collective forward movement. In contrast, American propaganda films promoted unlimited mobility through privately owned cars. In this vision of automobile mobility, certain expectations of collectivity and regularity could only be foregone. As American films like *American Working Women* and *Tuesday in November* illustrate, privately owned cars allowed audiences to imagine each individual moving independently, according to his or her own will. Each one possessed a right to elect his or her own delegates; thus, allegorically and theoretically, each one had a unique destination. This degree of flexibility, however, was not portrayed as unstable or hazardous but, rather, as bright and promising.

FIGURE 3.4 The election board chair (top) and the first voter (bottom) getting out of their cars in *Tuesday in November* (1945) (RG306-201). Courtesy of NARA.

In My Car: The Future of Private Ownership and the Modern Self

The bright images and assertive themes in these American propaganda films were, of course, linked to a utopian vision of this new mode of transportation—namely, the private car. This vision entailed not only the matter of private property but also a diverse array of issues tying back to the modern self, such as mobility as directed by one's free will, social status and mobility along the ranks, establishment of private spaces, and self-realization in an automobile-based society. As evidenced by General Douglas MacArthur's statement quoted above, the automobile was, from the very beginning, equated with the promise of private car ownership. In September 1945, when the U.S. Army landed on the Korean Peninsula, U.S. troops paraded in Jeeps among the newly liberated people (see fig. 3.5).[33] For those who had rarely seen such vehicles, the parade of Jeeps would have been a magnificent spectacle.[34] Even in Japan, people admired

FIGURE 3.5 U.S. troops parading in an armored car and a Jeep on September 10, 1945. From U.S. Army Signal Corps film footage (RG111-ADC-5245). Courtesy of NARA.

the strange vehicles and dreamt to "own one someday."[35] This new mode of transportation meant that a car could be owned personally, even though no one knew when that would be.

The Jeep, which was originally manufactured by Willys-Overland, gained its reputation as an all-purpose vehicle during World War II. In 1942, Willys-Overland began laying the grounds for "a market for a civilian version of the Jeep at the end of the war."[36] Postwar American society had already become an automobile-based economy, and Jeeps were a product that any civilian could purchase and possess. The war had played a significant role in advertising Jeeps for would-be buyers in civilian markets.[37] Therefore, when U.S. Jeeps were shipped from occupied Japan, they served a dual purpose as military vehicles in the Korean War and as advertisement for private car ownership in South Korea.[38]

Before the 1980s, Jeeps had a central role in South Korean car ownership and were viewed with "respect and admiration."[39] During the 1950s' vehicle recycling boom in the wake of the Korean War, South Koreans embraced, mimicked, and transformed American automobile culture, and Jeeps became a symbol of private car ownership. They were repainted black and used as private cars by "presidents, ministers, lawmakers, mayors, entrepreneurs, celebrities, and everybody."[40] The first Korean passenger car, the Si-bal, was manufactured to look like a Jeep, and its core components were imitations of those in an American Jeep engine.[41] The fact that those surplus Jeeps were seen as icons of private car ownership reflects the humble state of the South Korean auto industry at that time. Privately owned cars gradually came to be upheld as an ideal of economic success but were still inaccessible to ordinary people, and the rate of car ownership in South Korea remained low until the 1980s, when the number of registered cars saw a sharp increase (see table 3.1).[42]

On a discursive level, however, private car ownership became an object of admiration in the late 1960s. In a 1967 news article, the rosy future of "average life" was described with the newly coined term *maik'a* (my car).[43] The article predicted the future of a "consumer revolution" and the dawning of the my-car age. Another article in the following year predicted that the my-car age would arrive in South Korea in the 1970s.[44] This term appears to have been imported from Japan, where a *maikā* (my car) boom was already in effect around the time of the 1964 Tokyo Olympics.[45] However, the term had a different vernacular meaning in South Korea: while

Table 3.1 Number of Registered Automobiles in South Korea

	1947	1952	1957	1962	1967	1972	1977	1982	1988
Car	1,434	2,449	9,743	11,974	23,235	70,244	125,613	305,811	1,117,999
Truck	5,737	6,845	13,679	12,808	23,491	55,116	118,510	263,939	635,445
Bus	766	1,470	3,847	4,266	11,499	17,550	26,710	66,326	259,600
Total	7,937	10,764	27,269	29,048	58,225	142,910	270,833	636,076	2,013,044

Source: Ch'oe Un-sik, *Han'guk ŭi yuksang kyot'ong*, 254; Ministry of Transportation, *Kyot'ong t'onggye yŏnbo*, 102–5; Statistics Korea, *Number of Automobiles*.

my car was a term referring to an existing phenomenon in Japan, in South Korea, it was a slogan designed to mobilize people. Contrary to the optimistic forecasts in news articles, the my-car age did not arrive in South Korea until the late 1980s. *My car* was the "dramatic manipulation of a symbol, urging people to actively engage in the economic development" of Korea.[46]

P'aldogangsan of Tomorrow (1971), the third film in the *P'aldogangsan* series, is significant precisely for such symbol manipulation. In the film, Hŭi-kap appears as a guest on a television talk show and praises the dawning of a new era, one where the entire nation has access to the "one-day life zone," thanks to the construction of the expressways. As an example of this one-day life zone, he explains that he can receive fresh fish within a quarter of a day from his son-in-law in Pusan. After watching the show, the son-in-law visits him with the fish, driving his own car.[47] In this scene, the expressway is not the only object of emphasis. The fact that the son-in-law, a successful businessman, possesses a privately owned car underscores the attractiveness and pervasiveness of the my-car ethos in propaganda films. In this way, the *P'aldogangsan* franchise promoted a my-car utopia as a positive vision for the future. While the son-in-law's case is a symptom of that desire for cars, another scene expresses that desire in a more blatant manner. The old couple's granddaughter Chŏng-hŭi begins dating Sŏng-il, who is the couple's boarder. During their date, Sŏng-il drives a convertible with Chŏng-hŭi as a passenger. Their car takes the overpass in downtown Seoul. In fact, this scene is completely unrealistic, since such a car was beyond the means of a young, working-class boarder. Accordingly, this scene's portrayal of Seoul is not that of the present but that of a dream of the future.[48]

However, the adoration for my car should not be understood merely as a desire to possess a car. As evidenced by the transliteration of the possessive pronoun *my*, the my-car syndrome reflected the recognition of the first person. Acquiring more mobility by owning a car meant that the self also acquired a wider sphere of activity, and such an acquisition increased the available forms of movement. It also signified that he or she had obtained more freedom in choosing destinations.

One of the USIS Film Library holdings, *The Autobiography of a Jeep* (1943),[49] and a Korean-made USIS film, *I Am a Truck* (1955), both exhibit a significant tendency in American propaganda films from the reconstruction period, specifically in terms of recognizing the modern self. *The Autobiography of a Jeep* was made for the OWI during World War II by an American documentary filmmaker, Irving Lerner. Like many popular children's books in the wartime United States, this film uses the first-person point of view of a "talking Jeep."[50] *I Am a Truck*, directed by Kim Ki-yŏng in postwar South Korea, adopts the same style and uses first-person narration by a military truck. While these two talking automobiles differ in terms of their speech patterns and characters, they share a certain attitude toward the world—namely, confidence as an independent individual, or the modern self.[51] According to Kathleen German, the Jeep in *The Autobiography of a Jeep* reflects three ideal traits of the "American soldier—optimism, comradeship, and loyalty."[52] However, regardless of the vehicle's military background, its basic attitude mirrors the modern, liberal individualism of American society. The Jeep talks in a cheerful, outspoken voice, while its rhythmical motion and exhibitions of power bestow a sense of reliability in this small, self-contained unit. The personification of the Jeep not only projects a sense of intimacy between it and the audience, but it also promotes the ideal of an individual possessing free will and mobility. In turn, Kim Ki-yŏng's personified truck looks rather gloomy but is revealed as a strong-willed individual, engaging in reconstruction efforts in the war-damaged country. When the recycled American military truck declares, "Now I abandoned the desire to return to my country, for I love Korea very much," and "I made up my mind to stay and help the reconstruction of Korea," it testifies to how the ideal of free will in the modern self was adapted to the local version of American propaganda in South Korea.

In addition, it is important to remember that for all of its emphasis on the individual, the new mobility under my-car modernity was, in fact, oriented toward the nuclear family. One of the earliest news articles predicting the my-car age defined it as the age of "at least one car in every house."[53] In light of this definition, the individual self with free will was envisioned as the male breadwinner who might drive the family-owned car. In this regard, the cine-mobility of women driving cars in American propaganda films and Hollywood features did not just deliver images of the ideal female role in the nuclear family but, at the same time, provided potentialities of female agency that might undermine the family-centered my-car modernity. The car visualized her autonomy as an independent citizen, which may have gone beyond the propaganda authorities' intention. When *American Working Women* was adapted by USIS-Korea, the Korean version also included an introductory scene featuring a Korean man. While the USIS-affiliated Korean presenter introduced this film as one that "depicts how American women could successfully manage to do two jobs, that is, housekeeping and their own professional job," and while the original film's American narrator repeatedly remarked on how these American women's way of life was well organized because of American values, as a viewer, the woman's gestures are worth noticing in terms of their potentialities. Her facial expressions are so full of confidence, and they pricked at remnants of the male gaze inside myself as the present-day viewer, which prompts me to imagine that those same expressions dealt a more impactful blow to male Korean viewers at the time in the 1950s. This leads to the question: What about the female viewers? From the viewer's perspective, the affect of such gestures may or may not relate to the narrative or message of the film, but such an affect is definitely linked to the female figure's movement, as well as to that of the moving vehicle. One might even say that the affect, the gesture, and the movement of cinematic objects all came into being at the moment of screening. These elements, though designed by American propaganda authorities in South Korea and shown as part of a compulsory prefeature program, were not necessarily defined by the messages that the authorities wanted to send. Rather, these elements had an arbitrary relationship with any meaning the viewers might have pulled from their cinematic experience. One possible meaning could be related to the individual agency and autonomy of the female driver. Her car might symbolize the nuclear family as an ideal unit but could conversely embody her agency independent from the patriarch by fully controlling her own movement.

Conclusion

When Virilio claimed that "the history of battle is primarily the history of radically changing fields of perception" and that "once the cinema was able to create surprise, it effectively came under the category of weapons," a good deal of the mobility granted to cinema-weapons, particularly on the battlefields of perception, was generated by the most widely available mode of transportation.[54] In Korea, where there were ceaseless wars to win the hearts and minds of the colonial and postcolonial populations, the main vehicles that carried cinema-as-weapon were the train and the automobile. The shift from trains to automobiles indicated that there was a change in the perception of the world at the same time.

What is striking is the extent to which this shift was the result of the long-term U.S. military presence in South Korea, especially its efforts in film propaganda production and distribution. The cultural logic of locomotive modernity, which had been characterized by collectivity and regularity in mobilizing the public, made way for my-car modernity, which prioritized the modern self—in fact, the male head of a nuclear family unit—moving freely of his own will. This shift was stimulated by the blueprint of American auto culture, as well as by the actual automobiles that accompanied propagandistic exhibitions.

In light of these developments, the television show *Blooming P'aldogangsan* (1974–1975), the conclusion to the *P'aldogangsan* franchise, occupies a noteworthy place in the development of my-car modernity. By the time of the show's airing, the means of delivering propaganda was neither a train nor a Jeep. Audiences no longer had to gather in one place, since they could simply stay at home. The advanced technology of satellites enabled the maximization of mobility, and propaganda pictures could now reach people directly in their own homes. Much like private car ownership, television also provided the nuclear family with a sense of possession—namely, of a home theater at *maihom* (my home).[55] Such individuality of domesticity and everyday life suggests that the spread of automobile culture under U.S. power significantly affected the liberal technology of government after the dissolution of "railway imperialism" and its collectivity.[56]

However, we need to probe deeper into this utopian ideal of flexibility and private ownership under my-car modernity, particularly in terms of its actual effects. While the automobile ostensibly allows people to freely choose their own destination, when viewed in context, automobile society is anything but an autonomous utopia. Rather, it is the ceaseless circulation of products and labor, which rarely allows any respite from the circulation itself. In the rapid flow of the expressways, no individual car can turn, reverse, or stop. The only option is to maintain your speed so that you will not disturb the flow. Every potential accident and environmental disaster caused by automobile traffic is understood as an unavoidable side effect of utopia made flexible. In light of this, one might ask if there is an "actual" exercise of free will in automobile utopia. I would argue that my-car modernity is, rather, a "dictatorship of movement exerted on the masses,"[57] even as it leaves room to discern that a process for the "construction of a voluntaristic subject"[58] has existed in it.

CHAPTER 4

Birth of Happiness?

The Nationalization of Automobility

Ttosuni is a Korean term referring to a shrewd woman who is more than capable of maintaining her own livelihood. This once common term originates from a popular 1962 radio show, *The Birth of Happiness* (*Haengbok ŭi t'ansaeng*), and its cinematic remake, *Ttosuni: The Birth of Happiness* (*Ttosuni: Haengbok ŭi t'ansaeng*), which was a box-office hit the following year. The story is about a worldly woman with a strong northern accent and her fiancé, who is a rather weak-minded man, set in a town near the last stop for buses, called "a parking lot of ephemeral lives."[1] The woman, the second daughter of a bus company owner, is independent enough to leave her parents' home, resisting her father's old ideas and stinginess. Her measurement of success is rooted in getting back at her father for not recognizing her ability and manifests itself as a specific car model called the Saenara (New Country). By owning a Saenara, she thinks, she and her fiancé can start a taxi business, which will pave a golden road to success. When she finally achieves her goal, the couple brings the new Saenara to her parents' home and parades through the town surrounded by a crowd of neighbors.

While the success story of "industrious and pragmatically money-making" young people—particularly those who overcame the stubborn, old generation—was a popular trend in early 1960s South Korean cinema (especially since it resonated with the military junta's efforts to "eradicate old misdeeds"[2]), it is worth paying closer attention to the way this film draws a metaphoric connection between the possession of a Saenara and the owner's success in life. As discussed in chapter 3, beginning in the late 1950s, the automobile came to be seen as symbolic of an idealized future for the South Korean middle class, specifically under significant influence from the United States. Owning a Saenara, therefore, presented the hardworking couple as having entered the middle class, leaving behind the parent generation's old-fashioned way of life. The car's ambitious, new Korean name suggests that the middle class's idealized future is connected to the task of making a *saenara* (new country).

However, Saenara was, in fact, the licensed product of a Japanese car, Nissan's Bluebird. Before the automotive industry's rapid development in the latter half of the 1970s, the South Korean domestic auto market depended primarily on licensed production. Automobiles with foreign technologies and designs were imported and adapted for Korean brands.[3] Kia's Brisa, first released in 1975 with an original engine, and Hyundai's Pony in 1976, with an original body design, were the two historic models that opened the era of a relatively self-reliant automotive industry in South Korea.[4] Hence, the two decades between the ceasefire of the Korean War and the mid-1970s were a time when the foreign prototype of automobilized living was exhibited and desired yet barely accessed by the Korean public.

This chapter aims to document the Park Chung Hee administration's role in promoting automobility during this early stage of the South Korean auto industry, focusing on the government's engagement with media and popular culture. Park Chung Hee, who came to power through a military coup in 1961 and held the presidency until his assassination in 1979, oversaw an administration that exploited cultural representations of auto traffic and private car ownership to mobilize public support for the government and legitimize its dictatorship. This chapter examines the early and ambivalent stage of what would become a national industry, as it sat on the cusp of becoming an object of immense, national pride. It also examines the subsequent stage, where the nationwide expressway system was presented as an effective means of *nationalizing* automobility, which, in propaganda, was held up as the reward given in exchange for supporting autocracy.

Saenara: Visualizing the Will to Power

Since seizing power in May 1961, Park Chung Hee's junta, the Supreme Council for National Reconstruction (SCNR), presented an image of itself as actively promoting domestic auto industries. The Automobile Industry Protection Act, legislated in May and ratified in June 1962, was a part of such measures aimed at boosting the auto industry.[5] In particular, May 1962, when the Ninth Asian Film Festival and several other international events were held in Seoul, was a time when the automobile's flexible and convenient mobility was yoked to a blueprint for the prosperity of a cosmopolitan city, with "an unheard-of boom in the tourism industry," including the taxi industry.[6] Between April 20 and May 17, a total of 1,125 international visitors, including 300 international festival guests, visited Seoul, leading to a report of a 5.6–10.0 percent increase in annual profits for taxis in Seoul.[7] The Asian Film Festival was not only a "progeny of the U.S.-driven Cold War cultural politics" but also a golden opportunity for Park's junta to publicize their legitimacy by exhibiting cooperative relations with foreign allies.[8] It was also the first site to showcase the Saenara.[9] The Park junta allowed 248 new Saenara taxis, all of which were imported Nissan Bluebirds, to operate full-time in the city, while the other 2,700 existing taxis were restricted to a three-shift system.[10] The "snappy sedan taxi" upstaged old-fashioned, domestically produced taxis "made by hammer."[11] The Saenara became an icon of modern auto traffic and, at the same time, a promise that a national, self-reliant auto industry would be actualized by Park's new administration, buoyed by the belief that license production of a Japanese model would help the domestic company learn the basics of production.[12]

Saenara Motors was founded by a Korean Japanese entrepreneur on January 27, 1961.[13] While, within the year, the streets of Seoul had become "deluged with the five-color Saenara-Bluebird cars," as a news article criticized, the new company's dramatic success would have been impossible without strong support from the military government, such that this link between them was listed as one of the "four major scandals" during the Park junta.[14] Saenara Motors could import 400 completed Bluebirds as "tourist vehicles," including the aforementioned 248 units, exempt from taxation, and then would alter their declared purpose, indicating them as for "general use," so that they could be used as taxis without any further taxation.[15] Also, the timely legislation of the Automobile Industry Protection Act, which prohibited the import of completed automobile products but gave tax exemptions for imported automobile parts, helped licensed production companies become more adept at manufacturing. Accordingly, Saenara Motors completed its manufacturing factory in Pup'yŏng in August 1962 and began licensed production.[16]

This method of promoting Saenara automobiles critically strained the broader industry. The Si-bal (First Departure), the first domestically produced car (which was, in fact, a remodeled Willys Jeep with a domestic engine) that had dominated the South Korean taxi market since 1955, suffered a direct, heavy blow, with both the Saenara's cost-effective price and the limited number of taxi business licenses driving the replacement of Si-bals with Saenaras (see fig. 4.1).[17] As of January 1963, Saenara taxis in Seoul counted 1,050 only about six months after the model's first release, whereas the number of Si-bal taxis had dwindled from about 3,000 to 1,700.[18] In the Fortieth Plenary Session of the National Assembly of Korea on February 17, 1964, the opposition lawmaker Yi Sang-don addressed the issue that the junta encouraged taxi drivers to trade in used Si-bal taxis for new Saenara taxis, for the purpose of scrapping the former.[19] He doubted whether some 2,000 out of 3,000 Si-bal taxis had indeed been put out of commission by an administrative order from the military government, but the minister of commerce and industry had no immediate comment.[20]

Among critics, the Saenara, "a beauty dressed in Western style," was seen as having pushed out the Si-bal, "the thing that we had made ourselves."[21] Yi Sang-don argued that the series of tax exemptions for Bluebird parts was an "anti-state or anti-national policy," one that squandered foreign exchange holdings only to ruin the domestic auto industry.[22] Interestingly, the localization of automobile parts was apparently a goal shared by both Saenara critics and advocates, since this development was seen as a way to "join the ranks of advanced nations."[23] One of the advocates backing the Park junta's promotion of the Saenara, Min Pyŏng-u, who was then the president of the Foreign Technology Association, thought it a general trend to "import foreign product components first and gradually replace them with domestic components," but four years later, he lamented that Nissan was "so engrossed in moneymaking" that

FIGURE 4.1 Photograph titled *Saenara t'aeksi toip* (Introduction of Saenara taxis) (1962) (CET0035290). Courtesy of National Archives of Korea.

the South Korean subcontract manufacturer could not achieve the goal of "fully localizing production within five years."[24] Clearly, the Park junta's support for the Saenara generated difficulties for the Si-bal, in spite of its original intent.

As one of the four major scandals in the Park junta, the Saenara issue led to suspicions of illegal political funding. Three opposition parties inquired into the whereabouts of the enormous profits made by Saenara Motors when they doubled the price of imported products, going from 135,000 KRW (approximately 1,400 USD in 1962) per unit to 224,000 KRW.[25] This scandal, along with three others, ultimately linked back to Korea's Central Intelligence Agency (KCIA),[26] and an assistant deputy department head at KCIA was arrested on related charges.[27] However, former KCIA director Kim Chong-p'il, who was in office from May 1961 to January 1963, subsequently went abroad as a traveling ambassador, leaving many key questions unanswered,[28] and the investigation withered as the arrested KCIA agent was released.[29] Opponent party members in the

National Assembly raised the possibility of illegal "commissions" taken as "political funds."[30] Though the questions still remain unanswered, there are strong suspicions that the secret fund might have been used to form and launch Park's ruling party.[31]

While it seems a plausible conclusion that the Saenara scandal was a case of "the public [being] deceived by trickery and corruption," it is worth noting that it was not just a matter of "political corruption" but also of propaganda—media manipulation and visual presentation.[32] As mentioned above, localizing the automobile industry was intended to achieve self-reliant modernization, a vision shared by both the Park junta and its opponents. However, Park's government was more interested in *visualizing* its agenda to localize the industry. Rather than investing in the unsophisticated, outdated Si-bal, they thought it a more effective strategy to put many Bluebirds, "beauties dressed in Western style," on the streets. The 1963 film *Ttosuni* depicts enthusiasm for the Saenara as naturally given among people. When Ttosuni tells people, including her father, fiancé, and neighbors, about her plan to secure a Saenara as a cornerstone for her success, there is no disagreement on the value of purchasing the car. However, since the Saenara is a costly product for the young couple, Ttosuni and her fiancé, Chae-gu, have to raise money, the noisy farce that becomes the main plot for the entire film. They make and sell rat traps and rice cakes and, more interestingly, buy and resell truck tires. As a product placement of a South Korean brand, Han'guk Tire, the bundle of tires speaks to the importance of the automobile parts industry at the time, as well as to their potential exchangeability with a Saenara, a symbol of the localized automobile industry. When the couple eventually brings a new Saenara to their parents and gives them a trial ride, their neighbors show delight, as though the couple's success was that of the whole neighborhood. The film suggests that the embodiment of the government's agenda for self-reliant development—the Saenara—became visually dominant only within the year after its first release. Ttosuni, among several other female figures in South Korean cinema then, including Chŏng-hŭi in *Rice* (*Ssal*, 1963), presents the gestures of a financially and economically independent woman who even guides and controls her male partner. Her diligent and industrious body, however, in the last scene, is placed in the passenger seat of the car that her male, uniformed partner is driving.

"President Park Rode in a Jeep"

It is important to remember that 1963 was the year that Park Chung Hee was supposed to have transferred power to the civil branch of government, though, ultimately, he himself was elected as president after leaving the army that same year. After the series of international events in 1962 and 1963, the streets were full of Saenara taxis, a development seen as one indicator of Park's achievements under military rule. Indeed, Park tried to present himself as concerned about the new automobile company, particularly by visiting the Saenara manufacturing factory (see fig. 4.2).[33]

What, then, was the objective in linking the soon-to-be presidential nominee to the new automobile brand or automobility in general? It will

FIGURE 4.2 Photograph titled *Pak chŏnghŭi ŭijang saenara chadongch'a kongjang chun'gongsik ch'amsŏk hu sich'al* (Chairman Park Chung Hee's inspection after visiting the opening ceremony of the Saenara factory) (1962) (CET0029282). Courtesy of National Archives of Korea.

FIGURE 4.3 Untitled photograph of Park Chung Hee (in the center) and his men during the May 16 coup (May 18, 1961).

be helpful here to turn to an iconic photograph from Park's military coup (see fig. 4.3). While the photo is widely seen as depicting the coup on May 16, 1961, it is, in fact, a case demonstrating how photographic manipulation can affect the understanding of historical events. According to the former *Kyŏnghyang sinmun* journalist Yi Sang-u, the photo was originally taken on May 18, two days after the actual coup, when there was a procession of ROK Military Academy cadets supporting the May 16 coup.[34] More importantly, the main figure at the May 18 event was the man standing in the Jeep, out of the frame, and giving a speech, Chang Do Young, the first chairman of the SCNR installed by Park's group (see fig. 4.4, which shows the scene from a different angle).[35] Yi recalls that the iconic photo that did not include Chang Do Young (fig. 4.3) was not released until Chang's group had been purged, and Park became the chairman in July.[36] Therefore, this famous picture, one that conveyed the sense of urgency with which the coup leader and his men had stepped

FIGURE 4.4 Photograph titled *Kunsa hyŏngmyŏngwiwŏnhoe ŭijang changdoyŏng chungjang ŭi kyŏngnyŏsa* (Supreme Council for National Reconstruction Chairman Chang Do Young's pep talk) (1961) (CET0054899). Chang Do Young is standing on a Jeep, and Park Chung Hee is on the right. Courtesy of National Archives of Korea.

down from the Jeep to inspect the coup site, was, in fact, a photo of the then second in command on standby.

However, given that Park's group released this picture when Park took over leadership, it is likely that they wanted to promote precisely this kind of misconception. The two guardsmen on each side of Park were seen as "insignificant" at the time of the coup, but, with their bodies' fully in the frame, they seem to enter the spotlight.[37] Likewise, the Jeep in the background also came to carry special significance. As an apparatus that generated a sense of urgency during the military coup, the Jeep became an indispensable element in Major General Park's projected character, at a crucial moment in South Korean history, no less. By standing in front of a military Jeep, Park styled himself as a person with high levels of mobility and maneuverability, befitting the leader of young military officers who saw themselves as the right people to eradicate old misdeeds.

On the first anniversary of the coup, a newspaper recalled the "fatal hour" before the coup with an interesting description of Park in a Jeep: "506 unit commander Yi Hŭi-yŏng who received a mandate to shadow the revolutionary leader, Major General Park, followed him with two jeeps that had numbers starting with 5. . . . The vehicle carrying Major General Park wended its way through side streets to give an unknown chaser the slip."[38]

Indeed, Park was usually paired with a Jeep in the media. It was a tactic to present him as a strong personality, capable of making bold decisions and daring innovations. For instance, a news article in September 1962 reported: "Chairman Park Chung Hee suddenly imposed an inspection of the city of Seoul in a jeep at 1:00 P.M. on the 28th. Unprecedentedly, with no guard cars by his side, Chairman Park first inspected road construction site in Susaek. . . . Today, he took Public Information Officer Yi Hu-rak alone, and the constables at local police precincts realized that it was the Chairman's inspection only after he had passed through."[39]

It is worth noting that the expressions "suddenly," "unprecedentedly," and "only after he had passed through" paint the fact that Park was "in a jeep" as an image of an innovative leader maintaining high-speed maneuverability. Similar lines of discursive construction continued after Park won the presidency, detailing how Park "ran a jeep across the gravel that most sedans and buses cannot enter," "visited by a jeep without notice, only accompanied by a guard," and "transferred to a jeep and ran on a dusty road."[40]

The discourse around Park Chung Hee in a Jeep did not just help shape Park's projected personality but also linked Park's mobility in a Jeep to images of government-led civil engineering projects, particularly those that required huge budgets and social consensus. Park's drives frequently ran parallel with mammoth construction projects, such as the Kyŏngbu Expressway lines, a large-scale multipurpose dam in Andong, P'ohang Iron & Steel's industrial complex, and a tourist facilities complex in Cheju Island.[41] This discourse, therefore, situated the industrial landscape of South Korea in an inseparable relation with Park's own projected personality and mobility.

The Führer in a Postcolonial State

In the late 1960s, the government made significant efforts to generate a symbol of nationalized automobility—namely, with the construction of expressways. Construction of the Kyŏngbu Expressway, a pivotal line among five major expressways, began in 1968 and was completed in 1970. Policy makers saw the expressway as a necessary component of industrial modernization and, at the same time, as an indicator of achieving such modernization, one that would justify their legitimacy. However, since the majority of people at the time never saw or used the expressway, Park Chung Hee and his government were confronted with considerable opposition.

The Park government tried to develop a coherent narrative and linguistic strategies to construct counterdiscourses in government-produced documents, such as Park's campaign speeches for the sixth presidential election in 1967, official texts of speeches for construction ceremonies, and several white papers on expressway construction.[42] The blueprint for the "one-day life zone" enabled by expressways, as discussed in chapter 3, was a frequent point of discussion in government documents.[43] Those documents also frequently declared that the "era of the automobile" had "already come" following the global trend.[44]

Given that Park's expressway construction has transformed South Korean industry from railroad to automobile based, it is worth noting that the Park government, facing opposition to Park's promise of expressway construction at the time, fought back against such criticism by disparaging the railroad system. The construction of nationwide expressway lines involved high expenses, and many opponents expressed skepticism about the efficiency of a new traffic system. Moreover, the International Bank of Reconstruction and Development (IBRD), from which the government expected to acquire a loan, also expressed pessimism over the effects of expressway construction.[45] People knew that the railroad system had long held the role of bringing modernization about, a role it had held since the early twentieth century. The New Democratic Party, the main opposition against the ruling party, called for "the acceleration of conventional railroad lines and the double-tracking of the Seoul-Mokp'o line instead of expressway construction."[46]

The Park government responded to these criticisms by emphasizing the "outdated inefficiency" and the "saturated condition" of the railroad.[47]

They also stressed that the railroad could not quickly connect small towns, since it was "metropolis-centered."[48] Not only did they criticize the railroad's inefficiency, but the government also framed the expressway system as a matter of national significance, claiming that it would be the fruit of decolonization. Park Chung Hee's speech at the opening of the Kyŏngbu Expressway on July 7, 1970, sums up this strategy.

> Our initial aim in starting construction for this expressway lay, of course, in the economic and industrial areas. However, I had another goal in building the expressway, which was more important than economic and material ones. That is, I had a goal to put our nation's ability to the test through this expressway, to figure out how big our national potential was, how much energy our people had, and how skilled we were. Indeed, through this construction, we have verified that we have infinite national potential, we are the nation of infinite energy, and we have an iron will.[49]

He defined the construction of the Kyŏngbu Expressway as a test of Korea's "national potential," particularly by achieving what "others called reckless and unrealizable," and deemed it a great success despite the "unfortunate seventy-seven fatalities" that had accrued over the period of construction.[50] The grounds for this assessment included the completion of construction via "pure homegrown technology without foreign consultancy," the construction expenses that marked "just about a seventh" of Japan's, and the "two-and-a-half year construction period that covered one hundred kilometers more than" Japan's Tōmei Expressway, which, in turn, required seven years to complete.[51] In this way, "national potential" was judged from a quantitative comparison with the achievements of foreign countries, especially the former colonizer, Japan. Other types of government-related documents from that time also contain similar comparisons. For instance, then vice minister of construction Kim Wŏn-ki wrote in the *Journal of the Public Officials Benefit Association* that the Kyŏngbu Expressway set a record as the longest line in the East, "beating Japan's Tōmei and Meishin Expressways."[52]

By explaining expressway construction as synonymous with economic growth, the Park government condemned the railroad system as dilapidated and oversaturated.[53] This comparison highlights how the cultural logic of mobilization was reshuffled with the emergence of the expressway system and the dream of an automobile utopia. Interestingly, some of the government documents employed a dramatic narrative to devalue the existing railroad system as a vestige of Japanese colonialism and highlight the expressway as a national symbol of decolonization. *Han'guk kosok toro simnyŏnsa* (Ten-Year History of Korean Expressways), the Korea Expressway Corporation's 1980 edition of Park's posthumous commemorative book on the nationwide expressway system, compares the two systems thus:

> In our history of transportation, railroad construction in the 1900s and expressway construction in the 1970s are the two most groundbreaking events. However, these two historical events run counter to each other in various aspects. First, the construction of railroads was a privilege given to world powers by politicians who had already lost the ability to handle national crises, whereas expressway construction was made possible by the will of a leader who established the foundation of national restoration. Second, the construction plan did not arise out of our own necessity or belief, but merely, out of blind obedience to a global trend at the time of railroads, while the expressway was planned as a far-reaching blueprint bound up with statecraft. Third, the railroad was constructed out of others' money and technology, and eventually, became the property of others, whereas the expressway was constructed out of our own money and technology, and became our own property. Fourth, the railroad, as a result, produced a humiliating history of national ruin by advancing the invasion of Japanese imperialists. In contrast, the expressway produced a glorious history of the main artery of the nation, which has promoted the growth of national power and economic development.[54]

In this description, each transportation system acquires sociopolitical value that is the complete opposite of the other's. The juxtaposition of "humiliating" and "glorious" histories creates a diametrical opposition, one that explains what made the government reject the old system and build a new one, even with such heavy expenses. The fact that both systems served as means of modernization is not overlooked, since each modernization process is described, albeit as qualitatively different from the other. Under this framework, expressway construction becomes a national goal of decolonization. When criticized for inefficiency, particularly in its proposal to leave the railroad behind and develop an entirely new system, the discourse supporting expressway construction moved from a stage emphasizing the new system's efficiency to an entirely new stage, one that subjugated efficiency to national pride.

Another interesting feature in this discourse is an ambivalent attitude toward Adolf Hitler and the Third Reich. In several documents on expressway construction, including project logbooks and white papers, there is a recurring emphasis on President Park Chung Hee's individual belief and will. In particular, it is an oft-told tale that Park's experience on the Autobahn, during an official visit to West Germany in 1964, led to his sudden advocacy of expressway construction the following year.[55] In this cause-effect relationship, the Autobahn is presented as a model of successful industrial modernization. While construction of the Autobahn was explained as a coincidental byproduct of Hitler's ambitions for war,[56] Park often stressed that the German expressway system had miraculously rescued West Germany from defeat.[57] A research monograph on the expressway published at the time also pointed out that the Autobahn's construction was led "by Hitler" to "achieve three national projects, including 'solving the unemployment problem,' 'establishing military preparedness,' and 'modernizing the transport system.'"[58]

In these references to Nazi Germany, construction was usually recalled as a great undertaking that vastly improved the nation's economy, completely ignoring the undemocratic decision-making processes that underwrote construction, as well as the abysmally poor working conditions during construction. While the Autobahn project was "a hotly contested question within the cabinet," one that not even the armed forces supported, "Hitler ignored the Reichswehr's opposition" and caused "administrative chaos."[59] Working conditions were severely harsh and unjustifiable, involving arduous and risky tasks, poor food, and "extraordinarily depressed" wages, such that the "forced labor of ten-thousand prisoners of war" was approved to offset the shortage of workers.[60] The Park Chung Hee government's state papers only emphasized Hitler's own will and leadership in the project, from decision-making to completion, but did not recognize the despotic nature of such top-down mobilization.

These tactics used to frame Adolf Hitler and Nazi Germany thus are inseparable from the methods used to portray Park, particularly his will and leadership in constructing the expressways. "However, President Park had already secretly prepared for the construction project of basic nationwide expressway lines as a crucial matter of statecraft since the early 1960s. He had waited for proper conditions and perfect timing. This truth had been kept hidden until the official statement was released in April 1967.

Yet, people who had been close to him at that time later testified that they had sometimes heard his comments on the necessity of the expressway."[61]

This statement in a white paper, commemorating the tenth anniversary of the Korea Expressway Corporation's founding, negated other government documents that had identified Park's 1967 campaign speech as the beginning of the expressway project and moved that starting point back to the early 1960s, when Park had allegedly conceived of the idea. The grounds for this statement were only anonymous recollections, but by being included in a history of a government agency, one that oversaw expressway construction and management, this unverified history gained official status. The statement's impact was propelled by its emphasis on Park's greatness as an individual, one who could look into the future, even as the "proper conditions and perfect timing" had yet to arrive.

This discursive pattern appears frequently in the prefaces and forewords of other related government documents, such as construction project logbooks and white papers: "The birth of the expressway between Seoul and Pusan was enabled by the wise and prompt decision of His Excellency President Park Chung Hee."[62] "This is the product of His Excellency President Park Chung Hee's foresight and unceasing tenacity alone."[63] "It was conceived and planned by the great experience and knowledge of the late President Park Chung Hee, who personally made field investigations to select the most viable routes, and led the construction project in general, even visiting construction sites one by one."[64] "President Park is obviously a development-oriented *yŏngdoja* [führer]."[65]

In these statements, the expressway project is presented as something conceived, planned, and carried out entirely by Park Chung Hee himself, not by the state. This narrative divided people into two camps, those who celebrated the expressway project as a product of "foresight" and those who criticized it for being "short-sighted."[66] Ultimately, the narrative served to support top-down policy enforcement by a führer with foresight. While such records as "the longest line in the East" and "the two-and-a-half year construction period" legitimized the führer's leadership, the documents supporting him did not mention how working conditions worsened, how lands for road sites were illegitimately purchased, and how expressway construction led to uneven regional development.[67] These tactics resonate with those same documents' ambivalent attitudes toward the history of the Autobahn.

Discursive Construction of the Kosok Toro *(Expressway)*

Most likely, the term *kosok toro*,[68] the Korean equivalent of "expressway," "highway," or "Autobahn," was first used in an official capacity during the sixth presidential campaign in 1967, when Park Chung Hee was seeking reelection.[69] Park and his government began discussing the construction of national expressways as part of Park's campaign promises. According to a Korea Expressway Corporation report, the first use of *kosok toro* in a government document appeared in the appendix of the Grand National Development Plan Draft, which the Ministry of Construction had proposed to the Blue House in August 1967.[70] Given that then presidential candidate Park Chung Hee had used the term while on the Seoul campaign trail in April 1967, specifically in promising to push for the Grand National Development Plan's vision of "the Kyŏngbu kosok toro linking Seoul and Pusan" and "the Honam kosok toro linking Taejŏn and Mokp'o,"[71] the first official use of this term should, in fact, date to the 1967 election season.[72]

The 1963 opening of the Meishin Expressway's (J. Meishin kōsoku dōro) first section in Japan suggests the likely possibility that *kosok toro* was an adaptation of the Japanese *kōsoku dōro*.[73] On the other hand, it should also be noted that the word *kosok* (high speed) was effectively used in a lexical, semantic network of developmentalist discourses produced and distributed at the state level at the time. Park Chung Hee's speeches during the election year, covering budget announcements,[74] administrative policy speeches,[75] New Year's addresses, annual messages to Congress, and the inaugural address for his second term,[76] make constant mention of "high speed" in economic development and industrial modernization. These statements insisted that the task of modernization should be achieved immediately and that, to achieve high growth, the entire country's participation was needed. *Kodo sŏngjang* (high-speed economic growth) was one of the most important mottos in this speed-centered modernization project. Kosok toro was understood as a rationalized system that upheld the value of kosok by contributing toward high-speed economic development. At a press conference the day before the election, Park commented that the promise of expressway construction was "one of the basic blueprints for the modernization of the fatherland."[77]

In the meantime, the value of kosok was stressed ceaselessly during the expressways' construction. *Konggi tanch'uk*, meaning the reduction of construction time, was one of the most frequently repeated mottos at construction sites.[78] During the early stages of the project, the Kyŏngbu Expressway was slated for completion in five years, with one of the five sections being built each year. However, with the plan changes in December 1967, all sections began construction in 1968, with the completion date readjusted to August 30, 1970.[79] During this process, President Park issued an order that the government would not outsource work to construction companies who could not meet this new deadline.[80] Some companies even had to use quick-dry cement to meet these deadlines.[81]

Construction was drastically pushed ahead immediately after Park's reelection and the inauguration of his second term. It reorganized the country by completing several lines successively, including the Kyŏngin Expressway (the Seoul–Inch'ŏn line) in 1968, the Kyŏngbu Expressway (the Seoul–Pusan line) in 1970, the Yŏngdong Expressway (the line between the Singal Junction and the Saemal Interchange) in 1971, and the Honam and Namhae Expressways (the Taejŏn–Sunchŏn line and the Sunchŏn–Pusan line) in 1973.

The expressway was a system that was engineered fundamentally for high-speed economic growth, and it was simultaneously an actual goal to be constructed rapidly. This artificial structure—the embodiment of speed and a goal to be achieved with speed—came to be identified by the term *kosok toro*, not merely as a translation of a foreign concept but also as an outcome of discursive production.

The Expressway as a Rite of Passage

> "A mountain passed by. Houses passed by. Ceaselessly, everything was just passing by. Myŏng-pae felt the speed of the bus, [saying,] 'You may be thrilled when you die at the height of speed.'"[82]

How, then, was the discourse of the expressway shared and circulated in the public imagination? It may not be easy to grasp a general picture, but we can find clues by examining discursive features used in popular culture. "The Expressway" ("Kosok toro"), Pak Yŏng-jun's serial story, appeared in the *Tonga ilbo* newspaper from May 1969 to March 1970. Given that a story titled "The Expressway" was serialized during this period, one overlapping the construction period for the Kyŏngbu Expressway, we might speculate that the story could affect the public perception of the expressway at that time.

Pak, an established writer with almost thirty-five years of experience, began his literary career with a story titled "A Model Farmer" ("Mobŏm kyŏngjaksaeng") in 1934. His oeuvre after the Korean War exhibits recurring themes of "the rapid breakdown of traditions and morals, [and] the deviation from the existing value system, following direct contact with Western culture," and is understood as having pursued the disclosure, criticism, and overcoming of such ethical crises.[83] Accordingly, a series of his works from this period, including "Hospital Room of the Youth" ("Ch'ŏngch'un pyŏngsil"), "Blue Skirt" ("P'urŭn ch'ima"), and "Typhoon Zone" ("T'aep'ung chidae"), has been called "the stories of social conditions" (*set'ae sosŏl*).[84]

Clearly, "The Expressway" belongs to this group of works. This story can be read as a response to the wave of global student activism in the late 1960s, reflecting a distinct sensitivity to ethical crisis. The two protagonists, Myŏng-su and Sang-o, are suffering from the loss of an ethical direction. Myŏng-su is a college freshman, who begins an affair with the middle-aged Mrs. O, the mother of his brother's girlfriend, Hye-su. He continuously expresses disdain for the freewheeling lifestyles of Hye-su and her mother but, after a couple of short conversations, is tempted by Mrs. O. Both mother and daughter are portrayed as quite exceptionally modernized and unrestrained, not devoting themselves to their male partners. After a short-lived affair, however, Myŏng-su realizes that his love has come to nothing, and he himself is abandoned by Mrs. O. He decides to kill himself and gets in a taxi to take the expressway. Pak Yŏng-jun describes Myŏng-su's inner state thus:

> Black—in black, the darkest among the primary colors, the expressway anchors the surface to the ground, directly linking Seoul with Pusan. This stationary road is skewering lots of towns on its way. Hence, it pushes up its magical power onto the nation's modernization projects, including political, social, economic, and cultural issues. It casts the darkest and, at the same time, fanciest black magical power. . . . That is probably the reason

> why Myŏng-su has decided to die on the black expressway. When dying on the black expressway, even his blood will not show its true color. When dying on that unthinkably high-speed elsewhere, he will be able to burn his life down in the midst of modernization. He doesn't have to be pitiful even as he dies. He never has to feel pain.[85]

Myŏng-su's suicide attempt ends in failure. However, the description of his thoughts during the attempt illustrates the author's vision of the expressway. For Pak, the expressway functions as a means of purification, a role that stems from the nobility of its aim—modernization. After his suicide attempt, Myŏng-su conquers his frustration and begins dating a college girl around his age. The depravity of the middle-aged lady, who is Westernized and morally flawed, is completely washed away after his experience of speed on the expressway.

The other antihero, Sang-o, is a friend of Myŏng-su's elder brother, Myŏng-pae, and a womanizer. As a young businessman seeking to build up his own enterprise, Sang-o tries to stand on his own feet, independently of his father, who is the owner of a construction company. However, his business fails, and to make matters worse, he ends up cutting ties with Myŏng-pae over his affair with Hye-su, Myŏng-pae's girlfriend. At the end of all his wandering, he meets with his father and receives some advice.

> "Hitler is dead but his expressway remains." . . . In his mind, Sang-o pictured the black expressway that would penetrate the closest distance from Seoul to Pusan. The road embodying speed, the line on which all cultures concentrate—it appeared in close-up in his brain as the origin of the universe, rather than as a part of material civilization. He felt that dreams, hopes, and futures lay in it. . . . "Whenever you don't like the expressway, why not just visit any construction site? All the shapes and contents of architecture symbolize the culture of our times. That is to say, the purpose of construction is to plant culture in towns. You'll get interested when you go there and see it."[86]

Sang-o is a character who exhibits the anomie of the younger generation, one that bears no trust in the older generation. Accordingly, his drifting manifests as a rebellion against his father's generation. The expressway is implied as that which bridges all gaps and misunderstandings between the two generations. The expressway in Sang-o's mind is depicted as an ethical rite of passage, whereby the younger generation inherits their fathers' ideal of modernizing the fatherland. Notably, women are excluded from this succession, even though they are modernized. These women's modern lifestyles are perceived as decadence, while Sang-o, the licentious prodigal son, successfully returns to a moral way of life after passing the rite of embracing the value of expressway construction.

In this way, the representation of the expressway is rooted in the ideal of the modern nation-state, as well as in its masculine model of morality. It should be noted that this story references Adolf Hitler in glamorizing the expressway, while women's freewheeling lifestyles, as influenced by Western trends, are presented as the antipode of such glamorization.

Cine-Mobility of Being a Projectile

Pak Yŏng-jun's story gives us a glimpse of how early popular imagination envisioned the expressway as a built structure, but how was mobility *through* the expressway represented at the time? The visual strategies and discourses of expressway traffic in South Korean propaganda films might yield an answer to this question. Through the Motion Picture Law enacted on January 20, 1962, Park Chung Hee's junta mandated that every theater show a culture film before each screening, a move that had a significant role in shaping the military government's publicity. Under the Ministry of Public Information, the NFPC made a decent number of culture films and newsreels, all arguing for the government's construction policy and depicting dynamic images of construction sites. The expressway, a strange, new structure of transportation, was also something that could be effectively visualized in culture films. As culture films under the Japanese Empire showcased the cine-mobility of railway imperialism, the Park government's culture films homed in on the cine-mobility of a nationalized automobile traffic system.

Experiencing an expressway that did not yet exist, or that most people had yet to experience, in the theater was not only a form of entertainment, whereby people could consume a new culture, but also a training experience that disciplined viewers—namely, by introducing the new bodily senses that would be enabled by the expressway. In particular, the audience was subjected to vicarious audiovisual, or even synesthetic, stimuli from the experience of being on the cinematic expressway. This virtual ride helped the audience understand the unfamiliar traffic system, teaching them how it differed from other, more familiar experiences of motion.

In her essay on automobile cultures and the screen in postwar Los Angeles, Anne Friedberg discusses the relation between the "materiality and mobility" of automotive visuality and the "immateriality and stasis" of the cinematic spectator.[87] As one can infer from her identification of the automobile as a "viewing machine," the visuality of the automobile in motion is determined by visibility through its windshield, "a framing device," through which Paul Virilio thinks "cinema" goes on.[88] However, despite the "blunt equation between automotive mobility and cinematic visuality," the cinema as the "audiovisual vehicle" is premised on "the spectator as a 'sedentary' driver."[89] This paradoxical tension between mobility and immobility in automotive visuality was particularly strong in automobilized Western cities such as Los Angeles, where individual car owner-drivers gathered at drive-in theaters to watch fast-moving entertainment films with virtual driving scenes.[90]

How, then, should we understand automotive visuality in the culture films promoting expressway construction in South Korea? Unlike the audiences in Los Angeles, the majority of people in South Korea did not experience seeing through the windshield of a fast car on the expressway as part of their daily routines (see table 3.1 in chapter 3) but as something that could be received and "mediated through representation."[91] As a sedentary driver, the viewers of expressway culture films were mobilized to gaze at virtual movement on the screen. The immobility and virtual mobility of this cinematic experience prevailed over the actual mobility of automotive visuality. It is important to remember that the gaze was institutionally mobilized by the South Korean government through the mandatory screening of culture films. That is to say, the politically "summoned" aspect of a mobilized gaze needs to be discussed in greater detail, with close attention to the historical context of expressway construction under the Park Chung Hee government, as opposed to focusing on the relatively autonomous "mobile" gaze of an automobilized city.[92]

The automotive visuality of Korean spectators, who were mobilized as sedentary drivers, was shaped by virtual drives on the newly built expressway. Unlike commercial feature films with protagonists driving cars, culture films adopted a documentary style, whereby there was no fictional main character whose gaze mediated that of the audience or whose figure in a moving car became the object of the audience's gaze. In place of a fictional driver was a virtual driver. That is to say, the audience was positioned to look out from the windshield as if sitting in the driver's seat themselves. In a scene from *The Road to Reunification* (*T'ongil ŭi kil*), a 1970 culture film showcasing the opening ceremony for a 124-km line between Taegu and Pusan on the Kyŏngbu Expressway on December 29, 1969, the viewer is given the chance to experience a virtual test drive on the new line. The scene is set to give the sense of driving a vehicle rapidly on the open road, with no obstructions whatsoever. The test drive consists of several checkpoints, including the starting point with a placard, an overpass, a memorial gate, a couple of traffic signs on the right, and a tollgate marking the end point. These checkpoints indicate that the journey is continuously moving forward and progressing along a line of goals, with arrival at the tollgate signifying achievement of the final goal.

Notably, this visual journey is accompanied by an audio recording of the ruling politician's speech at the ceremony. After the narrator briefly introduces the speech and the start of the test drive scene, Park Chung Hee's recorded voice runs through the entire scene and over into the following scene, where his voice aligns with footage of Park's speech. The speech suggests a linear course of development—beginning with the construction of expressways, entering the checkpoint of an innovation in transport and distribution, and finally achieving the goal of an annual trade of six to seven billion dollars—which parallels the linear forward movement of the moving images. The virtual body of the audience as a projectile, or a bullet, in the experience of swiftly driving onward, embodies the politics of the mobilized proletariat in the industrial modernization project. A virtual bullet propelled toward a destination, the soldier-proletariat-audience serves a military-like, highly organized and disciplined action to achieve rapid and effective logistics for national interests. Similar parallelizations of virtual drives and narrated national objectives are exhibited in several other culture films, including *The Road* (*Kil*, 1967) and *The Road to Prosperity* (*Pŏnyŏng ŭi kil*, 1974).

The world as seen by a projectile also suggests a new vision, different from those of other traffic systems. The lateral view from a car in South Korean culture films on expressways, such as *Road to Kangwŏn Province* (*Kwan'tong ŭi kil*, 1975), a film that depicts Kangwŏn Province's major tourist attractions in geographical order, shares some similarities with the panoramic view from a locomotive. However, what defines projectile perception is the windshield view from the driver's seat, which gives the viewer a corporeal sense of heading toward a destination. Unlike the viewer-passenger in *Tokyo-Peking*, who glanced out the window or stepped out to look around the towns where the train stopped, the viewer-driver in *Road to Kangwŏn Province* can view the scenery before him or her from the driver's seat. In other words, projectile perception provides the viewer with an ontological sense of movement being merged with the viewer's own body rather than being carried by a vehicle that is distinctly separate from his or her body.

The cine-mobility of projectile perception entails certain political implications—namely, the dominion of forward movement. As Sobchack points out, cinema "projects and makes uniquely visible not only the objective world," such as the vehicle's movement on the expressway, "but the very structure and process of subjective, embodied vision," here manifested as the merged vision of a viewer-driver in expressway culture films.[93] The merged vision of camera and viewer-driver presents itself in a specific structure of cine-mobility. In particular, it directs the film-body-vehicle toward certain goals. The ontological signification of this forward movement is structured by a high degree of physical mobility that aims at the body-vehicle's arrival at a destination. In turn, the dominion of forward movement reveals the political logic of industrial modernization. The motility of a projectile not only forecloses in-between spaces, as the locomotive did in *Tokyo-Peking*, but also forecloses every landscape it leaves behind. The voice-over narration in *Road to Kangwŏn Province* mentions tourist attractions one by one and emphasizes the labor needed to establish accessibility to these sites but never mentions what the construction project left behind. While it stresses the three hundred days of construction needed to align the Tunnae Tunnel with the Yŏngdong Expressway, the film is clearly not interested in the costs residents near the tunnel had to pay, such as the impact the construction had on their lives, and the damage to the environment. There is no mention or consideration of these issues anywhere in the film, and they are simply foreclosed as if they did not exist. The forward movement of development and of the cinematic projectile are not only metaphorically linked with each other but also share the "subjective, embodied vision" that focuses only on the destinations. The structure of vision in cine-mobility becomes indistinguishable from the audience's subjective vision.

The Machine Space and Its Exterior World

The development of the high-speed traffic system also changed the viewer's sense of space. The establishment of Japan's railroad-based, modern transportation network led to the decline of smaller organized spaces like the *han* (clan) and the rise of large cities like Tokyo and Kyoto.[94] In a similar fashion, the opening of the Kyŏngbu Expressway boosted development of the area around Seoul, as well as of big cities like Pusan, recently connected by the new traffic system. Invoking Ernst Georg Ravenstein's laws of migration, however, the urban planner and historian Son Chŏng-mok criticized this shift as having led to the rapid downfall of rural areas, as well as small- and medium-sized cities in South Korea.[95] The resulting change, a kind of cognitive adjustment driven by the rapid automobilization of living spaces since expressway construction, shared some characteristics with the changes brought about by the spread of the railroad, such as the foreclosure of in-between spaces and the emergence of panoramic perception, as discussed in chapter 2. However, aiming at capillary networks connected to the national artery, the cine-mobility of automobiles reorganized the interrelation between humans and machines, the human perception of moving worlds and the moving self, and the system of mobility in a society now closer to the moving vehicle than the locomotive as sublime object ever was.

What, then, was the viewer's spatial sense of the national territory synthetically presented, in part, as these rationalized and homogenized spaces of networked traffic? The 1968 culture film *A Conversation* (*Ŏnŭ taehwa*), which was intended to cultivate the public's sense of order, particularly with its dialogue about the expressway, provides a clue to this question.

> **Old man #1:** You know, there was a great deal of fuss when they started building that expressway. Yet, once it took shape, it grew on me.
> **Old man #2:** They say that when it's completed next year, you can drive from Seoul to Pusan in half a day.
> **Old man #1:** Dear me! Times are changing so quickly that, maybe in a few years, they will say we can go to Pusan in the blink of an eye.
> **Old man #2:** You know what? If I were a bit younger, I would like to walk down to Pusan on that expressway. Ha-ha.
> **Old man #1:** Uh-oh, old chap. No way! Who would allow you to walk on that road?
> **Old man #2:** Men cannot walk on a road? Don't talk nonsense!

This dialogue, exhibiting an obvious collision between perceptions of road traffic systems, conveys the simple truth that people cannot walk on the expressway. The second old man's bewildered retort demonstrates that the new traffic system will radically transform the structural relationship between humans and space. Not only are people not allowed to walk on the expressway, but neither is it legal to park, stop, or drive under the minimum speed limit on these roads. Referencing Horvath, Choi argues that the Kyŏngbu Expressway emerged as *machine space*, an area where "the machine is normally given the right-of-way,"[96] which expanded "at the expense of *people space*."[97] This drastic reorganization of spaces into those where people could enter and those where they could not occasionally led to maladjustment. *Camera Dispatch* (*K'amera ch'uldong*), an investigative television news program on the major South Korean broadcaster Munhwa Broadcasting Corporation (MBC), reported that, as of June 26, 1987, nearly two decades after *A Conversation*, there was still a considerable number of people who jaywalked daily across Olympic Boulevard, a crosstown expressway in Seoul exclusively open for automobiles.

The machine space of expressways expanded from Seoul to Pusan, to Inch'ŏn, to Chŏnju, and to Kangnŭng, with effective logistics for industrial supplies, products, and manpower as the top priority. The expressway, on which one must operate one's vehicle without break, hindrance, or reduction of speed under a minimum limit, recalls the conveyer belt system in a factory. The traveler on the expressway becomes "the parcel" on a conveyer-belt-like distribution and circulation system.[98] The image of the expressway system that links farmlands, fish markets, and tourist attractions with manufacturing belts in *The Road to Prosperity* is nothing but the transformation of the whole country into a great factory. The scene of construction directly after the bus attendant's introduction of each site turns this virtual journey into a field trip to a factory. These representations of expressways in culture films restructure the nation's territories as rapidly operating industrial sites and subsequently redefine movement within these territories.

What about the image of the expressway in popular culture beyond the culture film? The long-lived, popular detective series on MBC, *Chief Inspector* (*Susa panjang*, 1971–1989), provides one evocative image of the expressway, resonating with the conveyer-belt imagery in government-sponsored culture films. The series first aired in March 1971, only months after completion of the Kyŏngbu Expressway. One of its earlier episodes, titled "The Expressway Drifted with Rolls of Bills" ("Kosok toro-e nalin chip'ye tabal"), used the expressway as the scene of the crime. With the subtitle "A Case of Child Abduction in Taejo-dong" ("Taejo-dong ŏrini yugoe sagŏn"), this episode dealt with the real story of a child who was abducted and killed on a sidewalk near the newly completed Kyŏngbu Expressway. The first two-thirds of the episode are devoted to portraying the psychological agonies and antagonism between the victim's parents, the kidnapper, and the investigative team, with several locations in Seoul used as key sets in the drama, including the victim's home in Taejo-dong, Sŏdaemun-gu, the site of the abduction, the headquarters of the investigative team, and the criminal's hiding place. The expressway first appears in a scene where the victim's parents drive to a place specified by the kidnapper to pay the ransom. Despite the investigative team's instruction that all contact from the kidnapper be reported, the parents, under great duress, decide to pay their child's ransom. The investigative team, while tailing them, realizes the parents' destination only when their car passes the National Cemetery, which is near the entrance to the Kyŏngbu Expressway. At this point, the script describes the following: "At this point, it was easy to guess that the place was some low hill near the Kyŏngbu

Expressway. It was not long before Mr. Chi's car turned down into the entrance for the Kyŏngbu Expressway at the southern end of Han'gang Bridge No. 3. The detective squad chief in the pursuit car suddenly smacked his fist into his palm. 'It must be the hill near that pass. Well . . . Detective Sŏ, they might catch wind of us. Follow them at a greater distance!'"[99]

The place where the kidnapper lures the parents turns out to be a hill near the shoulder of the road, between the entrance to the Kyŏngbu Expressway and the tollgate. For the investigative team, who have closely observed the parents and their actions upon receiving calls from the kidnapper, the expressway's shoulder outside Seoul is an unexpected venue, seen as an uncontrolled place made worse without any advance preparation. Neither the team nor the parents have any idea that the criminal was murdering the child at that very moment. The parents leave the money at the agreed-upon site and proceed to pass the tollgate, since they are not allowed to stop the car or make a U-turn on the expressway. The investigative team, right behind the parents' car, raids the site only to realize that the child is already dead. Ironically enough, the criminal is killed by the parents' car as it drives back in the opposite direction, running away from the investigative team.

> The criminal's body turned into a total wreck, as if he had been bombed that instant. The money was scattered and spread all over the asphalt. . . . Traffic was blocked and, in a second, dozens of cars lined up one after another in both directions. And the expressway patrols rushed at the road site with their sirens wailing. The rolls of five hundred won bills, which were three million won in total, wound up on the asphalt, and were blown like fallen leaves by a breeze. Chief Pak gave an order to the detectives. "Rake up the bills first. There are a lot of eyes on that amount of money."[100]

Here, the expressway and its extremities, where both the kidnapped child and the kidnapper died, are presented as a heartless space. As it suddenly halts operations, the expressway instantly becomes a line of congested traffic, much like a stalled factory conveyer belt with a queue of goods on it. The asphalt road with scattered, drifting bills is now a desolate space with no sign of life, except the anonymous eyes on the money. The invisible spaces between towns are depicted not only as anonymous but also as beyond police control. The expressway is characterized by the unceasing flow that cuts through those in-between spaces. Each site where that logistics flow is cut, an event that goes against the rules of the expressway, is merely a "non-place" without any authenticity.[101] The world outside the expressway is, thus, an unrecognizable, uncontrollable, and dangerous space that has been foreclosed.

Automobilization: A Trophy of Modernization

The kosok toro is, therefore, a result of propaganda and itself a discursive structure. Positive valuation of mobilized labor power in perfect order and rapid distribution, confidence in the subjugation of coloniality and the bright future of the nation-state, projection of moral consciousness onto the image of expressways—all of these are involved in discourse production around the expressway.

Therefore, ex post facto debates on the economic effectiveness of expressway construction can become mired in the same discourse production. For instance, Son's criticism, specifically that railroads would have been better suited to South Korea's demographics and geographical features, amounts to no more than speculation around the question "Which would have been the more 'effective' means of modernization?"[102]

Instead, demystification of these discourses, critical examination of the structure of statements organizing those discourses, and cultivation of alternative discourse systems would be the more meaningful steps in the present. Such steps will not only align with historical criticism of kosok toro discourses but also yield contemporary reflections on prevailing developmentalist discourses, which share discursive patterns with those of the past.

PART III

Post-Cine-Mobility

CHAPTER 5

Imagined Geographies of the World

Television, Aviation, and Koreanness

In July 1969, when Apollo 11 brought the first humans to the moon, USIS-Korea set up an outdoor television screen on the Mt. Namsan Park Bandstand and broadcast the historic event, from the rocket's launch on July 16 to the lunar landing on July 20.[1] On the night of the landing, more than 100,000 people gathered at the park to watch the televised event (see fig. 5.1).[2] It was also an indoor event. Television sets sold well at every store, and each house with a television attracted neighbors who wanted to watch the landing together.[3] This glittering media event was possible because South Korea had become a member of the International Telecommunications Satellite Organization (INTELSAT), an intergovernmental consortium of "free world" countries.[4]

This chapter examines the different ways in which USIS films and television shows from the late 1960s and 1970s represented the geographies of the "free world" to South Korean viewers and how they located those viewers' identities—namely, Koreanness—within that geographical imagination. In the 1970s, well into the age of television, the conveyor of propagandistic vision was neither a train nor a Jeep. Audiences did not have to gather in one place, as they could simply stay at home. The advanced technologies of satellites and aviation enabled a new degree of maximized mobility, and propaganda pictures now reached viewers directly. Much like private car ownership, television also gave the nuclear family a sense of possession. In this new media environment, the USIS television shows made for South Korean broadcasters were unique and

FIGURE 5.1 Outdoor screen from USIS-Korea televising the Apollo 11 lunar landing (1969). From *Tonga ilbo*, July 22, 1969, 7. © Dong-A Ilbo.

attractive to Korean viewers, who found their exotic foreign content appealing. Talk shows spotlighted the daily lives of Koreans in the United States, while documentaries depicted the modern progress of "free" Asian countries. Such programming narrowed the imagined geographic distance between Korean viewers and the outside world and positioned imagined Koreanness among the "free world."

It was a period not only of Koreans' fields of vision exploding through technology but also, following Marshall McLuhan's account, of the electrically visualized world *imploding*. The dialectic of explosion and implosion in the age of television suggested a departure from the more traditional way of perceiving the world, cine-mobility. However, South Korea's own aviation mobility, which would shape the new mode of visual mobility together with televisual visibility, significantly shaped the specific, local context of the divided nation under Cold War conditions, marking a deviation from McLuhan's notion of a "global village."[5]

To trace the genealogy of these imagined world geographies in the South Korean visualscape, this chapter navigates through images of the local and the global typical in USIS films, early USIS television images of the world, and the way certain translated, foreign, topological values were appropriated by South Korean media to situate a national identity on the imagined map.

Translation of "the Local" as an American Democratic Value

We can trace this genealogy back to a South Korean television series, *Blooming P'aldogangsan* (*Kkotp'inŭn p'aldogangsan*), which can be seen as a local counterpart to the foreign, televised images of the world. The series was aired on the Korean Broadcasting System (KBS) network from April 14, 1974, to October 5, 1975.[6] It was a television adaptation of the successful government propaganda film franchise *P'aldogangsan* (1968–1972), which was, as discussed in chapter 3, heavily influenced by the original creators' interactions with USIS-Korea. It aired daily, in a serialized drama format, racking up a total of 398 episodes and achieving high viewer ratings of over 40 percent.[7] While the cast had changed slightly,

Blooming P'aldogangsan shared the basic premise of the films—Hŭi-kap and Chŏng-sun traveling around the country to see their daughters and sons-in-law. In this light, the KBS television series successfully took over the role of cinematic propaganda formerly filled by the NFPC films. Moreover, it did so during a time when 82.8 percent of South Korean television viewers regularly tuned in to daily soap operas.[8]

Until *Blooming P'aldogangsan* concluded in October 1975, over eight years after the success of the original film, the entire *P'aldogangsan* franchise had been preparing for and celebrating the installation of the Yusin regime and actively served as the audiovisual embodiment of the regime. In this light, it is of particular importance that the franchise was understood as visualizing the nation's imagined geography. The term *P'aldogangsan* literally means "eight provinces, rivers and mountains," and refers to "the scenery from all corners of Korea." This franchise was the first attempt to compile and integrate representations of each region into a national narrative. The success of the original film in 1967 led to a considerable number of films with similar titles, such as *P'aldo Kisaeng* (1968) and *P'aldo Men* (*P'aldo sanai*, 1969).[9] While these films featured various genre film characteristics that differentiated them from the franchise films, they also shared a similar narrative structure, one that enumerated the characteristics of all the regions in South Korea and embraced these characteristics as indicative of the nation's diversity.[10] The *P'aldogangsan* franchise focused more on national unity than its spin-offs did, going on location to each region to introduce local residents, indigenous cultures, and industries.

Accordingly, it is this government-sponsored franchise that provided support for discourses of *han'guk-chŏk-in kŏt*, or "Koreanness," under the Yusin regime. The rhetoric of Koreanness was accompanied by that regime's critique of Western culture and Western-style democracy. The *P'aldogangsan* franchise successfully showcased a constructed vision of Koreanness as the antithesis of the West and, at the same time, as a postcolonial identity compromised by American hegemony under Cold War conditions. The social imagination of Koreanness implied certain geographical relationships between the Korean nation and the outside world, as well as among the various images of the local within the Korean nation. The *P'aldogangsan* franchise, with its narrative of traveling around the country and the world, effectively embodied the imagined geography carved out in the imagination of Koreanness.

The trajectories of key figures involved with the original *P'aldogangsan* film (1967) demonstrate the surfaces of emergence for this geographical imagination of the world. As briefly mentioned in chapter 3, the film's director Pae Sŏk-in and leading actor Kim Hŭi-kap both had experience working for or with USIS-Korea. They visited the United States together under the exchange program sponsored by the U.S. State Department. During their travels, the political visions expressed in American government-sponsored films and television shows, especially the visions of localism and federalism, were imported, translated, and appropriated into their worldviews, sowing the seeds for South Korea's cinematic imagination of an ideal nation-state and its outside world. These surfaces foreshadowed "the world in the image of a global village," composed of diverse national landscapes and ethnographic gazes on the self and the Other, specifically through "the new electronic interdependence" in the age of television.[11]

According to the American political scientist Harlan Han, localism and cosmopolitanism are often adversarial concepts representing the basic difference in attitudes toward American political systems, including city, state, and federal governments, formation of public opinion, and policy decisions.[12] Bill Kirkpatrick points out that the history of localism as a political ideology—"middle-class moral-reform movements acting on the belief that the small local community provided the ideal setting for spiritual and moral uplift"—has been a central doctrine of American democracy for more than two centuries, but the taste for local culture only formed in the first fifty years after the American Civil War.[13] "Loving stories of small-town life awash in local color, populated by the parsons and schoolmarms of places like Friendship Village, a literary cliché that critic Carl van Doren called 'the cult of the village,'"[14] dominated American literature from the late nineteenth and early twentieth centuries, and typical localist features, such as the Victorian small-town images depicted by D. W. Griffith and Mary Pickford's prototypical girl-next-door image, were formed in early Hollywood films.[15]

The film propaganda distributed by the U.S. Army and USIS-Korea also reflected these trends. Although these films marked the U.S. federal

FIGURE 5.2 A farmer riding a hay wagon in *Tuesday in November* (1945) (RG306-201). Courtesy of NARA.

government's deliberate attempt at propaganda, a considerable number of them were made with localist touches. The aforementioned film *Tuesday in November* is a good example. While it is clear that this film was produced to spotlight the triumph of the newly elected U.S. federal government in 1944, it is not incidental that the film was set in Riverton, a small city in California. From the opening narration that intones, "This is an American city, a city that is not very large, not very rich, not very old," to the images of a farmer riding a slow, horse-drawn hay wagon along country lanes, to the background flute music running through the scene with the public school principal, who serves as the chair of the election board for the town's fifteen thousand citizens, the film succeeds in illustrating a typical, slow-paced, peaceful, local American town (see fig. 5.2). The film shows local democracy as the basis for national democracy and provides justification for the U.S. federal government—that is, the film is a combination of American localism and federalism. As discussed in chapter 3, the film's first sequence depicts the election board greeting the voters, all of whom are neighbors with one another. The following animated scene shows how the U.S. administration is organized. Then, there are actual election scenes, with long lines of voters in a larger city, the election campaigns of the Democratic candidate Roosevelt and his Republican opponent Dewey, and the counting rooms. The film ends with a final scene of Roosevelt's victory and crowds celebrating in New York's Times Square. This film is a prime example of U.S. propaganda films used to introduce American democracy to foreign countries; it was chosen by the OCI of the U.S. Army Forces in Korea (USAFIK) to screen nationwide before the 1948 general election to establish the separate government of South Korea.

American propaganda agencies imported and released an abundance of films championing localism in South Korea. According to USIS-Korea's 1964 catalog for their film library, there were a considerable number of films that had localist touches. Some of them introduced New England as the birthplace of Puritan localism, including *New England*, *New England Calling*, *New England Farmer*, and *New England Portrait*, while other films depicted American local culture and rural life, including *American Village Storekeeper*, *Small Town USA*, *Creative Art in Rural America*, and *Country Store*.[16]

Small Town Editor (1952, produced by USIS), *Country Editor* (1954, produced by the Television-Radio Workshop of the Ford Foundation and released by USIS), and *Small Town Newspaper* (1956, produced by USIS as the second in the Reports from America series), were also localism-oriented public information films. As of 1964, the first two films were identified as available for public viewing and borrowing at USIS-Korea's film library.[17] Though many films in USIS-Korea's closed library of fiction and nonfiction films, including *Battleship Potemkin* (1925) and *Night Mail* (1936), were not listed in the USIS-Korea catalog for public use, it is likely that availability for *Small Town Editor* and *Country Editor* was even extended to staff during Pae Sŏk-in's work with USIS Liberty Productions between 1955 and 1958, as Pae himself stated that he frequently used the closed library.[18] Therefore, it is very likely that those films influenced Pae's USIS-Korea film of a similar theme, *Korean Editor* (*Chibang sinmun p'yŏnjipcha*, 1958), both directly and indirectly.

Small Town Editor introduces a local newspaper called the *Littleton Independent* in the town of Littleton, Colorado (see fig. 5.3). The film follows the day-to-day work life of the chief editor Houston Waring, moving from the collection of news materials to the selection of items of news value to the covering of cases. Waring covers trials in the district court, cases in the sheriff's office, a revised law for residents' security, newly installed night lights, and residents' concerns at town meetings. In bright and positive tones, the film depicts how the local newspaper and its editor intervene in local thorny issues, such as the pros and cons of establishing a community health center. Waring attends the town meeting and gives a speech on that matter as a guest panelist. After the newspapers are printed, the subsequent scene shows how the papers are distributed in the neighborhood by paperboys. The film's last scene shows the editor receiving feedback about the newspaper published that day.

Country Editor features a first-person narrator, who is introducing the town newspaper, *The Archive*, in Downingtown, Delaware County, Pennsylvania. With a population of just five thousand, Downingtown is perhaps most famous as the site where General George Washington engaged the British Army in the Battle of Brandywine during the American Revolutionary War. The chief editor and hero of the film, Bob McIlvaine, explains that his father was an architect who designed the Brandywine Creek Park, a historic site in the town. McIlvaine and his wife, Jane, are in charge of editing *The Archive*, but the newspaper is facing a financial crisis and is likely to be sold. The majority of the film is devoted to the coeditors' efforts to save the paper. To overcome the paper's financial problems, Bob tries to persuade local merchants to advertise in his paper. At first, he is unable to convince them of the newspaper advertisement's effectiveness. However, the local society ultimately recognizes his efforts to publicize local issues, and they grant the paper funds from the community chest. *The Archive* is taken off the auction block. In the final scene, the printing presses are shown back in full operation, churning out papers (see fig. 5.4).

Pae Sŏk-in's *Korean Editor* shows strong indicators of these two films' influence. The film shares similarities with *Small Town Editor*'s overall narrative construction, as well as with *Country Editor*'s use of a first-person narrator. The protagonist in Pae's film is the chief editor of the local newspaper, *Masan ilbo*, and the basic plot follows his daily routine, including interviewing reporters; attending local policy discussions; covering activities;

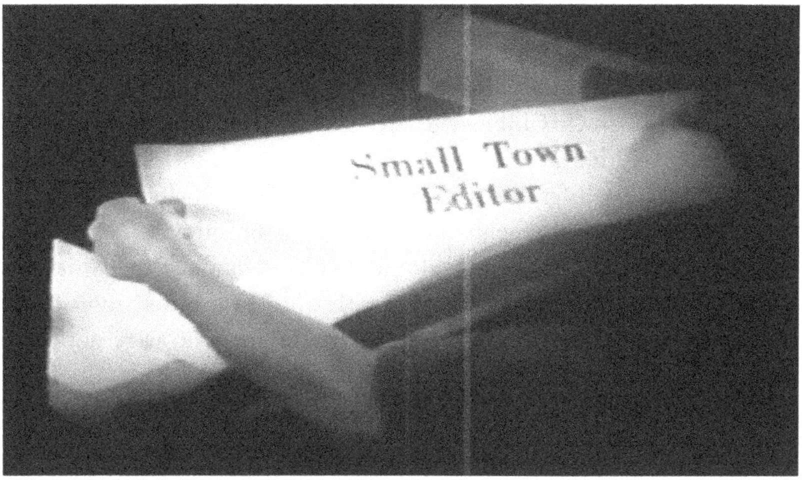

FIGURE 5.3 Opening graphics of *Small Town Editor* (1952) (RG306-5826). Courtesy of NARA.

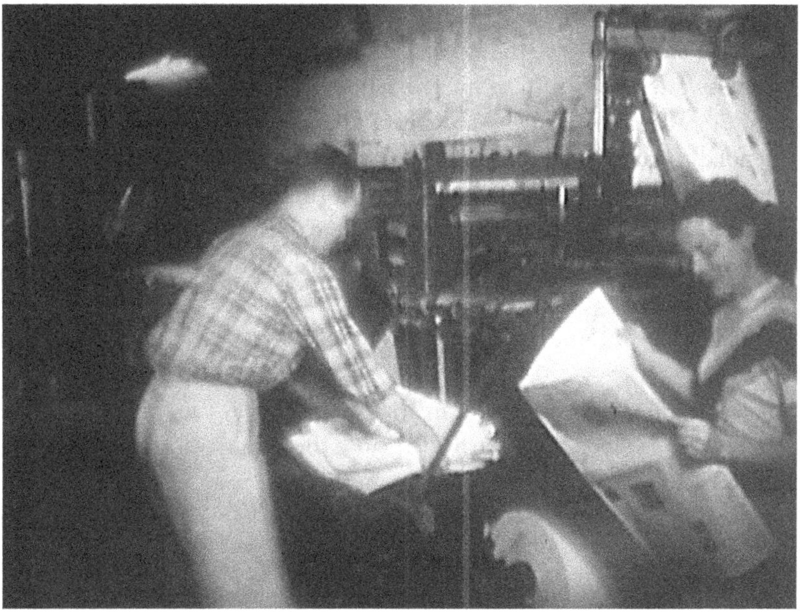

FIGURE 5.4 Scene from *Country Editor* (1954) (RG306-1346). Courtesy of NARA.

selecting, editing, and proofreading articles; and printing and typesetting the paper (see fig. 5.5). This schedule corresponds significantly with the one in *Small Town Editor*. In particular, the conference scene for renovating the Masan City Library recalls the establishment of the Littleton community health center in *Small Town Editor*, with the protagonist intervening in the conference as a public advocate and helping the others reach an amicable settlement. Furthermore, in an interview, Pae Sŏk-in discusses how much American film and culture had affected him. Pae, along with other filmmakers affiliated with USIS-Korea, were more aware of Hollywood-style production systems than those who were not affiliated but would still become his colleagues at the NFPC.[19]

On the other hand, *Korean Editor* features a number of details that contribute to the vernacularization of American localist values and that emphasize the value of "local media" beyond the mere adaptation of American films portraying local media outlets in American towns. For instance, in a sequence on reader feedback, the readers' letters include a request from a Chinese restaurant owner, who asks for help in driving beggar children out of his restaurant, as well as a tenant's complaint about his landlord's daughter playing the piano every night. There is also a scene that shows an informant asking the reporter to expose a group of violent creditors who are assaulting a debtor. These scenes with local issues are intended to garner the sympathies of Korean audiences by appealing to their emotions. In another scene, the editor refuses a bribe to avoid press coverage and is threatened for doing so. Background music creates a disquieting atmosphere, and over-the-shoulder shots of two figures, in turn, create a dramatic sense of urgency, as well as a sense that corruption was a "social evil" in South Korea during reconstruction after the Korean War.[20]

In an interview about his career at USIS-Korea, Pae specifies that he selected the *Masan ilbo* newspaper because the U.S. government was "delicate" about the matter. "Since the publication was neither leftist nor rightist, but centrist," the local newspaper was a suitable candidate, though his script still had to be translated and censored by the U.S. State Department.[21] These conditions were particularly relevant to the Eisenhower administration's policies, which sought to have moderate opponents in South Korea's political sphere, such as Democrats and moderates in the Liberal Party, maintain the status quo and keep the Syngman Rhee government's hard-liners at a remove.[22] The important point here is that

FIGURE 5.5 Two scenes from *Korean Editor* (1958) (RG306-3579). Courtesy of NARA.

localism, a principle of American federalism, was adapted out of necessity to meet the U.S. government's propaganda strategy for South Korea. This adaptation suggests that localism in American films, particularly *Small Town Editor* and *Country Editor*, and in *Korean Editor* have qualitative differences. I will address this issue later in discussing Pae's feature film *P'aldogangsan*.

Intellectuals Encountering the New World

While participating in the exchange program in the United States, Kim Hŭi-kap appeared on a USIS-produced television show called *Korea-America Today* (*Miguk-ŭi onŭl*).[23] On a special studio visit filmed in mid-January 1965, four months after he arrived in the United States, Kim gave his impressions of each region in the country. *Korea-America Today* was produced in Korean for a Korean broadcaster's cultural programming, specifically to introduce the American lifestyle by depicting the lives of Koreans studying there.[24] The show was moderated by Pak Chŏng-su and Yi Pŏm-chun, a couple who were pursuing their PhDs at the American University in Washington, DC.[25] The program's original format was a combination of documentary and talk show, and it invited Korean students or trainees in the United States to answer questions about their lives at the studio.[26]

These characteristics helped build imagined geographies in two ways.[27] First, they narrowed the imagined geographic distance between the United States and South Korea. The featured students and trainees, as well as their TV hosts, were all Koreans speaking Korean, which gave audiences a sense of kinship. Their efforts to adapt to the American way of life gave the impression of the program as providing firsthand, introductory accounts of American society, specifically for those not familiar with the country. It also played an important role in bringing American life to Korean audiences at a time when overseas travel was restricted. Second, the show builds an imagined geography of the United States. Opening with the logo of a stylized map of the United States, each episode introduces a specific American town and visually locates it on a map of its corresponding region (see fig. 5.6). This combination of images helps audiences build a strong sense of the geography of different American places, as well as of the nation as a whole.

FIGURE 5.6 Opening scenes and a map introducing American geography from *Korea-America Today* (ca. 1964) (RG306-5296). Courtesy of NARA.

In the special episode featuring Kim Hŭi-kap, filmed immediately after his travels across the United States, these characteristics significantly stand out. At the time of the special episode's airing, Kim could be still seen on South Korean screens, in films like *The Beauty Murder Case in Bath* (*Yokt'ang-ŭi minyŏ sakŏn*) and *Are All Potbellied People Presidents?* (*Pae-man naomyŏn sajang-inya?*), both of which were released in late 1964.[28] Such exposure, enabled by both the cinema's spatial nature as an anchored medium and the television's immediate nature as a floating medium, works to narrow the cognitive distance between the two countries by showing a South Korean celebrity, whose face audiences could still see on domestic movie screens, appearing on an American TV show. Pak Chŏng-su and Yi Pŏm-chun, who introduced the United States from a Korean's perspective in other episodes, now receive a visitor from South Korea as U.S. residents. After talking about his adjustments to American cultures and some anecdotes of conversations with Americans, Kim describes his travelogue of almost every major city in the country (see fig. 5.7). He covers Hawaii, with its "serene water and summery weather all the time"; Los Angeles, with its "endlessly vast lands but painful smog," Hollywood studios, and filming locations, with their "beautiful artificial jungle trees that looked natural"; San Francisco, with "very beautiful hilltops"; Niagara Falls, with "earthshaking rumbles"; Phoenix, with "the fertility of a desert-turned-farmland"; the Grand Canyon, with "majestic cliffs and countless gorges"; New Orleans, with "a flamboyant French style"; Miami, with Kim's "first helicopter ride"; and New York City, with "skyscrapers flying as high as planes"—all accompanied by a photo slide show. When Kim describes Washington, DC, the show devotes a full quarter of its run time to introducing the major tourist attractions in the capital city. This narrative structure, combined with the montage of stereotypical cityscapes, creates a tessellated picture of the country as a whole, yielding a format that could effectively help South Korean viewers develop geographic familiarity with the United States.

Another notable feature in this special episode is a specific group consciousness that the hosts and guest build together. It is clearly expressed in the following conversation:

Pak: Oh, by the way, where did you spend Christmas?
Kim: Christmas was incredibly exciting!

FIGURE 5.7 Kim Hŭi-kap's appearance on *Korean TV Special* (1965) (RG306-586). Courtesy of NARA.

[All laugh]

Kim: For Christmas, I was in New York City, at a party held by the Alumni Association of Kyŏnggi Girls' High School, uh . . . that party where all of us Koreans gathered. I joined the party. [Pointing at Yi] The chairperson of the association is here. I really appreciated that. [With a laugh]

Yi: Oh, well, it was also the first time for us to have such a party since we came to America. Listening to your talk and singing, it was a terrific night for us, wallowing in homesickness as we were.

Kim: [With a smile] Ah, thank you. So, who was that . . . ? The announcer of *Voice of America* . . . ? Mr. Hwang!

Pak and Yi: Right, you mean Hwang Chae-gyŏng. . . . Yes.

Kim: Yeah, he wrote the script. [Looking at Yi] We performed a one-act play, didn't we? The play.

Yi: Yes.

Kim: That old guy put mustaches here, my goodness!

Yi: [Laughing] You were almost frantic, looking for the mustaches.

Kim: Oh dear, the set was decent . . . I mean, almost perfect! I think I had a very exciting day.

Pak: Such an opportunity . . . yes. It's a very rare opportunity for us Koreans here, too.

Kim: Maybe at 5 A.M. . . . Yeah, I went to bed around five in the morning. [Laughing] I had a blast!

Pak: Oh, the next morning, you know, I took you for a sightseeing tour, didn't I?

Kim: Yes.

Pak: Well, would you please explain again with pictures?

In this scene, the boundary between the interviewers and the interviewee disappears, and these three people are revealed as having shared the same experience. When Yi, as chair of the Alumni Association of Kyŏnggi Girls' High School in the United States, discusses the party hosted by her association, and Kim talks about how he spent time with her alumnae and other Koreans there, their story calls attention to the moderator's distinct social status.[29] Given that there were only about twenty-five hundred Koreans in any course of study in the United States at the time,[30] the "Korean student group in America" represented a highly educated, select few, with Pak and Yi standing before South Korean television viewers on behalf of that group.[31] This scene, in which the three reminisce about an experience inaccessible to most Koreans, also emphasizes the geographical distance between South Korea and the United States, as well as the chasm between the wealthy, educated elites and the lower classes of South Korea.

This hierarchy between the elite and the common audiences is also exhibited in the life trajectory of Kim Hŭi-kap, who had the rare opportunity to travel around the United States. Kim and Pae Sŏk-in were among the second group of "Korean specialists" to be invited by the U.S. State Department for training. In the November 1964 issue of *Free World* (*Chayu Segye*), a USIS magazine published in Korean, Kim was described as "a buffoon like Charlie Chaplin, a jack-of-all-trades comedy actor like W.C. Fields, and a character actor like Victor Moore." He was praised for being "in an unutterable style of his own unique Korean appearance" (see fig. 5.8). The article went on to state that he was "well-known among foreigners" and that "many Americans in Seoul [went to] see his movies even without English subtitles."[32] While his folksy image greatly contributed to his popularity, the invitation from the U.S. State Department, the high praise from USIS-Korea, and his popularity among American residents in South Korea positioned him as the right person to introduce American culture to Koreans.[33] A meeting scene in *Korea-America Today*, which follows the Christmas anecdote, depicts Kim shaking hands with senior American diplomats in Washington, DC. This moment confirms that Kim Hŭi-kap, "an America expert," was also a member of the specialist group, mainly composed of highly educated elites. His image as an expert on the United States, or on the world, retained currency even after his return to Korea. Accordingly, Kim hosted a USIS-Korea television show, *Little Angels of Korea* (*Ŏrin ch'ŏnsadŭl*), in which he interviewed the Sŏnhwa Children's Dance Group about their tour in the United States in March 1967. In 1968, while he was touring the United States to film *The Land of Korea: P'aldogangsan 2* (*Sok P'aldogangsan: segye-rŭl kanda*), the first sequel to *P'aldogangsan*, he wrote a series of travelogues called The Nutcracker Face Reports Traveling around the World for a daily newspaper.[34]

The elite status of those who introduced Western culture to others recalls the hierarchies between the colonizer and the colonized and, moreover, is a role taken up by intellectuals in a colony. In an analysis of colonial elite intellectuals under the British Empire, Gyan Prakash

FIGURE 5.8 Article on Kim Hŭi-kap in *Chayu Segye* (1964). From *Chayu Segye* 13, no. 6: 6. Courtesy of NARA.

argues that those intellectuals had a kind of "second sight": they developed a way of seeing somewhere in between the "superstitious eye" of the colony and the "scientific gaze" of the empire.[35] This second sight was not the product of scientific training but, rather, of a performative process, such as "amazement and wonder" in encountering "the spectacle of science," as well as "the bewilderment experienced when confronted with alien knowledge while encountering the objects in the museum."[36] Kim Hŭi-kap's role was to show wonder at seeing the artificial South Sea Islands jungle set built for Ernest Borgnine's Hollywood feature, to show envy for the Hollywood production system that had advanced technologies "inconceivable" in South Korea, and to admire the dignity of American audiences "who tried to improve their culture as a means of scientific improvement."[37] His position and attitude were in line with those of the colonial elite intellectuals in Prakash's study. In other words, the elite status of both Kim and the television moderators not only created a social hierarchy between themselves and their Korean viewers but also revealed a regional hierarchy between their home country and the United States, which they encountered with amazement and wonder.

Negotiated Koreanness: Performed Localism, Translated Federalism

To return to the South Korean television series *Blooming P'aldogangsan*, as discussed in chapter 3, the franchise's main premise was an old couple traveling around the country to visit their daughters' families. The couple lives in Seoul with their youngest daughter, while their other five daughters are scattered all over the country. Interestingly, the daughters live in five different provinces: Ch'ungch'ŏng, Chŏlla, Southern Kyŏngsang, Northern Kyŏngsang, and Kangwŏn. The local culture and dialect of each region are consistently featured each time the parents visit one of their daughters. From Seoul to the DMZ, where their only son is completing his mandatory military service, the couple takes a long, roundabout trip counterclockwise. Their trip shares the same basic structure of Pae and Kim's journeys through the United States. Immediately after touring nineteen representative cities in the United States, Kim appeared on *Korea-America Today* and spoke of his experiences with the help of a slide show. The panoramic composition of the United States' local attractions, which were mostly stereotyped images, constructed an overall picture of that nation.

Clearly, the *P'aldogangsan* franchise had a strong attachment to local life and culture. In the panoramic exhibition of local sites on screen and television, local people were reimagined, exoticized, and emerged as both the ethnographic self and Other. Local specialties, attractions, and customs were exhibited as if they were in an exposition, and in so doing,

FIGURE 5.9 Photograph titled *Han'guk yŏnghwa p'aldogangsan kwallamgaek* (Audience queuing for the Korean film, *P'aldogangsan of Tomorrow*) (1971) (CET0057715). Courtesy of National Archives of Korea.

they built up the imagination of each region in South Korea, thanks to the unprecedentedly large budget provided by the government. As evidenced by the trend of "P'aldo" films, the representation of local identities proved attractive to viewers. Given the nationwide success of the *P'aldogangsan* franchise, viewers most likely consumed images of their own regions without objection (see fig. 5.9).

In this process of consuming local identities, the crucial factor was the way in which different local identities were combined and integrated into a single national identity. The localist vision in American government films presents an interesting point of comparison with *P'aldogangsan*'s representation of local identities. As mentioned above, images of "a typical, slow-paced and peaceful local American town" were frequently found in propaganda films from the United States. These images produced the imagination of stereotyped local living, filtering out any elements of conflict caused by differences and misunderstanding among different local communities. These differences are instead normalized and stereotyped to justify and facilitate cultural integration. Similar tactics are at work in the *P'aldogangsan* franchise. Each location is given a typical image to explain the site: Ch'ungch'ŏng presents a slow and easy pedestrian image, Chŏlla is depicted as pastoral scenery blended with the strong local dialect, Pusan (southern Kyŏngsang) exhibits crowded downtown streets and a huge outbound port, Ulsan (northern Kyŏngsang) is visualized as a scene of magnificent factory districts, and Kangwŏn is pictured as a sequestered fishing village. The dialects and customs of local communities are situated to season the show with humor and to encourage a sense of intimacy with the characters in each location. In particular, the protagonists' sons-in-law are presented as local stereotypes, making them more readily recognizable and digestible.

However, in terms of integration strategy, there is a major difference between these pseudo-localist stereotypes in *P'aldogangsan* and American localism. As Bill Kirkpatrick explains, American localism is rooted in the historical experience of forming the nation-state, which, in turn, was significantly shaped by the issues of Puritanism, the establishment of federal and state governments, and the Civil War.[38] The logic of integrating diverse local identities, therefore, depended on constitutional principles that formed in the course of pursuing a federal identity. *Tuesday in November* is a typical example of this kind of logic that links localism with federalism. Despite using many similar techniques to visualize local cultures, *P'aldogangsan* marks a distinct departure from its American localist counterparts. Pae Sŏk-in, the director of the 1967 original, likely learned of these techniques from the American government films he watched while working for USIS-Korea, which included such films as *Small Town Editor* and *Country Editor*. However, his film had a considerably different set-up that reshaped the task of integration—namely, familism. In particular, the family ties between the film's characters keep the audience from being too attached to or removed from specific regions. In turn, the shortcomings of the stereotyped local characters, such as the pinchpenny Pusan businessman, the loud and old-fashioned Chŏlla farmworker, and the needy and isolated Kangwŏn fisherman, were smoothed over in the course of the characters' family affairs. They, each of whom is a breadwinner of a self-contained nuclear family, serve to form a big, extended family, following the principles of the Park government's family policy that prioritized small, nuclear family units. As a metaphor of national integration, "seven households from different regions, professions, and social classes unite under the leadership of their father in Seoul"; the nation-state is likened to a family in this "political landscape."[39]

The family metaphor in national integration also led to a homogeneous imagery of national territory. The ending scene of *P'aldogangsan of Tomorrow* (1971), the third film of the franchise, depicts the Kim family taking a trip on an expressway. The newly constructed expressway is smooth and impeccable, an unending space on which the family's express bus rapidly glides. A series of views outside the bus windows enter and leave the frame at high speed. Then, turning its gaze inward, the camera rests on each passenger's face. The old couple from Seoul and the families of their seven children, each of which has come from a different region, take the same bus together and head toward an unknown destination. These relatives of different regional, occupational, and socioeconomic backgrounds spend time together in a harmonious, and even united, manner, a far cry from their daily routines at work. The individual times and spaces, as determined by each passenger's distinct social background, are all foreclosed as in-between spaces that the speedy vehicle leaves behind. In this cinematized trip on the expressway, the family occupies a time-space that is distinct from the outside. The surreal image of the family in harmonious coexistence on the bus is nothing but the new time and space made possible by the expressway. The national community, likened to a large family, lives in a vacuum on a projectile that does not stop until it reaches its destination. The vacuum is a rationalized, homogeneous space generated by industrialization and urbanization. Yi Hyo-dŏk advances the argument that the establishment of modern transportation networks gave rise to the homogenization of authenticities. The development of modern transportation technologies transformed local spaces as the "*resistance* to movement" into penetrable points, which led to the homogenization of authenticities.[40] The trip on the expressway at the end of *P'aldogangsan of Tomorrow* is a symbolic scene visualizing a homogenized space. The passengers on the express bus, as the old couple's relatives who live scattered throughout the country, perform as authentic locals from around the country. The *P'aldogangsan* series' premise of going sightseeing around p'aldogangsan, the scenery from all corners of Korea, was the stage for such "staged authenticity."[41] By being thus staged, the local authenticities become understandable, consumable, and thus penetrable. The slogan of the "one-day life zone" via the expressway, therefore, is none other than a homogeneous, penetrable territory of the nation-state.

Since the localist elements in American films were imported and circulated outside of their original context in South Korea, their federalist political vision, which emerged from the same context in the United States, also had to be arbitrarily translated. The regionally integrating leadership embodied by the father figure in *P'aldogangsan*, Hŭi-kap, points to a translated and transformed federalism. He is a rational but gentle, humorous character, one with economic means. His character marks a sharp contrast to the father figures that populated Korean cinema at the time, who were sincere but poor. Indeed, this new father figure was the model "hegemonic father."[42] It is interesting that this combination of familism and transformed federalism concluded in simple personalization. This emphasis of a fatherlike leader in the *translated* vision of federalism serves as a reminder of the *han'guksik minjujuŭi* (Korean-type democracy) slogan, which was stressed by the Park Chung Hee government during the Yusin regime. The slogan was a means of encapsulating the difference between the South Korean system of government and those of other democratic countries. The construction of "han'guksik" (Korean-type) discourses or images of Koreanness under Park's rule can give us clues to better understand the difference in perceptions between those within and those outside South Korea, specifically regarding evaluations of the Park Chung Hee period.

No matter how the real "han'guksik" was envisioned, there is no denying that its discursive structure was as the antithesis of the West.[43] Although discourse around the phrase stressed the uniqueness of South Korea, "Korean-type democracy" itself was not used to describe a certain tradition but was instead a synchronically coined term used to explain a recent development in the South Korean political system at the time, notably the enactment of the Yusin constitution.[44] It was an invention to locate the Korean self in geopolitical relationships, not a reflection of a tradition linking back to the past. This coined term shows that the crucial factor for public consent to a "state of exception" was, ultimately, representation.[45] The decision to advocate a Korean-type democracy was motivated by a desire to reject the democracy of others. Outwardly, such rejection was propelled by critiques of the political system—that is, the repression of the National Assembly, political parties, and opposition politicians. However, when combined with discourses on culture and history, Korean-type democracy became a self-appointed identity positioned as a moral and cultural antithesis. Accordingly, representation of the West in South Korean society was pivotal to figuring out the image of the idealized Korean self.[46] In other words, it became necessary to contextualize and historicize the process of shaping representations of the West and South Korea as its Other, together with the negotiations among social actors involved in these representations. Therefore, to better understand the representational issues that arose with the installation of the Yusin regime, we need to pay closer attention to the historical trajectory of representation formation leading up to the year 1972.

In this light, there is a symbolic weight to USIS-Korea closing its Liberty Productions film studios in 1967[47] and dismantling its film production department in the early 1970s,[48] during the early years of the Yusin regime. The closure seems to have been propelled by a combination of changes in U.S. foreign policy, including the Nixon Doctrine. However, given that the rhetoric of han'guksik democracy was rooted in criticism of Western-type democracy, the retreat of an American film propaganda production unit, which had been competing with the nation's own, was significant. At the very moment that USIS-Korea shut down its unmatched film studios in Sangnam and its influence started to decline, South Korea's NFPC successfully stepped up with the popular figure of *P'aldogangsan*, Kim Hŭi-kap, who embodied the ideal Korean self, then analogized as the führer of the Yusin regime, Park Chung Hee.

Television's Tactility and Aviation Mobility

On the other hand, the closure of USIS-Korea's film studios was also a decision made under a whirlwind of change in the mediascape. As evidenced by television's central role in USIS-Korea's celebration of the

Apollo 11 moon landing, the agency's withdrawal of film production in South Korea went hand in hand with its increasing use of the new medium. The Apollo 11 mission was "the televisual inauguration of an American-led global satellite network," and it confirmed the United States' victory over the Soviet Union in the space race.[49] Also important to the historical context of Cold War rivalry was television's place in global geopolitics, whereby television became the mainstream medium through this historic event in some American allied countries, particularly South Korea. The inauguration of the new medium meant the approaching twilight of an old one. For USIS-Korea, which closed its film production studios in Sangnam two years before the Apollo 11 landing, this pseudo-cinematic event in Mt. Namsan Park indicated the dawning of the age of television propaganda in South Korea.

However, this repositioning of audiovisual propaganda's center cannot be attributed to the overwhelming attraction of the new medium alone. Ironically, the change was also driven by the old medium's growth. Over the past decades, the South Korean government had recognized film as an effective means of propaganda, which led them to nurture film production agencies fully controlled by the government, including the Ministry of Public Information and its affiliate, the NFPC. During that same period, South Korea's film industry achieved success and self-reliance, especially after considerable support from American-led foreign agencies, such as USIS-Korea and the United Nations Korean Reconstruction Agency (UNKRA). Under these new circumstances, USIS-Korea's Liberty Productions films were no longer "sufficiently cost-effective," particularly when faced with competition from South Korea's governmental agencies and private productions.[50]

The use of television for propaganda, nevertheless, developed differently from film. USIS-Korea, which was a massive presence in the film industry, was limited to the role of subcontractor, to providing programs for South Korean broadcast stations, in the television propaganda industry.[51] The Motion Picture and Radio-Television Section of USIS-Korea developed a videotape production and distribution program in 1971, and its finished products were sent to each branch for distribution through local television broadcasters.[52] While USIS-Korea "hired Korean filmmakers to localize" America's propaganda efforts so that local filmmakers could adapt American styles for their films with Korean themes and language, the agency's involvement in television production was limited to using the new media platform to import American pictures, to bring the outside world into South Korean homes.[53] Adaptations of American television documentary shows, such as *Challenges against Pollution* (*Konghae-e tojŏn*, 1971); news shows dubbed in Korean, such as *Nixon Doctrine Program Review* (*Niksŭn tokt'ŭrin p'ŭrogŭraem ribyu*, 1969); and Korean correspondents' television interviews with foreign authorities, such as *Inquire Series* (*Taedam ssirijŭ*, 1970) and *Korean Reporter in Asia* (*T'ŭkp'awŏni pon asia*, 1970), made up the majority of USIS shows.

In the meantime, South Korea's entry into INTELSAT, coupled with the spread of television in the late 1960s and early to mid-1970s, turned public interest in the outside world into a new media trend that underscored television's sense of immediacy—that is, television news coverage by foreign correspondents. USIS television programs, such as *Inquire Series* (1970) and *Korean Reporter in Asia* (1970), were good early examples of this trend, and they were shot on location in the United States and in its allied Asian countries. South Korean broadcasters also began producing similar news shows in the early 1970s. KBS launched a show called *Overseas Report* (*Haeoe rip'ot'ŭ*) in April 1972 to air documentaries about foreign places all over the world, which were, in turn, filmed by the broadcaster's own correspondents.[54] This show eventually changed its title to *Correspondent's Report* (*T'ŭkp'awŏn pogo*) and became a regularly scheduled program.[55]

It is worth noting that these correspondent news shows made repeated use of aviation mobility to highlight the sense of immediacy, connectivity, and tactility. For instance, the "Taiwan: A Silent Revolution" ("Taeman: choyonghan hyŏngmyŏng") episode of *Korean Reporter in Asia* begins with an airport scene, where its correspondent enters the terminal at the Gimpo International Airport (then Kimpo International Airport), checks in at the airline counter, and boards the plane to Taipei (see fig. 5.10). This scene portrays the reporter as the primary bearer of news from the outside world, who personally travels to foreign countries, collects information, and, most importantly, communicates with the viewer at the same time. This sense of simultaneity was the object of the decision to televise the Apollo 11 mission the previous year. "Live broadcast" (*sirhwang chunggye*) and "on the air" (*saengbangsong*) were frequent catchphrases used to promote television shows covering the moon landing, which attracted viewers

FIGURE 5.10 Opening scenes of *Korean Reporter in Asia* (1970) (RG306-2376). Courtesy of NARA.

who expected that they would be able to witness the historic event in real time.[56]

The television coverage of the Apollo moon mission in 1969 and the correspondent news shows that emerged in the early 1970s were therefore similarly entwined with aviation mobility—that is, the cinematic conventions used for flight technologies, such as airplanes, satellites, rockets, and spaceflights—which marked the new age of a new medium in South Korea. The "implosive speed" of aviation let one "touch every part of the world" in one spot.[57] The new medium, television, was a tactile, electricity-enabled space that offered "a means of getting in touch with every facet of being at once" rather than a visual space like film, which had sequential, mechanical, and isotropic configurations.[58] This enhanced tactility of television was simultaneous, nonlinear, anisotropic, and, therefore, in sync with aviation mobility.

The airplane's implosive nature contrasted with the centralizing and hierarchizing force of the railroad and the expressway in Korea. For a considerable period, international flights were not a viable means of transportation for the majority of the Korean population but a medium that provided a sense of connection with the rest of the world. Until 1983, only a select group of Koreans could obtain travel visas for specific cases, and this group included diplomats, dispatched workers, and a small number of students studying abroad—only they could use airports as gateways to international travel. For the vast majority, the primary point of contact with global aviation mobility was media coverage of Korean officials or famous foreign visitors flying in and out of Gimpo Airport. Domestic flights were also seen as the territory of either "extravagant, pleasure-seeking tourists" or "someone traveling to do important work for the country or society."[59] When Korean Airlines first averaged over three thousand passengers a day, the media reported it as a result of the summer "vacation boom."[60] Thus, aviation mobility in South Korea in the 1960s and 1970s signified an opportunity to "touch every part of the world," an opportunity enabled by televisual representation, which allowed viewers to virtually connect with the outside world or with the world beyond the daily workplace routine. This development, together with the spread of television and increased opportunities to virtually experience aviation mobility through the small screen, resonated with what McLuhan has called an implosion.

However, implosion through television and aviation mobility in South Korean media did not necessarily lead to McLuhan's vision of a "global village," where "the human family" exists under the condition that "electromagnetic discoveries" recreate "the simultaneous 'field' in all human affairs."[61] Rather, the "simultaneous field" frequently manifested as fear and anxiety, drawing a line between the connected and the disconnected worlds. Since its early days in South Korea, air transportation proved frequently vulnerable to hijacking, hostile fire, or defection. Korean National Air (KNA) had its Douglas DC-3 aircraft, with twenty-nine passengers and four crew members aboard, hijacked on February 16, 1958, and this incident with North Korean spies led to serious business troubles for the first South Korean commercial airliner, which eventually closed in 1961.[62] When KNA's successor, Korean Airlines (KAL), had its YS-11 aircraft hijacked and taken to North Korea in late 1969, the incident was closely intertwined with the immediacy of television. In particular, the abducted crew members and passengers were brought to a press conference condemning the South on North Korean television,[63] and when they were released, their repatriation was broadcast live on South Korean television.[64] After their repatriation, another television conference was held on the South Korean side, denouncing North Korea for not releasing some of the abductees.[65] The fear and anxiety over this incident drove some passengers to cancel their flight reservations.[66]

In turn, when KAL flight 902 was shot down by the Soviet air defense on April 20, 1978, it grew into a media spectacle at the global level. When the pilot and navigator were released from Soviet detainment, they were allowed to leave for Denmark, and immediately after their arrival in Copenhagen, they appeared at a press conference.[67] Reporters from foreign broadcasters and newspapers, such as NBC and ABC from the United States and Japan's *Asahi Shimbun*, camped out at the Kastrup Airport lounge, while one of Denmark's television broadcasters recorded the conference and immediately distributed it to every other broadcaster in Europe.[68] Since the pilot, Kim Ch'ang-kyu, had managed to make an emergency landing on a frozen lake, a feat praised as being "beyond human power," his actions were seen as having "exhibited the best qualities of the heroic Korean captain who had solid aplomb and a sense of great athleticism among billions of television viewers, radio listeners, and newspaper readers all over the world."[69] This perception of simultaneity across the globe, as quoted from a column by Ch'oe Chŏng-ho, a South Korean professor in communication studies, illustrates how the idea of the "global village" manifested in the context of Cold War conflict, enabled by the televisual sense of immediacy and the spectacle of aviation mobility—a manifestation specifically as an environment where the Soviet Union and other Iron Curtain countries did not "simultaneously" exist. As a case in point, Kim Ch'ang-kyu and his fellow crew member took part in another television conference in Leningrad (now St. Petersburg) before being released from detainment, but this televisual event was only recalled in an interview on the South Korean side.[70]

The Twilight of Cine-Mobility

In the meantime, the alumni of the NFPC, the overdeveloped film production branch of the South Korean government, similarly jumped on the television trend of encouraging a sense of global connectivity and immediacy. With the success of *P'aldogangsan*, Pae Sŏk-in became a highly sought-after director and received many proposals for new film projects.[71] After leaving the NFPC, however, he chose to work on *Reaching the World* (*Chisang ch'oego-ŭi yŏjŏng: Segye-ro Ppŏnnŭn Han'guk*, 1968). This seventy-minute documentary was shot on location in eighteen countries across the Middle East, Southeast Asia, Europe, North and South America, and Africa.[72] Interestingly, the second film in the NFPC *P'aldogangsan* franchise, *The Land of Korea: P'aldogangsan 2* (1968), was filmed in sixteen cities abroad. It was directed by another NFPC director, Yang Chong-hae.[73] In this film, Kim Hŭi-kap boards planes to visit those cities in America, Asia, Europe, Africa, and the Middle East. After the panoramic images of local identities seen through *P'aldogangsan*'s semiethnographic gaze, these two films instead employed a full, uninhibited ethnographic gaze, its perspective and tactility enabled by aviation mobility. What is more, the regional hierarchy in *Korea-America Today* reappears in these depictions of the ethnographic Other.

However, this trend of filmic ethnographies in government-sponsored, or public information, films was a precursor to nontheatrical film production for television broadcasters. When KBS began filming the first

South Korean television film series, *The Front Lines of the Vietnam War* (*Wŏllam chŏnsŏn*), a coproduction by the broadcaster's television producer Im Hak-song and Hyŏndae Culture Film Production's director Kim Sŏng-in, in September 1970, it was promoted as being shot on-site in Vietnam and as hiring local actors.[74] KBS then began filming a television documentary series, *Korean Beauty* (*Han'guk-ŭi mi*), working with ethnographers, archeologists, geographers, and historians to document and broadcast South Korea's folklore, tradition, cultural heritage, natural landscape, and wildlife according to the vision of its producers, who began their careers in public information filmmaking.[75] The NFPC also provided broadcasters like KBS with its films, such as *This Is Korea* (*Igŏsi han'guk-ida*), which featured images of South Korea's industrial development, sceneries, and customs.[76]

The turn to film production for television broadcasters unfolded on an international scale. The NFPC produced a full-color culture film series, made up of individual eighteen-minute installments, for export purposes, which saw some success in 1970. Among the series' installments, *Korea* (*K'oriŏ*), an ethnographic account of South Korea's development, was exported to Japan's Fuji Television, while *The Hands of the Korean* (*Han'gugin-ŭi son*), a documentary about the originality of handicraft arts in Korea, was broadcast on Japan's NHK Television.[77] Japan's Nippon TV took a more direct route and filmed an episode of its popular ethnographic documentary show, *World Wonders—a Nonfiction Hour* (J. *Kyōi no sekai—nonfikushon awā*, K. *Kyŏngiŭi segye—nonp'iksyŏn awŏ*), in several rural locations and cultural heritage sites in South Korea, working together with South Korea's Tongyang Broadcasting Company.[78]

South Korean broadcasters also imported and aired foreign-made ethnographic documentaries, such as Taiwan Television's *Chinese Ancient Culture* (*Chungguk kodae munmul*), which was imported by MBC.[79] KBS began airing an animal documentary show, *Animal Kingdom* (*Tongmul-ŭi wangguk*), in June 1969.[80] This show was an adaptation of television nature documentaries imported from foreign television broadcasters, such as the BBC, National Geographic, and NHK. With the zoological and ethnographic gaze on wildlife in exotic, foreign countries, the nature documentary shows successfully secured space on television, replacing the educational and public information films shown in cinemas.

Ultimately, fewer and fewer people gathered at one spot to experience a shared cinematic sphere; instead, they chose to ride the electromagnetic flow of television at home, to get the sense of "touching every part of the world." This development heralded the twilight of cine-mobility. In this respect, it is worth noting that the emergence of television's post-cine-mobility regime accompanied such great interest in other parts of the world, in that the cognitive mobility turn was significantly interrelated with the dominant way of perceiving the outside world. Television's new cognitive realm of encountering world-as-gesture was defined by the immediate and haptic connections with the outside world through electromagnetic and satellite technologies that enabled a transcendental mobility.

CHAPTER 6

Technopia!

The Neoliberal Utopia of Automated Mobility

While the early post-cine-mobility regime in South Korea characterized itself as the proliferation of an individualized way of sensing the presented world-as-gestures through television's electromagnetic and satellite technologies, two waves of historical change on a global level in both economics and technology markets affected this cognitive mobility turn in the late 1970s and 1980s: neoliberalization and computerization. As David Harvey states, neoliberalism holds that "the social good will be maximized by maximizing the reach and frequency of market transactions, and it seeks to bring all human action into the domain of the market."[1] The tide of "creative destruction" through this process of neoliberalization in the late 1970s and early 1980s did not directly and immediately hit the domestic economic structure or "prior institutional frameworks" of South Korea but gradually challenged and menaced the dominant "way of life and thought" as well as "social relations."[2] The first computer in South Korea dated to 1967, but the early 1980s was the turning point in computer use, when microcomputers, or "personal computers," were commercialized.[3] It is undeniable that the rapid computerization in the 1980s and 1990s was tied with "neoliberalism's intense interest in and pursuit of information technologies" and South Korea was not an exception.[4] The impact of both neoliberalization and computerization on cognitive mobility did not appear in the form of a single visual medium, at least until the emergence of the early internet in the 1990s, but, rather, imbued everyday life with new rules of movement and a different attitude toward the visibility of information.

In the mid-1980s, the two biggest electronics companies in South Korea, GoldStar and Samsung, began circulating corporate image advertisements that emphasized their advanced technology. GoldStar created a slogan, "Technopia—Humans Meet Technology," in 1985, and continued using it in newspaper advertisements and TV commercials for a decade, until the company changed its name to LG in 1995 (see fig. 6.1).[5] The first advertisement in 1985 won the grand prize at a domestic competition that same year.[6] This provoked its rival company, Samsung, to rush into a similar campaign, "Human-Tech—Technology in Tune with Humans," the following year.[7] As the voice-over narration in Samsung Electronics' TV commercial in 1986 said, "Breaking open an age of automation to make humans feel more comfortable, we mount a challenge in the field of life sciences to make humans healthier. Forecasting natural disasters to make life safer for humans, our technology stays in tune with humans. That is Samsung's philosophy of Human-Tech."

Both these campaigns were understood as reflecting a shift in the two companies' processes of image making, specifically going "from making technology-oriented, competitive slogans, to putting an emphasis on the harmony between mankind and technology."[8] That is to say, the mid-1980s was a turning point, where the South Korean electronics market began identifying a humanistic value in its promotion of the utopian ideal of technological advancement.

What did humans have to do with technological advancement at the time? What drove the humanistic turn in the electronics advertising market? The term *automation* was frequently used by these electronics companies in their advertisement campaigns, and it is key to answering these questions. Automation in the Korean context has largely been studied in relation to the manufacturing industry and its management therein. For instance, studies have discussed the accelerated automation of production as a response to intensifying labor struggles in 1987.[9] These studies shared the major premise that in the manufacturing sector, the introduction of microelectronics and automation technology was a solution to the crisis of capital accumulation, specifically by increasing the relative surplus value.[10] As "the most refined application of the Fordist system of production,"[11] automation was regarded as inevitable in the technological

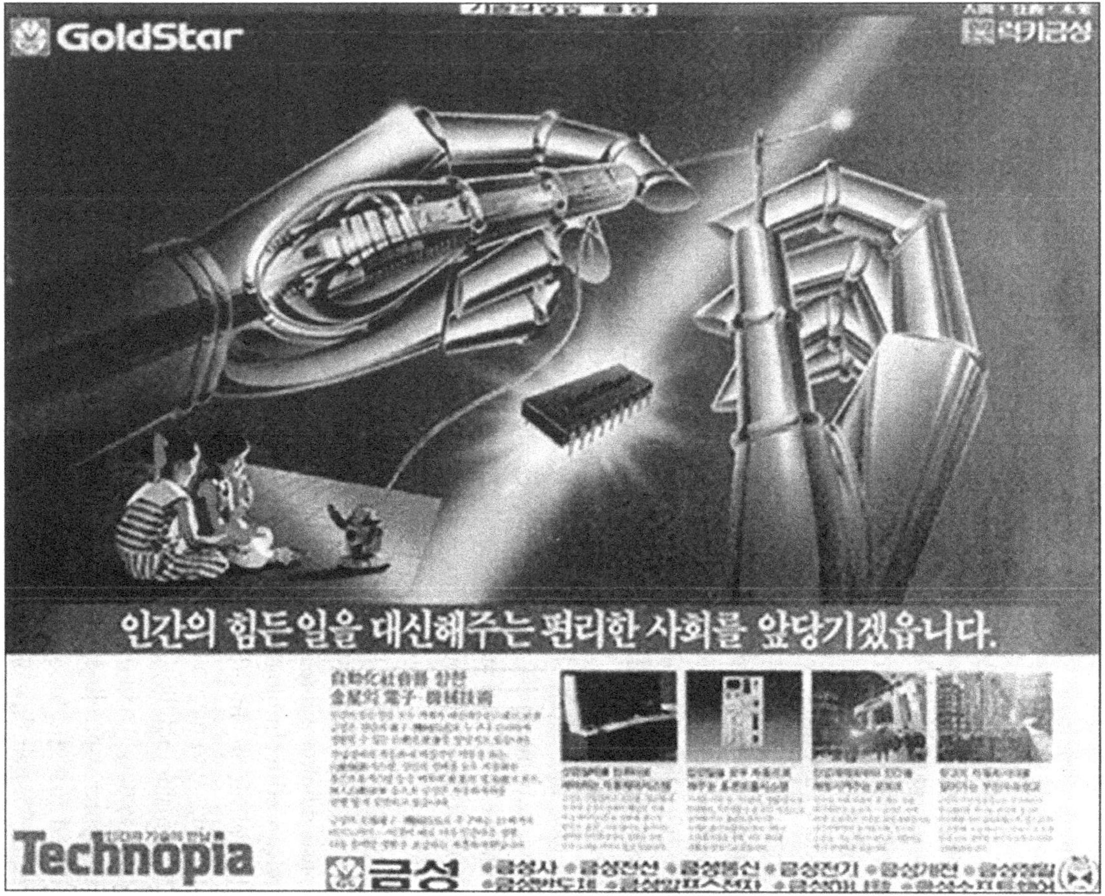

FIGURE 6.1 GoldStar advertisement (1986). Courtesy of LG Electronics Inc.

reconfiguration of the mass production system.[12] Seen in this light, the fancy imagery in the 1980s human-technology campaigns aligned with automation can be understood as having deployed a smoke screen to hide the possibility of high unemployment and promote the use of "labor-saving technology."[13]

However, this chapter attempts to question the widespread view that automation has primarily functioned to replace human labor. At the time, discourses on automation were circulated outside the manufacturing sector to a considerable degree. Since the late 1970s and the early 1980s, various types of unmanned machinery, including vending machines, elevators, escalators, and automatic doors, began permeating everyday life in Seoul and other big cities in South Korea. While the first uses of the term *chadonghwa* (automation) appeared in newspapers as early as the late 1940s, the popularization of automation in the 1980s was no coincidence.[14] The discourse of automation reflected the commercialization and commodification of advanced technologies in all areas of consumption at that time. Individual mobility rapidly increased through a series of liberalization processes, such as the partial easing of overseas tourism restrictions in 1981, the lifting of the curfew in 1982, and the popularization of private car ownership—all of these developments resonated with the maximized efficiency of automated mobility, by which I mean both the developments in actual human movement through automation technologies and the effects of such developments on societal values and beliefs, including the ideas of flexibility, transparency, and anonymity.

This chapter argues that the rise of automation systems and discourses pushed humans into a new mobility system shaped and promoted by these advanced technologies in the early stage of computerization and neoliberalization. In other words, the reassignment of human movement through automation technologies demonstrated the reorganization of the "one major mobility-system" across Korean society, corresponding to Korean society's economic transformation in the global economy.[15] The computer-controlled and programmed motion of machines not only reduced the sum amount of human labor but also put humans on the conveyor-belt flow of technologically enhanced enterprising systems. By focusing on longer-term changes from the late 1970s to the early 1990s in South Korea, I argue that the proliferation of automated or flexible modes of mobility in the 1980s should be understood as a gradual internalization process of the neoliberal paradigm—this process preceded the neoliberalization of the South Korean economy during the financial crisis in 1997, also known as the IMF crisis. And the incremental computerization and digitization throughout the 1980s and 1990s enforced a new principle in vision: transparency. The latter part of this chapter examines the shift in popular films' depictions of human bodies and their mobility during the 1990s before the IMF crisis. The films analyzed in this section expose the changed visual subjectivity in South Korean society, specifically through its response to global reform during the pre-IMF period.

Automation Fever in the 1980s

In a 1988 film directed by Chang Sŏn-u, *The Age of Success* (*Sŏnggong sidae*), automation is depicted as advanced technology that ruins a seasoning manufacturer who sticks to "natural" methods. As the voice-over narration for a fictional commercial in the film says, "No need to shake. You never need to taste the food. Automatically programmed, automatically launched, Compu-mi! Cutting-edge technology meets synthetic seasoning. Fully automatic Compu-mi!"

The protagonist loses his job in sales after losing an advertising war, in which his rival releases a TV commercial for a "fully automatic" seasoning machine. While the film's tone for this fake commercial seems satirical, the phrases it uses are similar to the advertising copies that frequently appeared in the electronics market around the early 1980s: Samsung's 1979 newspaper advertisement for a coffee vendor used the catchphrase "The days are past when female workers are needed to make coffee"[16]; a commercial for GoldStar's 1982 new television model "New High-Tech" emphasized that there was "no need" to turn off the machine before going to bed, since it would turn off automatically; and a 1983 advertisement of Daewoo's 2.5 kg automatic washing machine also claimed that there was "no need" for prewashing.[17] These advertising copies stressed the convenience of their goods and persuaded consumers that these new products would free them from tasks that previously required manual effort. In other words, their shared ideal lay in the nullification of human movement. The term *chadong* (automatic) was not only used in ads for new, computer-programmed products but was also frequently included in descriptions of the electronic workings of existing products. The line between cases where humans still had to apply their labor and those where machines substituted for human bodies became a focal point in a new marketing strategy.

As mentioned above, various automatic machines began pervading everyday life in Seoul and other big cities in the late 1970s. In 1978, over six electronics companies were in fierce competition to promote their imported vending machines, including automatic vendors selling coffee, tobacco, canned beverages, bus and metro tickets, and coin exchange.[18] The following year, a news article reported that there were over twenty-three hundred vending machines installed over the past year, with an average daily revenue of over 37 million won.[19] In December 1979, the Ministry of Construction announced a plan that would mandate the installation of a separate freight elevator in every high-rise apartment building.[20] This policy change highlighted how elevators had become widespread in South Korean apartment buildings by 1979. According to the Korea Elevator Safety Institute (KESI), the Housing Site Development Promotion Act, which was rolled out the following year, promoted the construction of high-rise apartment buildings and stimulated the elevator industry.[21] In a 1982 news article, a reporter criticized a new trend in fine dining restaurants in Kangnam, Seoul, which entailed excessive spending on interior design and landscaping, including the installation of automatic doors.[22] The "luxurious trend" of automatic doors also spread to transportation systems. In 1983, the National Railroad debuted automatic doors on the Saemaul Train's passenger cars, which was then the fastest class of train between Seoul and Pusan.[23] That same year, Hyundai Motors released a front-page newspaper ad for their brand-new bus, which had an automatic door system for exits.[24] Within only two years after that, the Seoul bus system was overhauled with automatic doors.[25]

Discourses on office automation (OA) and home automation (HA) also grew in popularity during the mid-1980s. Office automation was a part of industrial automation and became popular in the mass media in 1980. Historically, however, office copiers were in the domestic market as early as the 1960s,[26] while electronic calculators were introduced in 1973.[27] Indeed, automated equipment was far from rare, as highlighted by a columnist's essay on the widespread shift to electronic calculators and photocopiers in 1981.[28] Terms like *samu chadonghwa* (office automation) and *OA* were popularized in discourses from 1980 onward, spreading through a variety of academic events,[29] expositions,[30] and corporate campaigns that promoted the use of automatic machines in the workplace,[31] as well as through news media coverage that emphasized those terms.[32] *Kajŏng chadonghwa* (home automation), or *HA*, came paired with office automation and provided a blueprint for the future both at home and at work. Some headlines that built and contributed to discourses around this new development included: "Order tracking and stock-taking ready by machine";[33] "Computers swarm in—home automation revolution";[34] "The herald for the age of working at home";[35] "Electronic mail box transcending time and space";[36] "The beginning of an era of push button factories";[37] "The automation boom penetrates your home";[38] and "The third wave, My Com[puter] revolution—computerization of the home."[39]

It is worth noting that most of those discourses emphasized automation technology as a new object for management. Even in discourses on work efficiency, phrases were addressed to the businessman who would buy and use these new products. For instance, there was no room in such discourses for the female workers who would be replaced by automatic coffee vendors or the bus attendants who would lose their jobs over the introduction of automatic bus doors. Rather, readers were envisioned as the manager or owner of a bus company, one who would be enticed by how these new tools could solve various problems. The attractions of an automated utopia were, in other words, discursively produced as parts of the corporate, management system, as opposed to mass production systems.

Crash into the Automatic

In a 1982 film, *Hwa-sun*, the lead couple runs a mobile department store. *Idong paekhwajŏm* (mobile department store) was a specific form of independent business that emerged with the construction of the expressway system and that accelerated automobilization in South Korea. At first, it had been launched as a mobile branch service of a major department store,

Shinsegae.[40] Gradually, however, it became a type of individually owned pop-up store after Shinsegae withdrew from business in 1972.[41] *Hwa-sun* depicts how unstable and precarious the couple's life is on the road and ends with the husband's death in traffic. When the poor couple go to a hotel for the first time after years of sleeping in their truck, the elevator appears to them as an emblem of middle-class life. Faced with automatic movement however, the wife, Hwa-sun, instinctively warns her husband against a potential collision with an uncontrolled machine.

> **Hotel Manager:** There's the elevator going up.
> [Hwa-sun and her husband move toward the elevator. When the door opens, her husband enters the elevator first.]
> **Hwa-sun:** [To her husband] Please be careful with your neck!

Indeed, the automatic boom came with many collisions, falls, and jams that caused injuries and deaths. A 1985 news article covered three recent accidents, including one where passengers were using the newly installed automatic doors on buses. One passenger fell to her death when the door opened before the bus had stopped, while two other people were injured when the doors closed on them.[42] Elevators were also the site of many accidents. A news report in 1979 documented three recent, separate accidents.[43] The article affirmed that most accidents were caused by either mechanical failures or victims' carelessness. It then went on to describe some precautions when using elevators: "Passengers should not press buttons forcefully"; "Heavy goods should not be loaded onto passenger elevators"; "One should not jump or romp around in elevators"; "Young children should not take elevators without their guardians"; and "One should not attempt to force the elevator door open."[44] These guidelines indicated that the process of automation was not merely the replacement of human labor with machinery but the reassignment of human labor to a new mobility system. Humans now had to control their behavior and determine proper movement based on the machine's movement.

For example, in the bus transportation industry, bus attendants' labor was displaced and reassigned to each passenger's self-management. In May 1982, Seoul's bus industry proposed a bus service without female attendants, *annaeyang ŏpnŭn pŏsŭ*, to the municipal government,[45] which named the new one-man bus service, set to begin running on August 10, 1982, the *simin chayul pŏsŭ* (citizen's self-imposed bus ride).[46] Self-imposed tasks included preparing the fare or bus token, putting money into the fare box (see fig. 6.2), being informed of the bus routes and stops, and getting on and off in an orderly manner.[47] This was seen as "a breakthrough in the management of bus companies and profit improvement" by downsizing the number of bus attendants.[48]

The introduction of an automatic door solved problems and public discontent over single-door, one-man buses.[49] As a result, advocates of automation encouraged passengers to adjust to the automatic mode of mobility—this is labor reassigned from employed workers. Unexpected accidents occurred over the automatic doors, which were reported in the mass media and held up as a warning. Other kinds of automatic machinery spread over this same period, including vending machines, elevators, escalators, and office automation equipment. All of these assigned different types of self-regulated labor to their users, accompanied by specific rules of discipline that the users had to follow to avoid getting hurt or sustaining profit losses.

In this sense, the allegedly increased flexibility of human movement enabled by unmanned mechanical mobility did not always guarantee uncompromised convenience and relaxation. Instead, it sometimes amplified anxiety over technical errors and mechanical accidents. Automation's impact on behavior bears similarities to that wrought by the high mobility and flexibility of automobile traffic. Since the late 1960s, individual mobility rapidly expanded across South Korea with the development of automobile transportation, along with the improved circulation of commodities through expressway construction. However, this development changed people's roles in traffic circulation. People were encouraged to learn how to drive and to arm themselves with proper skills to prevent driving accidents. Learning to drive and obtaining a license were held up as prerequisites for "the 'my car' age."[50] According to a news report, a financial company had driving lessons for all of its employees so that they could sell products "with excellent mobility."[51] Likewise, some government employees were obliged to learn how to drive.[52] The push for employees to have driving skills meant that the increased autonomy and mobility of an individual in the flow of automobilization was guaranteed only after the individual's self-discipline and labor to get adjusted to the flow.

FIGURE 6.2 Citizen's self-imposed bus ride (1982). From *Kyŏnghyang sinmun*, Aug. 11, 1982, 11. © The Kyunghyang Shinmun Corporation.

The growth of self-service restaurants was another popular phenomenon in the 1980s. Equipped with semiautomated food production systems,[53] international fast-food chain restaurants began opening branches in Seoul in the 1980s. According to a column on the fast-food franchise, McDonald's discarded plans to open a branch in Seoul in the 1960s partially because Koreans did not like to eat while standing, moving, or working.[54] The columnist, Yi Kyu-t'ae, described how Koreans had changed markedly over the past two decades, such that by the 1980s, they liked imported food culture.[55] Accordingly, the first Burger King in Seoul opened in Gimpo International Airport in 1981, followed by Wendy's in Myŏng-dong in 1984, and McDonald's in Apkujŏng-dong in 1988.[56] The Japanese franchise Lotteria had already opened a branch through its affiliate, Lotte Department Store, back in 1979.[57]

As Yi Kyu-t'ae pointed out, newly imported food culture was a kind of nomadic culture.[58] These new restaurants imposed a series of necessary actions and movements on their customers. While the self-service system introduced efficiency and speed in restaurant management and food consumption, it was also accompanied by certain codes of behavior that customers were expected to follow, such as waiting in line to order, finding seats / moving trays by oneself, and cleaning up after oneself. Failure to follow these codes would lead to disorder among customers and loss of time. The 1988 film *Ch'il-su and Man-su* shows a scene where the protagonist (Ch'il-su) collides with a foreign customer at a Burger King in Seoul. Ch'il-su is a lower-class lacquerer, who fails to grasp proper conduct in the self-service restaurant. In contrast, his love interest demonstrates perfect understanding of the system, not only because she is one of the restaurant's part-time employees but also because she is a middle-class college student.

Automation and the Restructuring of Spaces

The all-at-once popularization of automation was no coincidence. It stemmed from the restructuring of urban spaces, mainly by promoting and legalizing high-rise apartments and commercial buildings. By 1981, more than 213 high-rise office buildings, with ten or more floors, had been built in Seoul over the previous decade. There were also 699 high-rise apartment buildings, likewise with ten or more floors, most of them built in the late 1970s.[59] A 1981 column describes this radical change over a short period:

> Until the mid-1960s, you could take in a grand view of Seoul on Namsan mountain. The first building that might catch your eye was the 8-story Pando Hotel in Sogong-dong, and there were only a few more buildings that were tall for their time, such as the Hwasin Department Store, the National Assembly building, and the Capitol building. However, after two decades of expansion, in 1981, it now takes quite a while to locate these buildings while standing on Namsan mountain. The 37-story Lotte Hotel replaced the Pando Hotel, and it is difficult to spot even the Hwasin and the National Assembly[60] because the high-rise buildings that sprang up everywhere in the 1970s block our view.[61]

These tall buildings required elevators and gondolas for both passenger and freight transport. Furthermore, since the partial revision of the Building Act on December 30, 1972, all buildings over 31 meters (approx. 102 feet) had to install an emergency elevator.[62] Therefore, the rapidly expanding apartment construction industry directly influenced the expansion of the elevator industry. After the Housing Site Development Promotion Act came into effect in 1980, the Chun Doo-hwan government announced the Fifteen-Year Construction Plan for Five Million Housing Units for those who were officially classified as homeless.[63] The official confirmation of both the 1986 Asian Games and the 1988 Seoul Olympics, respectively in 1980 and 1981, also significantly boosted demand for construction.[64] Under these circumstances, South Korea's ten-year average output for yearly construction from 1980 to 1989 exceeded 100,000 apartment buildings.[65] It goes without saying that the pace and scale of construction directly shaped the spread of elevators as a part of daily life.

Similarly, the vending machine industry greatly benefited from urbanization and increased high-rise construction in South Korea. According to a news article written in 1979, vending machines were popular in high-rise buildings with lots of traffic, including hospitals, high-rise office buildings, and department stores. Operation of these machines was usually overseen by such organizations as cooperatives and credit unions.[66]

In general, each high-rise building in Seoul was operating three to five vending machines at the time.[67] In turn, high-end department stores, such as Lotte and Shinsegae, were equipped with escalators and drew in customers with glass elevators with good views.[68]

The Kangnam area in Seoul was the main beneficiary of this urbanization process. It is "where many large-scale apartment complexes were built as part of the project to urbanize this part of the city in the late 1970s, where skyrocketing real-estate prices provided the highest expected profits."[69] Kangnam also functioned as the gateway to Seoul and connected the capital city to other regions via the newly built expressway system in the 1970s. Therefore, in the Kangnam area, automobility (maximized by expressways) converged with rapidly spreading high-rise apartment construction and its technologically driven automated mobility.

In a special episode of the popular detective show *Chief Inspector* (MBC) called "The Husband Is the Baggage, the Wife Is the Owner" (1977), television's characteristics underscore the spectacle of movement, frequently repositioning the leading actors by putting them on an expressway. The detectives move from Pusan to Seoul, Seoul to Taegu, and Taegu to Chinhae, to chase a couple who stole an express bus company's remittance after sneaking into the bus's luggage hold. It is worth noting this episode's premise: to steal the money, the husband hides inside the luggage, while his wife checks it in before she boards the express bus. The husband's transformation into cargo serves as an allegory for the conditions of individuals in the automobilized system. As the thieving couple's whereabouts are traced by using the express buses' passenger records, motels' guest registers, and former employers' personnel records, the couple themselves are passed along as a "commodity (parcel)" with tracking numbers.[70] In turn, the dry sequence of the express bus—boarding, in operation, and arrival—was likely included to introduce the Seoul Express Bus Terminal, which had newly opened in the Kangnam area, as well as to present a detailed picture of human logistics.[71]

It is worth noting that the show's own medium for distribution, the television, implies a point about the process of semiautomation in the auto industry. In the mid-1970s, mass factory production for the auto industry corresponded with the standardization of production. Most importantly, this correspondence introduced the Fordist system of labor management—a semiautomatic assembly system. Daewoo Motors first

FIGURE 6.3 Photograph titled *Hyŏndae chadongch'a ulssan kongjang* (Hyundai Motors Ulsan factory) (1976) (CET0037988). Courtesy of National Archives of Korea.

implemented the conveyor-belt system in 1972, with Kia following suit in 1973, and Hyundai in 1976 (see fig. 6.3).[72] One's role in the assembly line necessitated only simplified and standardized forms of manual labor, and these basic, minimum requirements for employment contributed to a rapid increase in the use of conveyor-belt systems. At the same time, workers on the assembly became deskilled and more easily replaceable.[73] In turn, the ceaseless circulation of the auto industry's semiautomated system encounters another flow in the medium of television.

Television, unlike cinema, is a machine that mediates a continuous, intermission-free flow of information. Viewers can get on this flow at any point in time. At each of these points, one is required to flexibly adjust to whatever is conveyed to them, whether it is a news show, a music performance, or a soap opera. These conditions also pertain to the environments and habits as changed by expressways. Through the construction of the nationwide expressway system, the "machine space" encroached upon the "people space," such that people could not enter without cars.[74] In television, much like passengers on an expressway, no one can stop or pause in the middle of the flow; while they can turn off the TV, walk away, or change the channel, these actions do not affect the flow itself, and there is only one option for them: to get on the flow again. I contend that such a loss of control over the conveyor-belt flows of traffic and television is closely linked to semiautomation in the manufacturing sector, as well as to the self-imposed ways of consuming automatic technologies. Individuals before conveyor belts are tasked with adjusting themselves to uncontrolled movements by developing techniques of "self-management."[75]

Electronic Mobility and Transparency

The automated teller machine (ATM) was one of the newly introduced, unmanned machines enabled by electronic connectivity in the 1990s. During this period, the spread of ATMs in South Korea traced and made visible the computer-based, machine-led flow, to which human mobility had been reassigned through the aforementioned automation fever, subsequently linking human mobility to its counterpart in the neoliberal economic system—the nonhuman, impersonal, electronic circuit of financial capital. Before the ATM, the online cash-dispenser (CD) network allowed its customers to withdraw money at any bank equipped with teller machines. The Chohung Bank (CHB) implemented this type of unmanned banking service as early as December 1979.[76] However, it was not until November 1988 that the CD network was operating nationwide across South Korea.[77] The following year, several major banks, including Kookmin Bank, Korea Exchange Bank, and CHB, began offering ATM services that also included a deposit function to their CDs.[78] But it took until 1990 before fully automatic banking services were introduced on a twenty-four-hour basis. That service was called *muin ŭnhaeng* (unmanned bank branches) or *muin chadonghwa k'onŏ* (unmanned automatic banking corner), with CHB installing its first ATM in Myŏng-dong, Seoul, in July 1990.[79] In October that same year, Commercial Bank of Korea installed an ATM in the same neighborhood. It ran twenty-four hours a day, 7 days a week, and was called *sambaegyuksiboil k'onŏ* (365-day corner).[80] The total number of CDs and ATMs in the nation then sharply rose from 5,150 in 1990 to 11,550 in 1993.[81]

As a news article noted, this new trend of unmanned banking services in South Korean banks served as preparation for opening the nation's financial market.[82] Not surprisingly, the computerization of banking, including ATM services, was included in an index of management rationalization set to be assessed by the Financial Supervisory Service.[83] As J. P. Pardo-Guerra points out, the late 1980s was a time of "the internationalization of finance," when financial "firms extended their reach throughout the globe," so that "high-reliability proprietary communications networks" at a global level were in high demand.[84] The movement toward financial automation, therefore, went hand in hand with neoliberal globalization, or its localized name, *segyehwa*, so coined by South Korea's Kim Young-Sam government as a means to concretely realize the spirit of the age.

The 1995 film *Tonŭl katko t'wiŏra* (*Millions in My Account*) illustrates how this new automation technology led to the reclamation of human movement and, more importantly, how machine-led mobility was indicative of the spirit of a coming neoliberal age, one defined by full transparency. The film centers on a hopeless, unemployed man, Ch'ŏn Talssu (Pak Chung-hun), who discovers that a group of hackers is using his previously inactive bank account to launder money. Talssu, who earns an irregular income working as a proxy for reserve forces training, is obliged to receive payments from one of his clients by wire transfer. On his way to the bank, he is accompanied by a waitress, Kim Ŭnji (Chŏng Sŏngyŏng), who wants to collect on his bill. Talssu has not been to a bank in such a long time that he does not know how to use an ATM, whereas Ŭnji is very familiar with the technology. When Talssu updates his account book, they realize that 10 billion won has been deposited into his account, on top of the client's remittance of 50,000 won. After some brief hesitation, the two collectively decide to withdraw 300 million won from the account, first to check if there is some error in the bank book and then to actually have the money in their hands.

Talssu's experience of both technological difficulty and electronic accuracy reflects ordinary Koreans' initial bodily experience with the ATM and of the affects generated through that experience. The immediate and uninterrupted operation of the ATM leaves no room for negotiation or procrastination. Individuals must adjust their bodily and affective reaction to the rhythm of electronic operation. In an essay relating the history of the ATM to the formation of neoliberal optical subjectivity, Mark Hayward calls the "fears and desires" in the newly changed relationship between client and the ATM as bank teller an "institutionalized form of depersonalization."[85] In postcolonial South Korea, where compressed modernity pushed citizens into a disciplinary system to avoid getting left behind the times, such "fears and desires" were also preceded by the correction of behavior or the transformation of the body.[86] For example, when Talssu hesitates, Ŭnji embarrasses him by saying, "Haven't you ever been to a bank?"

The couple's sudden fortune is, in fact, a satirical portrait of a wealthy society confronted with drastic financial restructuring. The Kim Young-Sam government issued an emergency order on August 12, 1993, to put the Real-Name Financial Transaction System into effect. This order prohibited any withdrawal of money from an account under a false or inaccurate name, unless the customer verified his or her real name within two months of the order's issuance.[87] As bank accounts with false or proxy identities had played a huge role in money laundering and illegal political fund-raising until then, the order's sudden and expedited enforcement was driven by the difficulty of political reform and the projected ineffectiveness of gradual implementation.[88] During the two-month verification period, banks were forced to report to the National Tax Service whenever clients made a one-time withdrawal of 30 million won or more, and for account holders with a balance of 50 million won or more, changes from false to real names prompted investigations into the source of clients' funds.[89] In the film, an attendant's remark to Talssu clearly confirms the impact of this order: "The only one in the world who can withdraw this money is you, Ch'ŏn Talssu." The original source of the transferred 10 billion won turns out to be a retired politician, whose portrayal recalls former president Chun Doo-Hwan, who was, at the time of the film's production, under investigation for a 180 billion won slush fund.[90] The ATM system's electronic accuracy, as depicted in the scene of Talssu's troubles with the new machine, goes in tandem with the transparency of the real-name system, which interrupted the attempt at money laundering. As a result, the old politician who stands helpless before the computerized financial system shares the same affective response as Talssu.

There were several other popular films featuring similar affective reactions to the irreversibility and magnitude of a computerized financial system in the mid-1990s. For example, the antagonistic husband of the female protagonist in *Days of Roses* (*Changmi ŭi nanal*, 1994) is devastated when he finds himself bankrupt, a direct result of an Australian bank's real client withdrawing the entire balance from the account he had been using under a borrowed name. A 1995 film, *Man with a Gun* (*Ch'ongjabi*), introduces the newly commercialized, mobile credit card reader in a scene where a bar owner comes to the protagonist's office to collect on bills and takes a card reader out of his bag, rendering the latter speechless. The computerization of bank systems also stimulated the popular imagination in other ways, namely by reenvisioning the Robin Hood figure as one who pursued corrupt politicians with the help of computers. In *Channel 69* (*Ch'aenŏl siksŭnain*, 1996), a group of hackers track a politician's slush funds and expose his secret in a television show that they broadcast by illegally modulating frequency. This politician, who has shown great interest in newly emerging internet technology as a tool to promote himself, stands before a television set, stunned by the information exposed. Together, these films dramatize the specific affective reactions of individuals encountering the machinelike immediacy and rationality of a renovated financial system—staring blankly at the machine, being at a loss for words, or standing frozen in confusion, while being overwhelmed, spellbound, or devastated.

It is important to remember that the reformation of the financial systems in the 1990s was a way to internationalize South Korea's economic structure, even as those changes were closely associated with domestic political reforms. In an essay written immediately after the two-month verification period for the Real-Name Financial Transaction System, Seoul National University economics professor P'yo Hakkil asserted, "Whether the Korean economy will succeed in the true meaning of internationalization in the years ahead is what will make or break the Kim Young-Sam government's New Economy policy."[91] According to P'yo, these new financial systems' transparency and rationality were needed to provide new global standards that would allow multinational finance capital to circulate smoothly. The old defects in the system, such as false-name accounts and outdated practices, were not merely the targets of social and political reforms but also the obstacles to neoliberal restructuring. In light of these conditions, it is worth noting that the Hollywood box-office hit *Ghost* (1990) also featured a story of computer-aided money laundering and how it fails when there is a real-name system in place. The film was released five years before *Millions in My Account*, and during the period when the real-name emergency order was in effect, a columnist wrote that this American film offered a glimpse of the future of the real-name financial system in Korea.[92] *Ghost* was one of several films distributed directly by United International Pictures (UIP), following the restructuring of South Korea's domestic film market in the late 1980s. Given that this film's distribution in Korea was another direct result of the local market adopting global standards, we might understand the film's dramatization of American society as having something of an instructive quality for Korean viewers, specifically by upholding financial transparency as a global standard that would soon be required.

Extended Visibility and Mobile Bodies in the Surveillance Society

Transparency in the age of financial automation was also a matter of visibility, of allowing the gaze through transparent windows.[93] Before the advent of automatic banking corners, customers visited their banks in person, only to have tellers conduct financial transactions for them. When the customer showed the teller her or his identification documents and bankbook, the teller was authorized to view the customer's records in the bank database, access to which was limited to the bank's employees, who could subsequently carry out the customer's financial transactions by proxy. Financial automation was an innovation for customers in that it increased the visibility of such information in bank databases. Customers using the ATM were able to access information simply by inserting their bankbooks or debit cards into the unmanned machine. "Instructions on the display" guaranteed customers such transparency at automatic banking corners, which were portrayed as "a dream bank," allowing customers to "conduct simple bank transactions on their own."[94] In a news article on a bank's new "direct banking" service, which enabled customers to open an account, issue a debit card, and get a bank loan on their own at an automatic banking corner, the service is explained as "the total self-banking system, where customers can directly conduct bank transactions just by touching the visual display with their fingers to communicate with bank tellers."[95] By allowing customers to see and work with database information, these devices of visualization guaranteed the automated mobility system in the bank.

The financial automation system made transparent was, in itself, a combination of visualizing devices. The maximized circulation of information made possible by recently established online network systems was another manifestation of maximized visibility. The pirate broadcaster-hackers in *Channel 69* reveal that the term *transparency* in the computer age signifies not only the disclosure of finance flow but also the transparent surveillance window on the observer. Digitization was necessary for data to be immediate and highly mobile in computer-based operations, but it also left individuals' information open to surveillance. Thus, transparency was a matter of the subject's visibility—that is, a matter of biopolitics. The 1995 film *Runaway* (*Rŏnŏwei*, 1995) shows how the individual's ability to observe and not be observed becomes the determining skill in the postindustrial city of Seoul, here portrayed as a space of hide-and-seek. In the film, Yi Tong-hŭi (Yi Pyŏng-hŏn, a.k.a. Lee Byung-hun) is the founder of a computer game production company, which is just about to release a three-dimensional shooting adventure game called *City Runner*, whose main theme is "the city as a labyrinth." After a one-night stand, Tong-hŭi and his partner Ch'oe Mi-ran (Kim Ŭn-jŏng), a freelancer illustrator, witness a murder in her apartment building's parking lot. Despite her reluctance, he reports the crime to the police, providing her home phone and his identity. The following day, the two are pursued by gangsters and driven to become fugitives. The city becomes a labyrinth for them, reconfiguring its spaces and necessitating a constant search for safe spaces, since their homes and offices are all known to the gang, and their telephone records are leaked by their friends and assistants. The only way to hide themselves safely is to remain anonymous in public spaces of transition, such as the metro and the public parks.

Interestingly, Tong-hŭi's knowledge of computer network systems, together with access to his friend's hacking program, functions as the counterstrategy in this game of pursuit. By hacking the Ministry of Health and Welfare's intranet, he discovers that the gangsters used the drug Kiniphine to anesthetize him and that the gang leader is the CEO of a pharmaceutical company that imports the drug.

> [A computer screen shows that access has been granted to the user, followed by the profile of the gang leader.]
>
> **Detective:** [Over the telephone] Yi Tong-hŭi, where are you? Is Ch'oe Mi-ran with you? Your friend Sin Chi-wŏn was attacked. He was stabbed to death.
>
> **Tong-hŭi:** I'll get right to the point. The murderer is Cho Tong-chin, the CEO of a drug company called Medi-World.
>
> **Detective:** Cho Tong-chin? Medi-World?
>
> **Tong-hŭi:** I just faxed you his personal record.

Upon receiving Tong-hŭi's report, the police summon and investigate the CEO. In the final sequence, however, Tong-hŭi and Mi-ran realize that one of the detectives is secretly connected to the gang and that he is the informant who leaked their whereabouts. The bidirectional use of surveillance is intriguing in that it gives individuals a form of agency that can be weaponized, specifically by visualizing the previously invisible with the help of advanced technology.

Digitized information circulated in any computer network system becomes transparent through the application of such self-taught skills. The self-proclaimed "kid cops" in the 1993 film *Kid Cop* (*K'idŭ k'ap*) similarly make use of visualizing devices by filming crime scenes with a portable video camera. The kid cops' bodies, made nimble and mobile by their rollerblades, expand the scope of visibility and improve their ability to navigate. In turn, *Channel 69*'s pirate broadcaster-hackers also tap into weaponized agency by collecting visual information on the corrupt politician and exposing that information across the nation. The computer technology that positively contributes to exposing a politician's corruption in *Channel 69*, however, serves a corrupt detective in *Runaway*. Technology itself is therefore depicted as morally unaligned and untethered to any single, specific form of control. Consequently, the knowledge needed to utilize computer technology is neither controlled nor distributed by the public sector but, rather, exists as a malleable option available to individuals and the free market. Such knowledge is acquired by self-reliant individuals who teach themselves.

Expansion of Non-Face-to-Face Relationships and Anonymity

Another significant change wrought by financial automation in 1990s South Korea was the spread of online sales and business—namely, home shopping services. Similar types of indirect sales, such as mail order and telemarketing businesses, predated financial automation, but the expansion of online computer networks and the advancement of automation technologies rapidly accelerated the development of home shopping services during this period. The telemarketing businesses promoted by some major department stores in the late 1980s also adopted early automation technologies, conducting transactions through computer systems or videotex. Crucially, however, these transactions still involved nonautomatic elements that obliged customers to pay in person or go to the bank to transfer money to the business's account.[96] The first instance of an online credit card transaction service being adopted for business was in August 1989, when Kyobo Bookstore Corporation's Hwanŭn Credit Card Service partnered with Korea Data Communication Corporation (DACOM). DACOM began an online sales service for bookstores, department stores, ticket sales companies, and travel agencies through Chollian II,[97] one of South Korea's most successful virtual terminal communication services for personal computers, called "PC communications."[98] This new type of commerce attracted increasing levels of attention over its convenience. According to DACOM's April 1992 report, "Survey on Chollian's Order & Reservation Service Use," the number of users more than doubled during the survey period of three months.[99]

Home shopping services grew dramatically when home shopping channels were allotted airtime on cable television networks. In 1995, South Korean cable television networks opened nationwide, and two home shopping channels, Hi-Shopping and HSTV, were officially added to those networks in October that same year, following two months of testing.[100] According to a special article on the first anniversary of home shopping channels, within one year, the number of customers grew to about 100,000, the market size to about 100 billion won, the average number of incoming orders to 1,000–1,300 per day, and the average sales to 50–60 million won.[101] The following year, sales for the two channels were, respectively, 5 times and 7.5 times the sales from the previous year, while the whole market grew 10 times in size.[102]

The spread of this kind of non-face-to-face commerce promoted the institutional spread of depersonalized relationships, as ATMs and automatic banking corners enabled an "institutionalized form of depersonalization," whereby people did not have to face tellers to do their banking. Visualization apparatuses at home, such as PC communications, cable television channels, and online credit card verification systems, increased both the transparency of commerce and the visibility of customers. Nevertheless, the increase of non-face-to-face, depersonalized relationships between seller and customer under this new type of commerce also indicated the emergence of anonymous relationships.

A scene at the metro in *Runaway* depicting two gangsters who helplessly stare at a departing metro train that loads the runaway couple, who are now anonymous among other passengers, therefore, can be interpreted as demonstrating a certain affective reaction, specifically to the technological system that facilitates transparency, proving that anonymity can lead to strategic dominance. In turn, *The Contact* (*Chŏpsok*, 1997), which depicts a pathological relationship with an anonymous Other, offers a great opportunity to more closely examine and discuss the representation of anonymous identities in 1990s South Korean cinema. Tonghyŏn (Han Suk-kyu), a radio producer, receives an online song request from a user called "Woman 2." Tonghyŏn has personal history with the song, "Pale Blue Eyes" by The Velvet Underground, so he suspects that Woman 2 is his ex-girlfriend. In fact, the woman, Suhyŏn (Chŏn To-yŏn, a.k.a. Jeon Do-yeon), is a telemarketer for a home shopping service, who suffers from a secret crush on her friend's boyfriend. At first, Suhyŏn acts as if she is a friend of Tonghyŏn's ex-girlfriend but then apologizes for the lie. The two become friends and set a time to meet offline, but sudden news of his ex-girlfriend's death puts an end to those plans. The memory of his unfulfilled love deeply wounds Tonghyŏn, and the news of her death causes him to suffer from communicative and social disorders. He hands in his resignation and decides to emigrate to Australia. The last sequence in the film portrays Suhyŏn's pathetically sincere efforts to meet him. However, Tonghyŏn's reaction to these efforts is pathological. In the final scene, Suhyŏn leaves multiple messages on his answering machine and continues to wait for him in front of a movie theater, but Tonghyŏn merely observes her anonymously through the window of a second-floor coffee shop the whole afternoon. After she leaves her last message through a pay phone behind him, deciding to give up and leave the meeting place, he finally steps outside and approaches her, ending the film.

The Contact topped the South Korean box office for all of 1997, drawing over 1.4 million viewers nationwide.[103] It is worth noting that a not insignificant number of reviews expressed empathy for the protagonists in the final scene: "They finally meet each other face to face. Jeon Do-yeon's dry, xerophthalmic eyes now grow moist, and viewers are also unable to hold back their tears. . . . Ah, after a long time, we see a love story that really pulls at the heartstrings."[104] Another review stated, "The film amicably depicts the process whereby a man and a woman with lonely hearts can fall in love through an online chatting service, without knowing each other's faces."[105] Yet another reviewer said of the film, "The male and female leads who are experiencing the bitterness of unrequited love—thus, living terribly lonely lives—see each other's faces for the first time in the last scene. However, audiences do not exhibit any resistance to this plot."[106] That is to say, the audience is not at all disturbed by the male lead's lengthy observation of the heroine but, rather, empathize with his hesitation and his desire to remain invisible until he is convinced of the relationship.

In this romance, not only are the couple's identities anonymous, but their everyday lives are also characterized by anonymity. Tonghyŏn's job is to transmit songs and stories to random people. He has opened up various ways to reach him for song requests, but as evidenced by his online conversation with Suhyŏn, his listeners are largely anonymous, such that they can easily hide or manipulate their identities. Suhyŏn's job as a telemarketer for a home shopping company also necessitates daily communication with many anonymous customers. Tonghyŏn's fellow producers do not understand his decision to play a twenty-minute piece of music, especially when the broadcasters want pieces that are under five minutes, to keep ratings high and to leave more airtime for their sponsors' messages. Similarly, Suhyŏn's efforts to help a customer with a love confession disturbs the ideal flow of smooth product distribution. Both must avoid unnecessarily intimate or irregular communications with their customers. The electromagnetic waves of the radio and the home shopping channel do leave little room for genuine connections, a sharp contrast to Tonghyŏn's ex-girlfriend's vinyl record of The Velvet Underground, which manifests an analog aesthetic of the past and appears to symbolize a genuine connection between the ex-lovers.

Therefore, the metro that preserves their anonymity is an extension of the electronic circulation that they participate in for work. As standardized components of the postindustrial knowledge economy, Tonghyŏn's and Suhyŏn's bodies flash by each other in an anonymous and automated circuit. Communications, however, are only collected and committed to memory as electronic signals to be accumulated in beepers and answering machines. Suhyŏn's ID as "Woman 2" implies that her identity is replaceable, indicating the nature of that anonymous flow in computer-mediated communications. The rise of computer-mediated communication in the late 1980s and the early 1990s, such as virtual terminal services, granted young Korean users anonymity, so they could secure access to virtual spaces without having to reveal their true identity. The individual's task was to adjust to the anonymous flow as much as possible, for if they did not understand the principle of anonymous circulation, they would be making their identities vulnerable by exposing themselves to anonymous others, or letting themselves be lost at sea. In other words, the autopoiesis of computer-aided technology compels people to further their knowledge and discipline themselves, in a way that echoes the impact of automated mobility via unmanned machines on human subjects. Therefore, anonymity equates to the individual's need for security and to stay firmly within the flow.

Anonymity, nevertheless, was an unattainable ideal in the age of financial automation. On the surface, it seemed like the anonymity of virtual spaces made individual participants invisible, but these spaces were, in fact, spaces of commerce, and consequently, the individual's identity was financial information that had to be more distinctly visualized. Even as her ID reflects her obsession with anonymity, and her identity remains unknown to her customers while she serves as a home shopping teller, Suhyŏn has a range of vision that allows her to see her customer's address, payment methods, the address of the woman her customer loves, and the fact that the woman does not want to accept his gifts. In this way, the anonymous flow was a kind of stage, on which each individual had to perform in the belief that it was indeed anonymous.

Another successful film released in 1997, *Beat* (*Pit'ŭ*), sets up interesting contrasts of pictures of individual mobility, reflecting an alternative affective reaction to this machinelike anonymous flow. Under immense levels of stress due to poor grades, a woman throws herself in front of a metro train. Her friend, the female lead, Romi (Ko So-yŏng), had been pretending that she had neglected to study yet still gained high marks with ease, so her friend's frustrations and suicide serve as a source of constant guilt. This type of suicide attempt has, in fact, been a rather frequent occurrence in the metro, and the scene's reflection of the trend suggests a link between the automatic (re)production of the competition-driven educational system and the metro's automatic, looping flow that shapes individual commutes in today's neoliberal era.[107] The South Korean educational system, which once guaranteed improved class mobility through a rapid and radical modernization process, nearly stagnated in the late 1990s and instead functioned as a machine automatically producing well-educated but standardized labor power. In the film, the suicide-led interruption of the automatic machinelike flow of the metro serves as a metaphor in terms of both its contribution to Romi's break from the autopoietic educational system and its exposure of a bigger picture, which is the new mobility system. Likewise, the male lead, Min, and his best friend, T'aesu, mark a deeper break with the metro, opting for motorbikes and further underscoring the young generation's reactions to the ever-automatizing flow of labor circulation.

Conclusion

Seoul's restructuring of spaces through massive construction projects, its nationwide spatial reorganization through the expressway system, and new media's increased flexibility and unceasing circulation have all converged toward a new subjectivity, one that was simultaneously exposed in a series of liberalization processes. Increased levels of individual mobility, enabled by these processes, fully resonated with the maximized efficiency of automated mobility. Under such flexibility and efficiency, the subject is positioned as an entrepreneur who evaluates the management value of new technology and imposes relevant codes of behavior on oneself to adjust to the new mode of mobility. In this way, the vaunted harmony between humans and technology featured in so many corporate advertisements was not intended to simply draw technology toward humankind but to restructure human mobility in the face of changes under electronic mobility.

How, then, can we define the subjectivity reorganized before this automated machinelike flow? One possibility is its identification as the "neoliberal homo economicus" or "manipulable man."[108] This subjectivity adjusts to new electronic movement that brings about greater effectiveness and innovation—a subjectivity that sees the value of automated circulation exclusively from the entrepreneur's perspective. A series of liberalization processes implemented in tandem with automation over the 1980s expanded the range of individual movement. Similarly, technological innovations in transportation sharply augmented the individual's ability to move. There was also significant restructuring in the "circulation of the labor force and consumers" with the establishment of a new mobility system.[109] That is, the restructuring was related to the increase in labor market flexibility that went hand in hand with globalization. Working subjects who could easily get on and off the labor market's conveyor belt, who could migrate further within the expanded range of circulation, were subjected to this kind of flexible mobility system. The economic restructuring after the 1997 financial crisis implemented "neoliberalism as a macroeconomic doctrine of state policy."[110] It enforced flexibility in the labor market by legalizing mass layoffs and nonregular employment. However, the reorganization of mobility systems since the 1980s shows that "neoliberalism configured as epistemology or social ethos" had already been in place before the crisis.[111] As films from the 1990s demonstrate, the human subjects who manage themselves on the conveyor-belt mobility system of automatic machines share similarities with those subjects who improve themselves with self-taught skills in the face of financial capital's nonhuman mobility. I argue that this kind of mobility system and the corresponding emphasis on self-management characterize the neoliberal technology of government in South Korea during the period of underdemocratized, new military rule. Most of the phenomena described began before the state-led, post-IMF crisis restructuring of the economy. Thus, I am not suggesting that automation technology was indicative of manpower's future in the post-Fordist era. Rather, I seek clues that the neoliberal ethos was not suddenly formed in reaction to this economic restructuring in 1997, arguing instead that it gradually grew out of an existing developmental ethos and was instilled as discipline through the advancement of technology and capitalism. In other words, South Korea's neoliberal governmentality should not be understood as the product of a sudden, historical break but, rather, as a historical accumulation of knowledge, ethics, and technology combined. The cognitive mobility of the time, which I have called post-cine-mobility, suggests a continuation of the vision-centered regime in the previous era. However, the visuality of this computerized neoliberal era does not just inherit the ocularcentrism of cine-mobility but also adopts an implosive vision that territorializes the bodily movement and, subsequently, personal data of the human subject in the name of efficiency and transparency.

EPILOGUE

Railroad Mobility in North Korea

At the peak of the nuclear crisis in early 2018, in an effort to ease military tensions, leaders from South and North Korea held their first Inter-Korean Summit in over a decade, the previous one dating to 2007. This historic meeting on April 27, 2018, was preceded by a series of diplomatic envoy and cultural delegation exchanges that occurred between February and April. South Korea's 120-member cultural delegation to Pyongyang was made up of popular musicians, government officials, reporters, and a tae kwon do demonstration team. It performed at the East Pyongyang Grand Theatre on April 1 and then at the Pyongyang Arena on April 3. Of great global interest was South Korea's K-pop girl group Red Velvet and their participation in the art troupe. They were the "biggest names" in the troupe, and some commentators believed that they could become "a subversive force in North Korea."[1] The North also appeared to take the so-called K-pop invasion seriously:[2] they did not let broadcasters air any live recordings of either concert, even strictly prohibiting diplomats and traders from watching and reimporting the recordings from another country.[3] However, according to well-informed sources, digital files of both recorded concerts spread rapidly via the North Korea–China cross-border black markets and were stored on USB flash drives.[4] The recent flurry of changing media environments in North Korea has indeed been remarkable. The advancement of digital technologies has made it possible to sneak South Korean television shows and Hollywood movies into North Korean homes with fewer risks of getting caught. The unusual digital media players manufactured in China, including *not'ŭt'el* (NoteTel), MP4 and MP5 players, are devices that not a few North Korean homes have to help people secretly watch forbidden shows.[5] Compared to the old VCD, DVD, and VHS players, these latest video playback devices are portable, have small displays, are rechargeable using electric condensers and car batteries, and, more importantly, are equipped with USB ports or SD card slots, so people can easily conceal and destroy problematic materials whenever necessary.[6] The growing popularity of these devices has forced the State Security Department to capitulate, so, in effect, personal possession of NoteTels has been decriminalized.[7] The latent ability of these small screens to disarm the government surveillance system is not only a clear matter of interest for the North Korean regime but also that of its antipodes. For instance, Thor Halvorssen, president of the Human Rights Foundation, noted that from 2014 through 2016, he and his organization had scattered more than a thousand USB flash disks onto North Korean soil, using drone technology.[8] Whether such acts of psychological warfare had worked or not, according to a former DPRK diplomat, the people in North Korea "chanted 'Hail to Kim Jong Un' during the day and watched South Korean movies under their blankets in the evening."[9] What exactly can we infer from this transboundary small screen spectatorship?

Interestingly, the Inter-Korean Summit in April 2018 affected not only the transboundary spectatorship of North Korea's digital media environment but also the realm of transportation mobility. In a speech for the country's seventy-third Liberation Day, South Korean president Moon Jae-in proposed an "East Asian Railroad Community," one that would encompass six Northeast Asian countries and the United States, modeled after the European Coal and Steel Community established in 1951, which later "gave birth to the European Union."[10] Moon gave this speech at a time when negotiations between Pyongyang and Washington still seemed uncertain,[11] but the plan for high-speed railways connecting the South and North had been proposed as early as the first summit in April,[12] and it was pushed forward through a series of workshop talks between the two Koreas.[13] These joint efforts, which seem to overly emphasize the economic value of railroad reconnection, recall the imperial powers' rivalry for control of railroad construction and management on the Korean

Peninsula over a century ago. The possibility of reunifying the railroad lines between the two Koreas would "give South Korea a land link to the rest of the Asian continent, potentially opening up hugely lucrative trading and infrastructure links,"[14] and help North Korea's ruling family achieve its longtime dream of "a state-of-the-art rail system linking its major cities with each other and the wider world."[15] Although the prospect sounds rosy, there is no denying the fact that the plan was driven by the "economic logic of capitalism," making some critics worry that it could potentially create "another mutant society on the northern part of the Korean Peninsula that has a splendid surface and a sick and rotten interior."[16]

However, it appears that the swift unfolding of the railroad reunification project is owing not only to the recent thaw between the two Koreas but also to the North Korean regime's own longtime emphasis on the railroad as the state's primary mode of transportation. On December 17, 2011, when North Korea's supreme leader Kim Jong Il died of a heart attack, he was reportedly "on his train, as he was conducting an 'on-site guidance tour' in an unspecified part of the country."[17] According to DPRK's *Great Dictionary of Korean* (*Chosŏnmal taesajŏn*), the on-site guidance tour, *hyŏnji chido*, is "a type of guidance conducted by a respected person by his or her visiting the spot in person,"[18] a term that has been exclusively attributed to the state's supreme leader since the 1960s. Accordingly, Kim Jong Il inherited the term only after Kim Il Sung's death.[19] This political act is understood as "one of the most revolutionary and plebeian ways to guide the public,"[20] since it aims "to grasp the exact state of concrete reality and people's ideals, in order to accommodate them when formulating and making policies," "to help the public understand the political lines and policies of the Workers' Party of Korea (WPK)," and "to set a positive example by guiding a specific unit."[21] Consequently, in the official commentary in *Rodong sinmun* (Workers' newspaper), Kim Jong Il's death on the train was praised as indicative of "a life of selfless service, conducting the on-site guidance tour even in the last moments of his life."[22]

Another phrase in the commentary evokes the symbolic connection between the tour as service and railroad mobility: "Majimak kkŭt'kkaji kŭi-nŭn inminhaeng ryŏlch'a-rŭl t'asigo inmin-ŭl wihayŏ pongmuhasiyŏtta" (On the train to the people, he served the people to the very end). According to a preface to a posthumous picture collection of Kim Il Sung, the phrase *inminhaeng ryŏlch'a* (train to the people) was "imagery" that Kim himself had adopted to express "his own plebeian method" for conducting on-site guidance.[23] The supreme leader's presence in remote areas all over the country, in defiance of poor traveling conditions, provided the basis for the leader's parental benevolence. It was "the train of great service, the train of miracles, and the train of victory," on which the supreme leader Kim Il Sung "carried the enormous belief and love that revered people as the sky, or as the teacher," so that he could "awaken the general public as the subject, and organize and mobilize their infinite energy."[24] Characterized thus, the train served as the means for the supreme leader to reach out to people and mobilize them.

The posthumous photograph collection of Kim Il Sung was published in 1997 to commemorate his achievements. It was titled *Inminhaeng ryŏlch'a-rŭl hamkke t'asigo* (Together Aboard the Train to People) and opens with a picture of Kim Il Sung on a train with his son, Kim Jong Il.[25] As one can infer from the title, this book was an attempt to show father and son together, implying that the imagery, the affiliation with the train to the people, had now passed on to the new supreme leader. Most likely, Kim Jong Il intended to inherit this successful imagery from his father. A 1995 song performed by the Wangjaesan Light Music Band, "Tallinŭn pulbit" (A running glow), incorporates lyrics that indicate how the imagery of inminhaeng ryŏlch'a was already associated with Kim Jong Il, only a year after Kim Il Sung's death: "The window of a night train with a sweet whistle / Brimming over with a merciful glow / Commander goes out to people this night again / Miles and miles of love continue / That glowing light on the train to the people / A running glow that carries love."[26]

The 2016 novel *The Field Train* (*Yajŏn ryŏlch'a*) is a posthumous fictionalization of Kim Jong Il's final year and, interestingly, portrays the same ritual for inheriting the imagery:

> "Changgun-nim [Commander], according to the weather report, it is expected to be windy and very cold this week due to cold continental high pressure. The snowstorm will abate tomorrow morning, but it will be the coldest this year."

> "Taejang [General], don't worry too much. I'm fine. Have I ever avoided cold or hot weather when conducting the on-site guidance service? I have never postponed any scheduled on-site tours whether it rained or snowed. I'm well trained, so don't worry."[27]

Despite his assurance to Kim Jong Un, Kim Jong Il dies in the field train the following day, as he reportedly did in reality. The novel's final two chapters employ a laudatory tone to praise the late supreme leader's "selfless" devotion to the service of meeting people in person. Seeing the sorrow-stricken faces of workers and farmers who came from distant areas to Pyongyang to mourn his father's death, Kim Jong Un, the successor, realizes that his father's visits to remote industrial sites and farming villages have powerfully influenced people. This propagandistic novel reaffirms the late ruler's legitimacy and dedication through the imagery of inminhaeng ryŏlch'a, and at the same time, it constructs a narrative of growth, whereby the new ruler understands and inherits that imagery from his father and grandfather.

This state-led process of upholding the railroad as a symbol in the North marks a sharp contrast with the political meaning attached to the railroad in the South, which saw a radical transition from rail- to automobile-based industrialization, as discussed in chapters 3 and 4. According to Byung-min Ahn, the railroad is the "best means of transportation to control the public by virtue of its ability to limit the free movement of people," as well as "the most appropriate traffic system that guarantees extensive, scheduled, and stable transport," qualities that likely serve as the grounds for DPRK's preference for the railroad.[28] Moreover, it is worth paying attention to article 2 of DPRK's Railways Act, which states that "the railroad is an honorable trophy from the revolution to fight for the nationalization of major industries."[29] On August 10, 1946, the North Korean Provisional People's Committee passed a law to nationalize the railroad industry, including trains, tracks, facilities, transport networks, and manpower, along with other key industries that were previously owned by the Japanese.[30] Given that the Park Chung Hee government in South Korea denounced the railroad as "a vestige of Japanese colonialism," promoting the expressway as an alternative attainable through "sole national potential" (see chapter 4), article 2 of DPRK's

Railways Act clearly demonstrates that the two Koreas took markedly different paths for historicizing transportation systems in the postcolonial era.

The information we might glean about spectators in the DPRK is undoubtedly limited. However, the cases in South Korea that we examined in chapters 2 and 3 demonstrate, in no uncertain terms, how machine-led mobility's accelerated speed and maximized connectivity ultimately demand submission to the system of acceleration itself, a development that Virilio identified as a "dictatorship of movement."[31] In the era of inminhaeng ryŏlch'a's cine-mobility, it was possible and necessary for North Korean audiences to encounter, as a world-as-gesture, a portrait of the supreme leader Kim Il Sung attached to the front of an approaching locomotive, a scene that features in the opening and ending sequences for the film *The Locomotive Engineer's Son* (*Kigwansa-ŭi adŭl*, 1971). In the era of NoteTels and possible bullet trains across North Korea, linking South Korea and Russia, it looks remotely possible that the same portrait would come to viewing subjects in a similar manner.

Notes

Introduction

1. The "scopic regime" was a concept originally coined by the film theorist Christian Metz, but Martin Jay expanded the concept to indicate the "dominant, even totally hegemonic, visual model" of an era. He criticized the prevalent view that the modern scopic regime had a singular hegemonic form, Cartesian perspectivalism, and suggested that there had been plural, different scopic regimes contesting with one another. Jay, "Scopic Regimes of Modernity," 4.

2. Photographic media, especially film, were regarded and used by both colonial authorities and postcolonial militarist governments as tools for propaganda. They were also frequently used by the military as means of exerting influence over colonial people's hearts and minds. In colonial Korea, "since the shock of the March First Movement in 1919, the Japanese Government-General encouraged the founding of propaganda agencies and organizations, as well as the spread of propaganda activities using visual media, especially documentary films, until the end of [Japanese] rule." Jung, "Japanese Colonial Information Control," 45. The U.S. Army Military Government in Korea, in cooperation with the U.S. Army Signal Corps, actively maintained film propaganda production and distribution units to hold a dominant position over leftist Korean filmmakers during the American occupation. Han Sang Kim, "Uneven Screens, Contested Identities," 31–61.

3. Aside from colonial authorities' use of film as propaganda, early cinema in Korea was largely a part of imperial expansionist projects. The first known public film screening in Korea took place around 1903, conducted by an American electric tram company partly for the purpose of ingratiation. Similarly, some of the earliest screenings were part of promotional events for the British-American Tobacco Company. Dong Hoon Kim, *Eclipsed Cinema*, 25–26; Kang Chun-man, "Han'guk tambae ŭi yŏksa," 190–91. The nascent market for theaters with regular motion picture screenings presented a serendipitous business opportunity for Japanese colonial settlers in Korea. Chŏng Chong-hwa,

#Chosŏn yŏnghwa ranŭn kŭndae, 37–38. "Most films shown to Korean audiences at the time were of foreign origin," offering "the viewing public access to foreign, modern, and exotic worlds outside Korea." An, *Parameters of Disavowal*, 5. Alternatively, we might even posit a surrogate aspect of spectatorship, in light of subimperial South Korea's surrogate labor in Vietnam and other parts of Southeast Asia. See Jin-Kyung Lee, *Service Economies*.

4. Heidegger, *Off the Beaten Track*, 67.

5. Heidegger, 67.

6. W. J. T. Mitchell, "World Pictures," 54–55.

7. Timothy Mitchell, *Questions of Modernity*, 18. See also Hughes, *Literature and Film*, 4–5.

8. Martin Jay critiques this distinct viewer-picture division—that is, the subject-object division—as a monolithic generalization of the modern scopic regime, one that insists on that regime as singular.

9. Gunning, "Whole World within Reach," 33.

10. Ball, "Paranoia in the Age," 119.

11. Michel Foucault included "technologies of sign system," "technologies of power," and "technologies of the self" in the four main types of technologies he defined, adding to the technology in widespread use, such that it has been separated from the art of living, which he called "technologies of production." Foucault, "Technologies of the Self," 18.

12. Benjamin, *Gesammelte Schriften Band II 2*, 662, as cited in Doherty, "Test and Gestus," 458.

13. Doherty, 458.

14. O, *Pŭrehit'ŭ ŭi kyoyukkŭk*, 145.

15. O, 150.

16. Doherty, "Test and Gestus," 458–59.

17. Marx, "Theses on Feuerbach," 95 (italics added).

18. Agamben, *Means without End*, 55.

19. Agamben, 55.

20. Baumbach, *Cinema/Politics/Philosophy*, 229.

21. Jihoon Kim, "Biopolitics, Montage, and Potentialities," 76.

22. Jaeho Kang, *Walter Benjamin*, 160.

23. I use the term "territory" here, instead of "age" as in Heidegger's original phrase, to stress the geographical dimension of heteronomous spectatorship, as well as to emphasize the nuance of the world being a virtual "arena" or "stage" of the gestural performance.

24. Sobchack, *Carnal Thoughts*, 60 (italics in the original).

25. Ethnomethodology is "the study of the 'ethnomethods' that people use to make sense of what others do and particularly of what they say," normally "without giving any conscious attention to" those methods in everyday life. Ethnomethodological experiments, including interactional vandalism, are designed to breach tacit rules in daily social interactions and conversations. They include acts like maintaining one's private space and avoiding "any gestures that might be taken as too intrusive"—acts that reveal both the arts of "micro-level interactions" and the "forces that operate on the macro level," such as "class, gender, and racial structures." Giddens et al., *Introduction to*

Sociology, 116, 124–28. I adopt this term to argue that the cinematic viewer in a heteronomous and induced spectatorial environment is invited to an unintended, experimental situation, which may vandalize the tranquility of her or his own society's tacit rules of everyday social interactions or lead her or him to observe/learn new social behaviors/attitudes on the screen, specifically by being made to encounter world-as-gestures.

26. Garfinkel, *Studies in Ethnomethodology*, 36.

27. Garfinkel, 36.

28. Garfinkel, 37.

29. Garfinkel, 37.

30. Cheah, "World as Picture," 195.

31. It goes without saying that the drive of cine-mobility does not stop at global and macro-level politics. Rather, it extends to micro-level cultural politics. For instance, enhanced social/physical mobility through the automobile as represented in films had different connotations for female audiences in colonial and postcolonial Korea. See chapters 1 and 3.

32. I use the term *lanterna magica* as a metonym to designate the precinematic model of cine-mobility that had a heteronomous or induced setting.

33. Kittler, *Optical Media*, 70–88. See also Friedberg, *Window Shopping*, 23.

34. Chow, *Entanglements*, 25.

35. Jay, *Essays from the Edge*, 57–58.

36. Jay, 58.

37. Jay, 53–54.

38. Jay, 54.

39. Jay, 58.

40. For more details about this itinerant film exhibition, see chapter 1.

41. In the case of Mokp'o, it is highly likely that moviegoing culture emerged in the mid- to late 1920s, after the two first Korean theaters, the Mokp'o Theater and the P'yŏnghwagwan, opened respectively in 1926 and 1927. Before that, there had been some theaters for Japanese residents in Mokp'o, which served mostly noncinematic purposes. Among them was the Sangbanjwa, which opened in 1908 and showed films occasionally. Mokp'o was urbanized earlier than many other provincial towns, since it was a port town with over one thousand Japanese households, some having settled there as early as 1911. Wee, "Cultural Hybridity in 1920s," 39–45.

42. Jay, *Essays from the Edge*, 55–56.

43. Jay, "Scopic Regimes of Modernity," 5.

44. Jay, *Essays from the Edge*, 53.

45. Dong Hoon Kim, *Eclipsed Cinema*, 25–26.

46. Jay, "A Parting Glance," 613.

47. Jay, 613.

48. According to Thomas, "modernity itself can be understood as a colonialist project in the special sense that both the society internal to Western nations, and those they possessed, administered and reformed elsewhere, were understood as objects to be surveyed, regulated and sanitized." Thomas, *Colonialism's Culture*, 4.

49. This methodological concern about archival film studies and the qualitative sociology of visuality will be elaborated in my second book project.

50. Klein, *Cold War Cosmopolitanism*, 3–5.
51. Klein, 5–7.
52. Ryang, *Reading North Korea*, 8–13.
53. Henry, *Assimilating Seoul*, 13.
54. Ryang, *Reading North Korea*, 4.
55. Such conversations have already been initiated and expanded by scholars including, but not limited to, Tsuchiya Yuka, Hadi Parandeh Gharabaghi, Bret Vukoder, and Aysehan Jülide Etem, who have explored the on-site and mobile film propaganda activities of the U.S. Information Agency in Japan, Iran, Vietnam, Turkey, and many other Asian countries; Jie Li and Hongwei Thorn Chen, who have shed light on mobile film units in Mao's and the Kuomintang's China; and Sandeep Ray and Sangjoon Lee, who have historicized the cinemas of (re)colonized or postcolonial Southeast Asia. Tsuchiya, "Atoms for Peace"; Gharabaghi, "*American Mice Grow Big!*"; Vukoder, "Filmic Aesthetics and Technologies"; Etem, "American Marshall Plan Film"; Li, "Cinematic Guerrillas"; Chen, "Cinemas, Highways"; Ray, "Two Films"; Sangjoon Lee, "Asia Foundation's Motion-Picture."
56. Kwon, *Intimate Empire*, 14–15.
57. Kwon, 10, 16.
58. Hughes, *Literature and Film*, 2.
59. Chung, *Split Screen Korea*, 3, 8.
60. Fortuitously, recent Korean film studies show an inspired interest in mobilities. See, for example, Chung and Diffrient, *Movie Migrations*; Choe, *Tourist Distractions*; and Yi Yŏng-jae, *Asiajŏk sinch'e*.
61. Jay, *Essays from the Edge*, 57.
62. Lamarre, *Anime Machine*, xiii–xix.
63. Sobchack, *Address of the Eye*, 9.
64. Merleau-Ponty, *Visible and the Invisible*, 155, as cited in Sobchack, 3.
65. Merleau-Ponty, *Sense and Non-Sense*, 52.
66. "Since relatively few Korean [viewers] at this time had experienced riding in the trains," for many, it was only virtual. Kelly Y. Jeong, *Crisis of Gender*, 23.
67. Hughes, *Literature and Film*, 11–12.
68. Urry, "'System' of Automobility," 25–39.
69. This is a modification of the term "train-cinema interface," which came about in conversation with Thomas Lamarre, who suggested that the visual mobility regimes be named by epoch.
70. Virilio, *Speed and Politics*, 30, as cited in Beckman, *Crash*, 23.
71. Moon, *Militarized Modernity*, 17–18.
72. Eckert, *Park Chung Hee*, 3.
73. Williams, "Archives of Liveness," 290.
74. This modified term came up in conversation with Yusung Kim, who suggested closer attention to the viewing subject's maximized immobililty.
75. Kyung Hyun Kim, *Virtual Hallyu*, 4–5.
76. Foucault, "Subject and Power," 785 (italics added).

1. In a Loop, on the Track

1. Hyun-hee Park relates *Sweet Dream* to Henrik Ibsen's *A Doll's House* (1879), first translated into Korean in 1921, in terms of the play's influence on the discourse of new women in colonial Korea. Hyun-hee Park, "Enlightenment and Disenchantment," 60–64.

2. As I discuss in chapter 3, I follow John Urry's definition of the term *automobility*: "Automobility is a source of freedom, the 'freedom of the road.' Its flexibility enables the car-driver to travel any direction along the complex road systems of western societies that link together most houses, workplaces and leisure sites. . . . But this flexibility is necessitated by automobility. . . . Automobility is thus a system that *coerces* people into an intense *flexibility*." Urry, "'System' of Automobility," 28.

3. Holmes, *Burton Holmes Travelogues*, 75–76.

4. While the exact year is still in debate, Moon Im Baek presumes that Holmes's first visit to Korea was 1901, based on his autobiography, his travelogues between 1899 and 1901, and news articles. Moon Im Baek, "Study of Travelogue," 61–63, 68–75.

5. Holmes wrote in his travelogue that he arrived in Seoul on a train from Chemulpo. Baek defines his visit to Seoul as "a new arrangement of time and space through a new technology—his own film camera—right at the moment when 'America with her electricity' was bringing modern infrastructures, such as railroads, trams, electricity, and water supplies to Korea." Holmes, *Burton Holmes Travelogues*, 14, 112; Moon Im Baek, 83.

6. Holmes, 75–76.

7. Min Suh Son's doctoral dissertation deals with the electrification of Seoul at the end of the nineteenth century and its role in the modernization of the city. Min Suh Son, "Electrifying Seoul," 105–6.

8. Korean Society for Railway, *Han'guk ch'ŏlto kŏnsŏl paekyŏnsa*, 78–83.

9. Korean Society for Railway, 83–107.

10. Korean Society for Railway, 91–107.

11. Anne Friedberg introduces a compound term, "a mobilized virtual gaze," to refer to the specific perspective that cinema as an apparatus developed. It can be defined as "a received perception mediated through" the cinematic representation that was historically "rooted in other cultural activities that involve walking and travel." Eunwoo Joo analyzes the tracking shots in *Keijo* and explains, "The gaze of the camera that looks through the subjects incorporates the 'mobile vision' that was routinized in not only Western metropolises in the nineteenth century but also Japan's imperial capital and colonial Chosŏn's capital in the early twentieth century." Friedberg, *Window Shopping*, 2; Joo, "Cinematic Representation," 75.

12. Hyun-hee Park, "Enlightenment and Disenchantment," 69–74.

13. Kelly Jeong examines the representation of railroads in colonial Korean literature, including Yi Kwang-su's *Heartless*, Yŏm Sang-sŏb's *Before the Cheers*, and Ch'ae Man-sik's *Muddy Water*, reading railroads as emblems of colonial modernity. Kelly Jeong, *Crisis of Gender*, 23–26.

14. Fujitani, *Splendid Monarchy*, 25.

15. Wang-moo Lee, "Daehan Empire," 285.

16. So-young Kim, "Imperial Tour," 160–61.

17. Wang-moo Lee, "Daehan Empire," 60; So-young Kim, 165. Since Sunjong's father, Emperor Kojong, had opposed the Protectorate Treaty publicly, the resident-general tricked him into relinquishing the throne in 1907. Eckert et al., *Korea Old and New*, 236–41.

18. Fujitani, *Splendid Monarchy*, 24–28.

19. Christine Kim, "Politics and Pageantry," 846–47.

20. While kings of the Chosŏn dynasty paid limited visits to people living near Seoul, Sunjong's southbound tour covered Taegu, Pusan, and Masan, and the subsequent northwest-bound tour reached Kaesŏng, Pyongyang, and Ŭiju. So-young Kim, "Imperial Tour," 166–75. Both tours were nationwide events made possible by the completion of the Seoul–Pusan line in 1905 and the Seoul–Sinŭiju line in 1906. Tourism Sciences Society, *Han'guk hyŏndae kwan'gwangsa*, 243–45.

21. Wang-moo Lee, "Daehan Empire," 62, 291–92.

22. Wang-moo Lee, 65. In the elementary school textbooks published by the Japanese government-general in Korea during the 1910s, for instance, the following contents were included with illustrations: how Kyŏngŭisŏn connected to the South Manchuria Railway, why a late passenger was not allowed to ride in the train, and how railroad lines were arranged on the Korean Peninsula. Pak Kyŏng-su, "Kŭndae ch'ŏlto rŭl t'onghae pon singminji Chosŏn mandŭlgi," 261–70.

23. Bok, "Study of the Role," 253–54.

24. Bok, 254.

25. *Maeil sinbo*, Apr. 25, 1916, 2.

26. *Maeil sinbo*, Apr. 25, 1916, 2; May 25, 1916, 3; June 13, 1916, 3.

27. *Maeil sinbo*, Apr. 25, 1916, 2; May 12, 1916, 3.

28. *Maeil sinbo*, May 25, 1916, 3; June 13, 1916, 3.

29. *Maeil sinbo*, Apr. 25, 1916, 2.

30. *Maeil sinbo*, May 2, 1916, 2. The media used the term *paegwan* usually to refer to the act of visiting and seeing royal places, such as palaces and tombs. *Tonga ilbo*, Aug. 25, 1920, 2; Aug. 21, 1923, 4. *Pae* is the Korean pronunciation of the Chinese character *bài*, which means "to pay obeisance," while *gwan* is *guān*, meaning "to look at." Paton, *Dictionary of Chinese Characters*, 6, 45.

31. Foucault, *Discipline and Punish*, 203–5.

32. *Maeil sinbo*, Apr. 25, 1916, 2.

33. *Tonga ilbo*, Apr. 15, 1921, 2.

34. *Maeil sinbo*, June 1, 1916, 2.

35. *Tonga ilbo*, Oct. 23, 1921, 3.

36. Han Sang Kim, "Culture Film Screening," 36–37.

37. *Tonga ilbo*, June 5, 1925, 5; July 13, 1925, 3.

38. *Tonga ilbo*, Apr. 26, 1925, 3; Dec. 3, 1928, 4.

39. Choong-sil Jeong, "Tongyeong Youth Corps' Film," 101–3; *Chosŏn ilbo*, Aug. 27, 1921, 4; *Tonga ilbo*, Oct. 2, 1922, 4.

40. *Maeil sinbo*, Apr. 28, 1916, 4; May 2, 1916, 2.

41. *Maeil sinbo*, May 4, 1916, 2.

42. *Tonga ilbo*, Sep. 21, 1926, 2.

43. *Tonga ilbo*, July 29, 1934, 2.

44. *Tonga ilbo*, Apr. 15, 1921, 2.

45. Schivelbusch, *Railway Journey*, 52–69.

46. Fujitani, *Splendid Monarchy*, 28.

47. Kirby, *Parallel Tracks*, 1–3.

48. Lamarre, *Anime Machine*, xiii.

49. Foucault, *Security, Territory, Population*, 42–44.

50. Urry, "'System' of Automobility," 29.

51. According to Hyun-hee Park, *Sweet Dream* was most likely produced as a "traffic education film" or "traffic propaganda film," with the support of the Kyŏnggi Provincial Police Department. Hyun-hee Park, "Enlightenment and Disenchantment," 44–58. The film's opening sequence credits the *Sŏn-Man Traffic Times* for sponsorship, so it is likely that the film was also involved in promotion efforts for Nai-Sen-Man tourism (see chapter 2).

52. Kramer, "Film Forays," 102–3; Li, "National Cinema," 81.

53. Li, 81.

2. *Cinematic Railway Tourism in the "New Order in East Asia"*

1. High, *Imperial Screen*, 101.

2. Han Sang Kim, "Culture Film Screening," 36–39.

3. *Tonga ilbo*, June 13, 1931, 3; Nov. 1, 1931, 7; Nov. 15, 1938, 4; Apr. 20, 1939, 7; *Chosŏn ilbo*, Aug. 18, 1935, 2; July 9, 1939, 3; Aug. 8, 1939, 3; Aug. 30, 1939, 3.

4. Han Sang Kim, "Culture Film Screening," 36–39.

5. *Tonga ilbo*, Mar. 11, 1938, 2.

6. *Chosŏn ilbo*, Jan. 18, 1938, 2.

7. *Tonga ilbo*, May 20, 1938, 2.

8. *Tonga ilbo*, Mar. 11, 1938, 2; Feb. 2, 1939, 7; *Chosŏn ilbo*, Oct. 26, 1939, 2.

9. *Tonga ilbo*, May 20, 1938, 2; Dec. 8, 1938, 5; Feb. 2, 1939, 7; May 29, 1940, 2; *Chosŏn ilbo*, Mar. 12, 1939, 2; Oct. 26, 1939, 2; Dec. 15, 1939, 4.

10. Kushner, *Thought War*, 38–39.

11. Kushner, 44.

12. Beom Suk Kang, "Critical Approach to Visualism," 109; Kavanagh, "Ocularcentrism and Its Others," 454.

13. Crary, *Techniques of the Observer*, 13.

14. Jean-Louis Comolli, "Machines of the Visible," 122, as cited in Friedberg, *Window Shopping*, 15 (emphasis added by Friedberg).

15. Friedberg, 16.

16. Virilio, *War and Cinema*, 1.

17. Virilio cites Sun Tzu and states, "Military force is based upon deception." Virilio, 7.

18. Lim, "Globalization of Memory."

19. In his talk, Lim quoted Du Bois's essay "The Negro and the Warsaw Ghetto," originally cited in Rothberg, "W. E. B. Du Bois in Warsaw," 172: "The result of these three visits, and particularly of my view of the Warsaw ghetto, was not so much a clearer

understanding of the Jewish problem in the world as it was a real and more complete understanding of the Negro problem."

20. Gunning, "Whole World within Reach," 27.
21. Gunning, 38.
22. Crary, *Techniques of the Observer*, 14, 48.
23. Gunning, "Whole World within Reach," 38.
24. Gunning, 39–40.
25. Lasker, *Propaganda from China*, 9–10.
26. Lasker, 9.
27. Tetsudō-in, *Official Guide*.
28. Gi-jae Seo, "Modern Japan," 73–91.
29. Kyoung Hoon Lee, "Colony and Tourist Resort," 87.
30. Nakane, "Cheguk ilbon ŭi mansŏn kwan'gwangji wa kodo kyŏngju ŭi p'yosang," 60–61.
31. Osa, "Senji ka no 'manshi' shisatsu ryokō," 284–95.
32. Kwag, "Enjoyment and Narrative Appropriation," 234–35.
33. Kyoung Hoon Lee, "Colony and Tourist Resort," 94–95.
34. Kyoung Hoon Lee, 91–92.
35. Lasker, *Propaganda from China*, 120.
36. Min-ju Han, "Politics of Representation," 355–58. Ellie Choi interestingly unfolds the subjectivity of this quasi-imperialist impulse into "a rationalized subject conversant in both *minjok* nationalism and Tokyo modernity." Ellie Choi, "Memories of Korean Modernity," 667.
37. *Chosŏn ilbo*, Apr. 9, 1938, 2.
38. *Chosŏn ilbo*, Apr. 9, 1938, 2.
39. As the film's first episode ("Tyosen) begins with the narration, "We are now in Tyosen," it is possible that an episode on Japan is missing. However, given that the "Tyosen" episode is smoothly linked to the film's opening sequence, with the background music playing through both, it is also possible that there was no episode on Japan.
40. While the Korean Film Archive's version of the film, which was transferred from the Planet Bibliothèque de Cinéma in Osaka, Japan, in 2004, has the "Tyosen" episode only, Toho's version also includes both the "Manchoukuo" and "North China" episodes (as of 2008). However, two final scenes in the "Tyosen" episode are missing from the Toho version. This chapter examines both versions, which complement each other.
41. Okawa, "Image of Chosun."
42. Kanneh, "Feminism and the Colonial," 346.
43. Said, *Orientalism*, 206.
44. Duara, "Nationalism, Imperialism, Federalism," 52–53; Dubois, "Rule of Law," 296.
45. Jin, "East Asian Railway Networks," 133–34; Dubois, 296.
46. Duara, "Nationalism, Imperialism, Federalism," 53.
47. Jin, "East Asian Railway Networks," 133–34.
48. Seok-Won Lee, "Paradox of Racial Liberation," 519–25.
49. Morris-Suzuki, "Invention and Reinvention," 764.
50. Sang-woo Lee, "Greater East Asia," 164.

51. Harvey, *Condition of Postmodernity*, 244–46.
52. Harvey, 254.
53. Schivelbusch, *Railway Journey*, 52–69.
54. Spivak, *Critique of Postcolonial Reason*, 6.
55. Urry, *Tourist Gaze*, 1–3.
56. Gunning, "Whole World within Reach," 39.
57. Bruno, "Bodily Architectures," 107.
58. Bruno, 107.
59. Gunning, "Whole World within Reach," 39.
60. Gunning, 39–40.
61. Gillespie, "Tourist Photography," 343–66.
62. MacCannell, "Staged Authenticity," 589–603.
63. Amad, "Visual Riposte," 53.
64. Agamben, *Remnants of Auschwitz*, 37–39.
65. Agamben, 39.
66. Hansen, *Cinema and Experience*, 53–54.

3. My Car *Modernity*

1. Han Sang Kim, *Choguk kŭndaehwa rŭl yuram hagi*, 56–59.
2. Urry, "'System' of Automobility," 26–28.
3. Böhm et al., *Against Automobility*, 3.
4. Han Sang Kim, *Choguk kŭndaehwa rŭl yuram hagi*, 10–24.
5. Kim Hŭi-kap, *Ŏnŭ kwangdae-ŭi sarang*, 215–54.
6. *Chosŏn ilbo*, Aug. 1, 1961, e4.
7. Kim Hŭi-kap, *Ŏnŭ kwangdae-ŭi sarang*, 215–54.
8. This series adopted the real names of the performers as the names of its characters.
9. Fujitani, *Splendid Monarchy*, 24.
10. Han Sang Kim, *Choguk kŭndaehwa rŭl yuram hagi*, 45–48.
11. U.S. Army Forces in Korea, "History: Public Information Dept."
12. Stewart, "Report on the History," 1947.
13. The U.S. public information agency's operation of local centers and mobile screening units should be examined in terms of early cinematic spectatorship in rural areas. While the culture of moviegoing had already been established in Korea before the liberation, it was confined to urban areas, mostly Seoul. Traveling film exhibitions were the alternative in local villages. Even during the mid-1950s and the 1960s, mobile screenings played a key role in offering cinematic experiences to local people. Wee, "Film Exhibition Practices." That is to say, unlike Seoul, which had already formed commercial film markets in the 1900s, rural areas had yet to form these markets and permanent theaters. Thus, mobile screenings, conducted both by propagandists and showmen, defined the early cinematic experience of rural audiences. Automobiles, including Jeeps, played a crucial role in establishing spectatorship for mobile screenings and showcasing their attraction to rural audiences.
14. Ohtsuka, *Jeeps over the Pacific*, 136.

15. *Kyŏnghyang sinmun*, Feb. 3, 1949, 4.

16. Chŏn, *Kojong K'aedillak ŭl t'ada*, 246–51.

17. Shimokawa, *Japanese Automobile Industry*, 104–5; Toyota Motor Corporation, *75-Year History through Text*.

18. U.S. Department of the Army, "Outgoing Classified Message."

19. Acheson, "To Amembassy Pusan."

20. As of December 1951, the total number of mobile units assigned to Korea was nineteen: three units in Pusan, three in Taegu, three in Taejŏn, three in Seoul, one in Chŏnju, and three in Kwangju. Furthermore, two units were held for operations in new branches, and one unit was used by the Motion Picture Production Center. Conners, "Report on USIE Korea."

21. Conners.

22. Muccio, "To Secretary of State."

23. Muccio, "Transmitting Report."

24. Foucault, *Discipline and Punish*; Foucault, *Security, Territory, Population*.

25. Han Sang Kim, *Choguk kŭndaehwa rŭl yuram hagi*, 40–44; Moon, *Militarized Modernity*, 2, 64–66.

26. After the establishment of the Republic of Korea in August 1948, the U.S. Army transferred public information efforts from the OCI to the USIS, a U.S. civilian agency. Han Sang Kim, "1945–48 nyŏn chuhanmigunjŏng mit chuhanmigunsaryŏngbuŭi yŏnghwasŏnjŏn," 177–212. During and after the Korean War, the USIS Film Department continued film propaganda activities directed at South Koreans, including traveling film exhibitions and regular screenings at local branches. For these screenings, USIS Korea produced introductory footage for American-made films so that audiences could more readily embrace the unfamiliar foreign cultures depicted in those films. There is a sequence, for example, introducing *American Working Women* with a Korean host in traditional costume. *Harapoji Introduction Series*, a moving image record housed in NARA, RG306-5857.

27. Murphy, *Eisenhower Interstate System*, 73–88.

28. There are several books on the cultural effects of the expressway system. See, e.g., Gudis, *Buyways*; Kay, *Asphalt Nation*; Seiler, *Republic of Drivers*.

29. Sibul, "Forging Iron Horses," 227.

30. Sibul, 227.

31. U.S. Army Forces in Korea, "Report of Activities."

32. Han Sang Kim, "1945–48 nyŏn chuhanmigunjŏng mit chuhanmigunsaryŏngbuŭi yŏnghwasŏnjŏn."

33. Chŏngŭmsa, *Sajin ŭro ponŭn kwangbok 30-yŏnsa*, 16–17.

34. During World War II, midsized motor vehicles were rarely seen in the Japanese Empire. In colonial Korea, taxi businesses had flourished in urban areas during the 1920s and early 1930s but declined soon after the outbreak of the Second Sino-Japanese War in 1937, as the colonial administration converted most automobiles into military vehicles. Ch'oe, *Han'guk ŭi yuksang kyot'ong*, 248–50. Under these circumstances, it appears that people in the Japanese Empire were often "impressed and even amazed with" the design and performance of enemy Jeeps, a development reported in the media from distant battlefields. Ohtsuka, *Jeeps over the Pacific*, 2–4.

35. Ohtsuka, 136.
36. German, "Economic Convergence," 95.
37. German, 95.
38. Ohtsuka, *Jeeps over the Pacific*, 160.
39. Nelson, *Measured Excess*, 93.
40. Chŏn, *Kojong K'aedillak ŭl t'ada*, 246–51.
41. Chŏn, 251–57; *Kyŏnghyang sinmun*, Oct. 1, 1955, 3.
42. Nelson, *Measured Excess*, 93–101.
43. *Kyŏnghyang sinmun*, Mar. 27, 1967, 4.
44. *Maeil kyŏngje*, Sep. 24, 1968, 4.
45. Ministry of the Environment, *Heisei 14-nenban junkangata shakai hakusho*.
46. Kim Hyŏng-guk, *Tosi sidae ŭi Han'guk munhwa*, 125.
47. Han Sang Kim, *Choguk kŭndaehwa rŭl yuram hagi*, 63–64.
48. Han Sang Kim, 78–79.
49. The USIS Film Department also established a film library for internal use by employees, incorporating such monumental film works as *The Battleship Potemkin* (1925) and unreleased American-made propaganda films. Korean Film Archive, *Han'guk yŏnghwasa kusul ch'aerok yŏn'gu sirijŭ*, 35–36. Korean filmmakers who were affiliated with the USIS Film Department could view these films to learn advanced techniques and new trends in filmmaking. It appears that some American-made propaganda films affected certain Korean-made USIS films directly, specifically in terms of narrative structure and filming styles, as was the case with *The Autobiography of a Jeep* (1943) and *I Am a Truck* (1955). Han Sang Kim, "Cold War."
50. Han Sang Kim; National Film Preservation Foundation, *Treasures from American Film*, 119–20.
51. Han Sang Kim.
52. German, "Economic Convergence," 97–98.
53. *Maeil kyŏngje*, Sep. 24, 1968, 4.
54. Virilio, *War and Cinema*, 7–8.
55. *Maihom* was also a transliterated word from English, indicating a privately owned home. It gained popularity in the media in the late 1960s. *Maeil kyŏngje*, July 11, 1967, 5. See Han Sang Kim, "'My' Sweet Home."
56. Davis, "Railway Imperialism in China."
57. Virilio, *Speed and Politics*, 83.
58. Jin-kyung Lee, *Service Economies*, 33.

4. *Birth of Happiness?*

1. *Kyŏnghyang sinmun*, Oct. 27, 1962, 6.
2. Yi Yŏng-mi, "Ttosuninŭn tonŭl moa sajangi toeŏssŭlkka?," 157.
3. Sinjin Motors, which took control of Saenara in 1965, entered into a technical partnership with Toyota the following year and established a joint company with General Motors in 1972. A few domestically developed automobiles, such as Si-bal, also relied on imitation.
4. *Wŏlgan nae ch'a*, Mar. 1986, 19–26.

5. *Kyŏnghyang sinmun*, May 22, 1962, 1. Several other laws regarding auto traffic legislated under military rule included the Automobile Hypothecation Act (ratified on Dec. 2, 1961), the Road Act (Dec. 27, 1961), the Private Road Act (Dec. 27, 1961), the Automobile Transport Business Act (Dec. 30, 1961), the Road Traffic Act (Dec. 31, 1961), the Road Transport Automobile Act (Jan. 10, 1962), the Automobile Accident Compensation Security Law (Oct. 1, 1962), and the Toll Road Act (Jan. 5, 1963). *Kyoch'egye*, Sep. 1983, 136–37; Oct. 1983, 134; Nov. 1983, 135–36.

6. *Kyŏnghyang sinmun*, May 20, 1962, 2.

7. *Kyŏnghyang sinmun*, May 20, 1962, 2.

8. Sangjoon Lee, "Asian Film Festival," 231.

9. *Kyoch'egye*, Oct. 1983, 136.

10. *Kyŏnghyang sinmun*, May 20, 1962, 2.

11. *Kyoch'egye*, Nov. 1983, 134–35.

12. Min, *Ssalgapkwa chŏngch'iwa*, 265–68.

13. *Wŏlgan pijinesŭ*, Aug. 1962, 94–96.

14. The four major scandals involved suspicions over "a stock manipulation that led to a market crisis," "unjust enrichment and embezzlement in the construction of the Walkerhill hotel," "off-the-books money transactions in the approval process of the importation of Pachinko gambling machines," and preferential treatment for Saenara Motors. *Tonga ilbo*, Feb. 25, 1963, 3.

15. *Kyŏnghyang sinmun*, May 24, 1962, 1; National Assembly LJ-40-6, Feb. 5, 1964, 17–18.

16. *Kyoch'egye*, Nov. 1983, 135.

17. *Tonga ilbo*, Feb. 25, 1963, 3; National Assembly PS-40-12, Feb. 17, 1964, 7–8; *Newsis*, Sep. 11, 2014.

18. *Kyoch'egye*, Nov. 1983, 135.

19. National Assembly PS-40-12, Feb. 17, 1964, 7.

20. National Assembly PS-40-12, Feb. 17, 1964, 7–12.

21. Sangach'ulp'ansa, *Chaebŏldŭl 1*, 339; *Kyoch'egye*, Nov. 1983, 135.

22. National Assembly PS-40-12, Feb. 17, 1964, 7.

23. Min, *Ssalgapkwa chŏngch'iwa*, 265.

24. Min, 267–68.

25. *Kyŏnghyang sinmun*, July 24, 1963, 2.

26. *Kyŏnghyang sinmun*, Feb. 25, 1963, 1.

27. *Tonga ilbo*, Mar. 26, 1963, 7.

28. *Tonga ilbo*, Feb. 25, 1963, 1.

29. *Chosŏn ilbo*, Apr. 12, 1963, 7; *Kyŏnghyang sinmun*, Dec. 25, 1964, 3.

30. National Assembly PS-40-12, Feb. 17, 1964, 8–17; *Kyŏnghyang sinmun*, Feb. 17, 1964, 1.

31. *Tonga ilbo*, Feb. 25, 1982, 5; *Han'gyŏre*, Nov. 2, 1995, 22.

32. Cho, "Study on Korean Films," 184.

33. *Kyŏnghyang sinmun*, June 9, 1962, 1; Aug. 27, 1962, 7.

34. Yi Sang-u, *Pak chŏng-hŭi sidae*, 13.

35. Yi Sang-u, 14–15.

36. Yi Sang-u, 14–15.

37. Yi Sang-u, 13. They were Major Pak Chong-kyu on the left and Captain Ch'a Chi-ch'ŏl on the other. They later served as the chief officer of the presidential security respectively from 1964 to 1974 and from 1974 to 1979.

38. *Kyŏnghyang sinmun*, May 20, 1962, 1.

39. *Kyŏnghyang sinmun*, Sep. 28, 1962, 1.

40. *Kyŏnghyang sinmun*, Dec. 13, 1963, 1; Apr. 18, 1975, 1; June 15, 1977, 1.

41. *Kyŏnghyang sinmun*, May 21, 1968, 1; Apr. 18, 1975, 1; *Tonga ilbo*, Dec. 11, 1975, 2; *Maeil kyŏngje*, June 10, 1977, 7.

42. White papers are usually published by the government, "used as a means of presenting government policy preferences prior to the introduction of legislation." Chapin and Deneau, *Citizen Involvement*, 33.

43. Key National Expressway Planning Inspectorate, "Kukka kigan kosok toro kŏnsŏl ŭi ŭiŭi," 9; Key National Expressway Planning Inspectorate, "Sŏul-pusan kan kosok toro nŭn wae kŏnsŏl hayŏya hanŭn'ga," 10; Ministry of Public Information, "Kosok toro," 2; Ministry of Construction, Republic of Korea, and Korea Expressway Corporation, *Sŏul-pusan kan kosok toro kŏnsŏlji*, 78–89; Ministry of Construction, Republic of Korea, and Korea Expressway Corporation, *Kosok toro hyogwa chosa pogosŏ*, 1–3.

44. Korea Productivity Center Pusan and Kyŏngnam Regional Headquarters, *Kyŏngbu kosok toro ŭi kyŏngjejŏk hyokwa*, 23; Korea Expressway Corporation, *Han'guk toro kongsa simnyŏnsa*, 38.

45. Korea Expressway Corporation, 139–41.

46. *Chosŏn ilbo*, Jan. 9, 1968, 1.

47. Korea Productivity Center Pusan and Kyŏngnam Regional Headquarters, *Kyŏngbu kosok toro ŭi kyŏngjejŏk hyokwa*, 30–31.

48. Korea Productivity Center Pusan and Kyŏngnam Regional Headquarters, 23.

49. Presidential Secretariat, Republic of Korea, *Pak chŏng-hŭi taet'ongnyŏng yŏnsŏlmunjip che7chip*, 212–13.

50. Presidential Secretariat, Republic of Korea, 211–12.

51. Presidential Secretariat, Republic of Korea, 212–13.

52. Kim Wŏn-ki, "Kyŏngbu kan kosok toro kaet'ong ŭi ŭiŭi," 34–39.

53. Korea Productivity Center Pusan and Kyŏngnam Regional Headquarters, *Kyŏngbu kosok toro ŭi kyŏngjejŏk hyokwa*, 30–31.

54. Korea Expressway Corporation, *Han'guk kosok toro simnyŏnsa*, 123.

55. Korea Expressway Corporation, 117–18.

56. Korea Productivity Center Pusan and Kyŏngnam Regional Headquarters, *Kyŏngbu kosok toro ŭi kyŏngjejŏk hyokwa*, 21.

57. Presidential Secretariat, Republic of Korea, *Pak chŏng-hŭi taet'ongnyŏng yŏnsŏlmunjip che5chip*, 258; Korea Expressway Corporation, *Han'guk kosok toro simnyŏnsa*, 117.

58. Kim Tŏk-hyŏng, *Kosok toro wa kukka paljŏn*, 1.

59. Zeller, *Driving Germany*, 56–57.

60. Zeller, 60–61.

61. Korea Expressway Corporation, *Han'guk toro kongsa simnyŏnsa*, 50.

62. Korea Expressway Corporation, *Yŏngdong kosok toro sin'gal-saemal kan kŏnsŏlji*, preface.

63. Ministry of Construction, Republic of Korea, and Korea Expressway Corporation, *Sŏul-pusan kan kosok toro kŏnsŏlji*, preface.

64. Korea Expressway Corporation, *Han'guk kosok toro simnyŏnsa*, preface.

65. Korea Expressway Corporation, 115.

66. Ministry of Construction, Republic of Korea, and Korea Expressway Corporation, *Kosok toro hyogwa chosa pogosŏ*, preface.

67. Son Chŏng-mok, "Tosi 50nyŏnsa 12," 109–12.

68. Korean Expressway Corporation explains that *kosok toro* is semantically connected to the high-speed way, "linked to America's 'expressway' and '(super) highway,' Japan's 'kōsoku dōro,' and China's 'gaosu gonglu' as synonyms." In contrast, they say that the "German 'Autobahn,' Italian 'autostrada,' French 'autoroute,' and English 'motorway' are linked to one another in a meaning group referring to the motor vehicle way." Korea Expressway Corporation, *Han'guk kosok toro simnyŏnsa*, 65–66. It seems that the corporation misunderstood the etymology of "highway," which, in fact, means a "main road from one town to another." Harper, "Highway."

69. The idea of introducing expressways in Korea traces back to the 1930s, while ideas and an actual construction plan were bounced around in 1940 for an expressway linking Sinŭiju and Pusan, one that would have been named Minami toro (Minami way), after the Japanese governor-general Minami Jirō. Korea Expressway Corporation, 46. Some other early names for the expressway included *hubang kiji chŏllyak toro* (strategic road for rear military bases), which was proposed by the military in 1958 but halted amid the chaos of the April Revolution; *yuryo toro* (turnpike), which appeared in a government document in 1966; and *haiwei*, which was merely a combination of letters transliterated from the English "highway." Ministry of Home Affairs, Republic of Korea, Public Information Attaché, "Pugang kwa pŏnyŏng ŭi silk'ŭ rut'ŭ," 160–65; Korea Expressway Corporation, 91; *Chosŏn ilbo*, Apr. 13, 1962, 3.

70. Korea Expressway Corporation, 91.

71. Presidential Secretariat, Republic of Korea, *Pak chŏng-hŭi taet'ongnyŏng yŏnsŏlmunjip che2chip*, 1072–88.

72. The press used this term earlier in 1965, which seems to have been influenced by the construction of the Meishin kōsoku dōro (expressway) in Japan (*Chosŏn ilbo*, Apr. 6, 1965, 2).

73. According to the pictorials in the twentieth anniversary white book for the Japan Highway Public Corporation, it is very likely that an old name, *dangan dōro* (bullet road), instead of *kōsoku dōro*, had still been in use in Japan as of 1959. However, at the 1963 opening ceremony for the Meishin Expressway's first section, the one between the Rittō Interchange and the Amagasaki IC, the term *kōsoku dōro* was used. Japan Highway Public Corporation, pictorial pages.

74. "1967 is the first year of the Second Five-Year Economic Development Plan, following the achievement of the First. We are standing at a crucial juncture where we have to urge the establishment of a self-supporting economy and accomplish step by step the national task of modernizing our fatherland as soon as possible." Park's budget announcement for the 1967 fiscal year, *Tonga ilbo*, Sep. 8, 1966, 1.

75. "At the IBRD's World Bank board meeting on this year's economic issues a few days ago, this 10% growth in G.N.P. was the basis for recognizing South Korea as an

exemplary country that has achieved the most stable and high-speed growth among developing countries." Park Chung Hee, "Chungdan ŏmnŭn choguk kŭndaehwa tojŏnge yŏnggwangi," 6–7.

76. "We should increase the pace of our 'great advance' toward the modernization of our fatherland with indomitable will and courage." Park Chung Hee, "Che 6 tae pak taet'ongnyŏng kakha ch'wiimsa," 7.

77. Korea Expressway Corporation, *Han'guk kosok toro simnyŏnsa*, 122.

78. *Han'guk kyŏngje*, Aug. 7, 2008, 1.

79. Ministry of Construction, Republic of Korea, and Korea Expressway Corporation, *Sŏul-pusan kan kosok toro kŏnsŏlji*, 55.

80. *Chosŏn ilbo*, June 6, 1969, 1.

81. *Ik'onomisŭt'ŭ*, Jan. 13, 2009, 26.

82. Pak Yŏng-jun, *Manu Pak Yŏng-jun Chŏnjip 13*, 130.

83. Yu, "Yŏksa wa ilssang e taehan 'yullijŏk' t'usi," 295.

84. Yu, 295–97.

85. Pak Yŏng-jun, *Manu Pak Yŏng-jun Chŏnjip 13*, 117.

86. Pak Yŏng-jun, 144.

87. Friedberg, "Urban Mobility," 186.

88. Friedberg, 184–85; Virilio, "Third Window," 188.

89. Friedberg, 186; Virilio, 109.

90. Friedberg, 186–87.

91. Friedberg, *Window Shopping*, 2.

92. Verhoeff, *Mobile Screens*, 44–45.

93. Sobchack, *Address of the Eye*, 298.

94. Yi Hyo-dŏk, *P'yosang konggan-ŭi kŭndae*, 227–34.

95. Son Chŏng-mok, "Tosi 50nyŏnsa 12," 116–17.

96. Horvath, "Machine Space," 169.

97. Byung-Doo Choi, "Gyeongbu Expressway," 202.

98. Friedberg, *Window Shopping*, 56.

99. Yi Ch'ŏl-hŭi, *Susabanjang (1)*, 63.

100. Yi Ch'ŏl-hŭi, 68–69.

101. Augé, *Non-Places*, 34.

102. Son Chŏng-mok, "Tosi 50nyŏnsa 12," 117.

5. Imagined Geographies of the World

1. *Tonga ilbo*, July 16, 1969, 3; *Kyŏnghyang sinmun*, July 21, 1969, 7.

2. *Kyŏnghyang sinmun*, July 22, 1969, 3.

3. *Tonga ilbo*, July 17, 1969, 7.

4. *Kyŏnghyang sinmun*, Jan. 21, 1967, 5.

5. McLuhan, *Gutenberg Galaxy*, 31.

6. *Kyŏnghyang sinmun*, Apr. 13, 1974, 8; Oct. 1, 1975, 6.

7. Han Sang Kim, *Choguk kŭndaehwa rŭl yuram hagi*, 122.

8. *Kyŏnghyang sinmun*, Apr. 25, 1975, 4. According to the same news report on April 13, 1975, 87.4 percent of the 1,680 households in Seoul, surveyed from March 31

through April 6 by the Korean Public Relations Culture Institute (Han'guk kwangbo munhwa yŏn'guwŏn), owned television sets and watched television for 4 hours 43 minutes a day on average. *Kyŏnghyang sinmun*, Apr. 25, 1975, 4. It was almost quadruple the values from 1970, when there were about 230,000 television sets and a total of 1,029,483 households in Seoul, meaning that 22.3 percent of households owned television sets. *Maeil kyŏngje*, Dec. 5, 1970, 6; Seoul Development Institute, *Chip'yo-ro pon sŏul pyŏnch'ŏn*, 15.

9. Others included *P'aldo Sons-in-Law* (*P'aldo sawi*, 1969), *P'aldo Daughters-in-Law* (*P'aldo myŏnŭri*, 1970), *P'aldo Swordsmen* (*P'aldo kŏmgaek*, 1970), *P'aldo Scrooges* (*P'aldo noraengi*, 1970), *P'aldo Girls* (*P'aldo kasinai*, 1970), *P'aldo Housekeepers* (*P'aldo singmo*, 1970), and *P'aldo Woman Soldiers* (*P'aldo yŏgun*, 1970).

10. In one of these spin-off films, *P'aldo Men* (1969), the "P'aldo" narrative is used to show a national identity that resisted Japanese imperialism during the colonial period. The local imagery in this film, as in *P'aldogangsan*, is used to identify a hierarchy structuring the central and the local society. However, comic accents and gestures for each locality replace any serious local values, which were used to achieve national integration in *P'aldogangsan*. Another film from the following year, *P'aldo Daughters-in-Law* (1970), does not use the P'aldo narrative to identify the hierarchy. Rather, the narrative is used as a comedic device when the old protagonist, In-kap, exhibits his collection of "eight daughters-in-law" from different regions in the country. In a travesty of panoramic local images, the hierarchy between the central and the local society is presented as vanishing. Most likely, these P'aldo films downplayed the serious agenda behind the central-local hierarchy, an important theme in *P'aldogangsan*, by presenting local characteristics as a comic farce.

11. McLuhan, *Gutenberg Galaxy*, 31–32.

12. Han, "Attitudes Toward Federalism," 65–74.

13. Kirkpatrick, "Localism in American Media," 45.

14. Kirkpatrick, 44.

15. Kirkpatrick, 44–45.

16. USIS-Korea, *USIS Film Catalogue 1964*, 2–232.

17. USIS-Korea, 55.

18. Korean Film Archive, *Han'guk yŏnghwasa kusul ch'aerok yŏn'gu sirijŭ*, 35–36.

19. Korean Film Archive, 42–45.

20. A term used by the voice-over narrator in *Korean Editor*.

21. Korean Film Archive, *Han'guk yŏnghwasa kusul ch'aerok yŏn'gu sirijŭ*, 78–80.

22. Yi Ch'ŏl-sun, "U.S. Policy Toward Korea," 275–342.

23. It should be noted that the literal meaning of the show's Korean title was "America's today," which can be understood as "America as seen from the South Korean perspective." Its English title in NARA's catalog, *Korea-America Today*, sounds rather neutral, implying that the show depicts the relationship between the two countries.

24. Pak Chŏng-su, "My Overseas Studying Years," 9.

25. They both received their doctorates in the Science of International Politics at the American University in 1965. *Tonga ilbo*, June 17, 1965, 6.

26. Of the total three episodes at NARA, one episode covering Michigan State University in Lansing shows Korean students' daily lives, including coursework, lab experiments,

dormitory life, leisure time, and graduation ceremonies. These students majored in a variety of subjects, including sociology, political science, business administration, agriculture, chemistry, and metal engineering. Another episode introduces the facilities at the U.S. Naval Hospital in Oakland, the Naval Postgraduate School in Monterey, and the Defense Language Institute in Monterey, California. It shows Korean army surgeons working or learning at the U.S. Navy's medical and educational facilities, inviting them to the studio, and asking them about their experiences of American life.

27. The concept of "imagined geographies" comes from Edward Said's theories on Orientalist and colonialist discourse. Said, *Orientalism*, 49–73.

28. In his memoirs, Kim Hŭi-kap states that he had to push ahead with appearances in films, to go to the United States upon fulfilment of his contracts in 1964. Kim Hŭi-kap, *Ŏnŭ kwangdae-ŭi sarang*, 215–16.

29. The Kyŏnggi Girls' High School was one of the top-ranked schools in South Korea during the period when a high school entrance examination system was still in place. *Tonga ilbo*, Feb. 3, 1978, 3.

30. Office of Research, "Communication Fact Book."

31. While Yi headed the Alumni Association of the Kyŏnggi Girls' High School in the United States, Pak was chair of the Korean Students' Association in Washington, DC. After returning to Korea, Pak was appointed lawmaker five times and held various posts in succession, including the minister of foreign affairs and trade. Yi was also elected to the National Assembly in 1973 and became a professor at Ewha Women's University and the dean of the Graduate School at Sungshin Women's University. Pak Chŏng-su, "My Overseas Studying Years," 9; *Kyŏnghyang sinmun*, Dec. 26, 2003, 17; *Tonga ilbo*, July 15, 2011, 27.

32. *Chayu Segye*, Nov. 1964.

33. *Han'gyŏre*, May 20, 1993, 9.

34. *Chosŏn ilbo*, May 26, 1968, 5.

35. Prakash, *Another Reason*, 17–48.

36. Prakash, 17–48.

37. Kim Hŭi-kap's expression used in his comments on Hollywood in *Korean TV Special*.

38. Kirkpatrick, "Localism in American Media," 44–45.

39. Han Sang Kim, *Choguk kŭndaehwa rŭl yuram hagi*, 53.

40. Yi Hyo-dŏk, *P'yosang konggan-ŭi kŭndae*, 233–34.

41. MacCannell, *Tourist*, 91–108.

42. Han Sang Kim, *Choguk kŭndaehwa rŭl yuram hagi*, 45–48.

43. In his special statement on October 27, 1972, ten days after declaring martial law, Park attributed the nation's instability and developmental inefficiency to the attempts "to imitate the democracy of others prematurely" and demanded that the country establish a "Korean-type democracy that best suits our society." *Tonga ilbo*, Oct. 27, 1972, 1.

44. According to Jung In Kang, Park's criticism of Western democracy had been discursively constructed by moving from "administrative democracy" (1961–1963), to "national democracy" (1963–1972), to "Korean-type democracy" (1972–1979), whereby each of these discourses reflected continuous engagement with the mechanism of government.

Jung In Kang, "Analysis of Park," 287–321. However, the emphasis on "things Korean" was a new attitude that emerged in the late 1960s and early 1970s, and it was accompanied by the promotion of national culture and history. Won Kim, "Competition concerning Appropriation," 185–235.

45. Interestingly, the perception of the Korean self was first incorporated into discourse production, specifically of government-led democracy, at the very moment when parliamentary democracy was shut down, and "the state of exception was institutionalized." Agamben, *State of Exception*, 1–31; Chŏng Kŭn-sik, "Social Control and Resistance," 83–130.

46. Investigation of the Park Chung Hee government's written or verbal definition of the West, however, may not yield a comprehensive explanation of representations of the West at the time. Representations cannot merely be explained as reflections of transcendental meaning or as carriers of their creators' intent. Rather, it is important to consider representations as public and social products, shaped by "social actors who use the conceptual systems of their culture and the linguistic and other representational systems to construct meaning." Hall, "Work of Representation," 11.

47. *Maeil kyŏngje*, June 2, 1967, 3.

48. Alan C. Heyman, interview, Jan. 2012.

49. Schwoch, *Global TV*, 1.

50. Marks, "Telegraph Sent to Manila."

51. Bunce, "Monthly Report."

52. Hemsing, "Audit Report."

53. Han Sang Kim, "Cold War," 552.

54. *Maeil kyŏngje*, Apr. 13, 1972, 6.

55. *Tonga ilbo*, Oct. 18, 1972, 8; Oct. 19, 1972, 5.

56. *Kyŏnghyang sinmun*, July 12, 1969, 5.

57. McLuhan, *Understanding Media*, 185.

58. McLuhan, 12, 249.

59. *Kyŏnghyang sinmun*, Sep. 4, 1967, 1.

60. *Maeil kyŏnje*, Aug. 11, 1969, 3.

61. McLuhan, *Gutenberg Galaxy*, 31.

62. *Kyŏnghyang sinmun*, Mar. 8, 1958, 3; Aug. 26, 1962, 6.

63. *Tonga ilbo*, Feb. 16, 1970, 1.

64. *Tonga ilbo*, Feb. 14, 1970, 2.

65. *Maeil kyŏnje*, Feb. 24, 1970, 7.

66. *Maeil kyŏnje*, Dec. 12, 1969, 3.

67. *New York Times*, Apr. 30, 1978, 1.

68. *Kyŏnghyang sinmun*, May 1, 1978, 7.

69. *Kyŏnghyang sinmun*, Apr. 25, 1978, 1.

70. *Kyŏnghyang sinmun*, May 1, 1978, 1.

71. Korean Film Archive, *Han'guk yŏnghwasa kusul ch'aerok yŏn'gu sirijŭ*, 145–50.

72. *Kyŏnghyang sinmun*, July 8, 1967, 8; *Tonga ilbo*, Nov. 7, 1967, 6.

73. Yang had been taught by Syracuse University instructors when the International Cooperation Administration and the United States Operations Mission sponsored a

project to bring American film specialists to educate filmmakers in Korea. [Anonymous], "Personnel Breakdown." Like Pae, he was also invited to the United States by the State Department in 1964.

74. *Tonga ilbo*, Sep. 12, 1970, 6.
75. *Kyŏnghyang sinmun*, Apr. 16, 1974, 8.
76. *Maeil kyŏngje*, Sep. 10, 1973, 8.
77. *Kyŏnghyang sinmun*, Apr. 25, 1970, 2.
78. *Tonga ilbo*, Feb. 17, 1971, 5.
79. *Tonga ilbo*, Feb. 14, 1974, 8.
80. *Tonga ilbo*, June 5, 1969, 8.

6. Technopia!

1. Harvey, *Brief History of Neoliberalism*, 3.
2. Harvey, 3.
3. National Institute of Korean History, *Kŭnhyŏndae kwahak kisul kwa salmŭi pyŏnhwa*, 278–79.
4. Harvey, *Brief History of Neoliberalism*, 3.
5. *Tonga ilbo*, Apr. 14, 1996, 11.
6. *Maeil kyŏngje*, Oct. 28, 1985, 10.
7. *Maeil kyŏngje*, Mar. 16, 1989, 7.
8. *Yŏnhap nyusŭ*, Jan. 7, 1991.
9. Yi Sang-yŏng, "Kukkaŭi nodongjŏngch'aekkwa kongjang chadonghwa," 93–120; Yi Ŭn-chin. "Chadonghwaŭi hyŏndan'gye," 107–22; Pak Sŭng-hŭi, "Kongjang chadonghwae ttarŭn nodonggwajŏngŭi pyŏnhwa," 123–51; Kim Chang-ho, *Chadonghwa kisul hyŏksingwa koyong*; Pak Hyŏng-jun, *Hyŏndaenodonggwajŏngnon*.
10. Yi Sang-yŏng, 110–11; Pak Sŭng-hŭi, 127; Pak Hyŏng-jun, 61–65.
11. Sugrue, *Origins*, 130.
12. Pak Hyŏng-jun, *Hyŏndaenodonggwajŏngnon*, 64–65.
13. Palladino, "When Militancy Isn't Enough," 196–220.
14. *Tonga ilbo*, Aug. 12, 1949, 1; *Chosŏn ilbo*, Oct. 24, 1949, 2.
15. Urry, *Mobilities*, 51.
16. *Maeil kyŏngje*, Sep. 21, 1979, 8.
17. *Tonga ilbo*, Nov. 22, 1983, 12.
18. *Tonga ilbo*, July 1, 1978, 2.
19. *Maeil kyŏngje*, June 23, 1979, 7.
20. *Maeil kyŏngje*, Dec. 19, 1979, 7.
21. Korea Elevator Safety Institute, *Han'guk sŭngganggi palchŏnsa*.
22. *Kyŏnghyang sinmun*, Nov. 9, 1982, 7.
23. *Maeil kyŏngje*, Jan. 5, 1983, 11.
24. A front-page ad promoting a bus with an automatic door made by Hyundai Motors in 1983. *Kyŏnghyang sinmun*, Aug. 4, 1983, 1.
25. *Maeil kyŏngje*, May 1, 1985, 10.
26. *Tonga ilbo*, June 2, 1960, 2; *Maeil kyŏngje*, June 6, 1967, 6.

27. *Maeil kyŏngje*, Sep. 30, 1972, 8; Apr. 5, 1973, 6.

28. *Tonga ilbo*, Mar. 2, 1981, 9.

29. The first record of an academic event of this kind was the Seminar on Word Processing for Office Automation, jointly held by the Korea Institute of Science and Technology and the U.S. Embassy in Korea on November 25 and 26, 1980. Since 1982, many academic events emphasizing the necessity of office automation were held by either business machine manufacturers or related groups, such as the Korea Management Association and the Electronics Industries Association of Korea. *Maeil kyŏngje*, Nov. 20, 1980, 3; Mar. 15, 1982, 8; Apr. 2, 1982, 8; Mar. 17, 1983; Mar. 19, 1983, 11; Apr. 18, 1983, 8; July 18, 1983, 5.

30. In the early and mid-1980s, there were a variety of expositional events, including the Office Automation Equipment Show held at the Capitol building by the Ministry of Government Administration in November 1982, the OA Equipment Traveling Exhibition organized by major business machine manufacturers, and the Office Automation Equipment Fair held at the Korean Exhibition Center. *Maeil kyŏngje*, Nov. 23, 1982, 1; Mar. 15, 1983, 1; June 22, 1985, 6; *Tonga ilbo*, Nov. 15, 1983, 10.

31. The first corporate campaign to promote office automation in Korea appears to be CJ's 3-O campaign in 1981. *Kyŏnghyang sinmun*, Oct. 28, 1981, 5. According to a *Maeil kyŏngje* special series on corporate strategies in Korean companies, which was published in issues from January and September 1983, several big companies, such as LG (then Lucky GoldStar), Doosan, and Kumho, launched similar office automation campaigns. *Maeil kyŏngje*, Jan. 7, 1983, 7; Jan. 13, 1983, 7; Sep. 10, 1983, 7; Sep. 22, 1983, 7; Sep. 24, 1983, 7.

32. KBS broadcast a special program called *The Office Automation (OA) Revolution* on May 2, 1983. *Kyŏnghyang sinmun*, May 2, 1983, 12. *Maeil kyŏngje* published a special serialized feature titled "OA: What's the Status of Office Automation?" in June and July 1984. *Maeil kyŏngje*, June 26–July 18, 1984, 8. *Tonga ilbo* also ran a feature, "Automation Waves Rolling In," in October and November that same year. *Tonga ilbo*, Oct. 29–Nov. 6, 1984, 5.

33. *Tonga ilbo*, June 4, 1983, 5.

34. *Kyŏnghyang sinmun*, Aug. 3, 1983, 3.

35. *Tonga ilbo*, Oct. 30, 1984, 5.

36. *Tonga ilbo*, Nov. 2, 1984, 5.

37. *Tonga ilbo*, Nov. 5, 1984, 5.

38. *Maeil kyŏngje*, Sep. 17, 1985, 9.

39. *Maeil kyŏngje*, Mar. 5, 1986, 11.

40. *Maeil kyŏngje*, Nov. 17, 1969, 2.

41. *Maeil kyŏngje*, Mar. 9, 1972, 8.

42. *Tonga ilbo*, Mar. 21, 1985, 7.

43. *Maeil kyŏngje*, June 9, 1979, 8.

44. *Maeil kyŏngje*, June 9, 1979, 8.

45. *Kyŏnghyang sinmun*, May 19, 1982, 6.

46. *Kyŏnghyang sinmun*, July 27, 1982, 1.

47. *Kyŏnghyang sinmun*, Aug. 11, 1982, 11; *Maeil kyŏngje*, Aug. 12, 1982, 2.

48. *Maeil kyŏngje*, Aug. 12, 1982, 2.

49. *Kyŏnghyang sinmun*, Aug. 4, 1983, 1.

50. An advertisement for a driving school in *Han'guk ilbo*, July 27, 1969, 3; *Kyŏnghyang sinmun*, Jan. 22, 1969, 6; June 16, 1969, 5; Jan. 13, 1978, 7; *Tonga ilbo*, July 9, 1973, 4; *Chosŏn ilbo*, Aug. 10, 1968, 2.

51. *Maeil kyŏngje*, May 6, 1977, 3.

52. *Kyŏnghyang sinmun*, Nov. 17, 1978, 6.

53. Neurnann, "Risks to the Public," 4–23.

54. *Chosŏn ilbo*, Apr. 10, 1988, 4.

55. *Chosŏn ilbo*, Apr. 10, 1988, 4.

56. *Tonga ilbo*, Feb. 25, 1981, 2; Jan. 28, 1985, 2; *Maeil kyŏngje*, Mar. 29, 1988, 14.

57. *Maeil kyŏngje*, Nov. 5, 1979, 6.

58. *Chosŏn ilbo*, Apr. 10, 1988, 4.

59. *Tonga ilbo*, Sep. 7, 1981, 9.

60. As of March 2016, it is now the Seoul City Council building. Originally, it was Pumin'gwan, a municipal theater built by the Seoul city government under the Japanese government-general in 1935. As of 1981, when this column was written, the building was an annex to the Sejong Center for the Performing Arts.

61. "High-Rise Life," *Tonga ilbo*, Sep. 7, 1981, 9.

62. Act No. 2434, effective July 1, 1973.

63. Gelézeau, "Changing Socio-Economic Environments," 295–321; Korea Elevator Safety Institute, *Han'guk sŭngganggi palchŏnsa*.

64. Korea Elevator Safety Institute.

65. Gelézeau, "Changing Socio-Economic Environments," 295–321; Ministry of Construction and Transportation, *Ap'at'ŭ chugŏ hwan'gyŏng t'onggye*.

66. *Maeil kyŏngje*, July 23, 1979, 7.

67. *Maeil kyŏngje*, July 23, 1979, 7.

68. *Maeil kyŏngje*, Nov. 6, 1973, 6; Sep. 9, 1980, 6; *Tonga ilbo*, Mar. 11, 1982, 5.

69. Gelézeau, "Changing Socio-Economic Environments," 295–321.

70. Friedberg, *Window Shopping*, 56.

71. *Kyŏnghyang sinmun*, Dec. 30, 1976, 7.

72. Kim Hyŏng-ki, "Han'guk tokchŏmjabonŭi undonggwa nodonggwajŏngŭi pyŏnhyŏng," 41–90.

73. Kim Hyŏng-ki, 41–90.

74. Horvath, "Machine Space," 167–88; Byung-Doo Choi, "Gyeongbu Expressway," 181–218.

75. Gordon, "Governmental Rationality," 1–52.

76. *Tonga ilbo*, Dec. 1, 1979, 2; *Kyŏnghyang sinmun*, Mar. 20, 1982, 4.

77. *Maeil kyŏngje*, Nov. 4, 1988.

78. *Tonga ilbo*, Jan. 11, 1989.

79. *Maeil kyŏngje*, July 20, 1990.

80. *Kyŏnghyang sinmun*, Oct. 31, 1990.

81. *Maeil kyŏngje*, Jan. 4, 1994.

82. *Kyŏnghyang sinmun*, Oct. 31, 1990.

83. *Kyŏnghyang sinmun*, Feb. 19, 1992.

84. Pardo-Guerra, "Financial Automation," 575.

85. Hayward, "ATMs, Teleprompters and Photobooths," 205–6.

86. Chang Kyung-sup calls compressed modernity "a social situation in which economic, political, social, and/or cultural changes occur in an extremely condensed manner with respect to both time and space, and in which the dynamic coexistence of mutually disparate historical and social elements leads to the construction and reconstruction of a highly complex and fluid social systems." Chang, "Individualization without Individualism," 38.

87. *Han'gyŏre*, Aug. 13, 1993, 1.

88. P'yo Hak-kil, "Chinjŏnghan kukchehwa e sahwalgŏllin han'gukkyŏngje," 51–52.

89. *Han'gyŏre*, Aug. 13, 1993, 1.

90. *Han'gyŏre*, Oct. 7, 1995, 2.

91. P'yo Hak-kil, "Chinjŏnghan kukchehwa e sahwalgŏllin han'gukkyŏngje," 54.

92. Yi Hyŏng-yŏl, "Kŭmyungsilmyŏngjewa yŏnghwa sarang ŭi yŏnghon," 190.

93. For a classic discussion of transparency and visibility in the surveillance society, see Lyon, *Electronic Eye*.

94. *Tonga ilbo*, July 20, 1990, 21.

95. *Maeil kyŏngje*, June 2, 1996, 1.

96. *Tonga ilbo*, July 14, 1988, 5.

97. *Tonga ilbo*, Nov. 25, 1989, 19.

98. Chollian was the first virtual, terminal-based, commercial computer network service in South Korea and began offering its services in 1985. Similar services, such as HiTel, NowNuri, and Unitel, gained considerable popularity in the early to mid-1990s. It was not until the mid- to late 1990s when the current form of the World Wide Web was commercialized in Korea.

99. *Han'gyŏre*, Apr. 23, 1992, 8.

100. *Maeil kyŏngje*, Aug. 1, 1995, 11; *Tonga ilbo*, Sep. 29, 1995, 35.

101. *Maeil kyŏngje*, Aug. 27, 1996, 47.

102. *Maeil kyŏngje*, May 7, 1997, 19.

103. *Maeil kyŏngje*, Dec. 13, 1997.

104. *Tonga ilbo*, Aug. 29, 1997.

105. *Kyŏnghyang sinmun*, Sep. 4, 1997.

106. *Maeil kyŏngje*, Oct. 4, 1997.

107. *Han'gyŏre*, Oct. 4, 1996.

108. Gordon, "Governmental Rationality," 43.

109. Urry, *Mobilities*, 51.

110. Song, "Family Breakdown," 37–65.

111. Song, 37–65.

Epilogue

1. Elise Hu, "K-Pop Stars Red Velvet Set to Perform in Pyongyang This Weekend," NPR, March 30, 2018, https://www.npr.org/sections/parallels/2018/03/30/597872371/k-pop-stars-red-velvet-set-to-perform-in-pyongyang-this-weekend.

2. Motoko Rich and Su-Hyun Lee, "Can North Korea Handle a K-Pop Invasion?," *New York Times*, March 30, 2018, https://www.nytimes.com/2018/03/30/world/asia/north-korea-k-pop-red-velvet.html.

3. Chu, *P'yŏngyang chabonjuŭi paekkwajŏnsŏ*, 171.

4. *Tonga ilbo*, Apr. 10, 2018, A3.

5. Jieun Baek, *North Korea's Hidden Revolution*, 169–70; Chu, *P'yŏngyang chabonjuŭi paekkwajŏnsŏ*, 186–89.

6. Jieun Baek, 169–70; Chu, 187–89.

7. Chu, 188.

8. *Tonga ilbo*, July 22, 2016, A25.

9. *Chungang ilbo*, Dec. 28, 2016, 3.

10. Moon Jae-in, "Address by President Moon Jae-in on Korea's 73rd Liberation Day," *Cheong Wa Dae*, Aug. 15, 2018, http://english1.president.go.kr/BriefingSpeeches/Speeches/61.

11. James Griffiths, "South and North Korea Want a Peace Treaty: What Happens if the US Doesn't?," CNN, Aug. 24, 2018, https://www.cnn.com/2018/08/22/asia/north-korea-south-korea-peace-treaty-intl/index.html.

12. Sohn Ji-young, "Koreas Hint at Possibility of High-Speed Railway Connecting South and North," *Korea Herald*, Apr. 27, 2018, http://www.koreaherald.com/view.php?ud=20180427000663.

13. Jung Min-kyung, "Koreas Agree to Conduct Joint Study on Railway Cooperation," *Korea Herald*, June 26, 2018, http://www.koreaherald.com/view.php?ud=20180626000810.

14. Griffiths, "South and North Korea."

15. Ju-min Park and Jane Chung, "Korea Detente Revives North Korean Leader's Bullet Train Dreams," Reuters, Aug. 30, 2018, https://www.reuters.com/article/us-northkorea-southkorea-railroad-analys/korea-detente-revives-north-korean-leaders-bullet-train-dreams-idUSKCN1LE2TO.

16. Kim Chong-ch'ŏl, "Ch'ŏldoyŏhaeng-ŭi kkum-to choch'iman" (The Dream of a Railway Journey Is Good, But . . .)," *Han'gyŏre*, June 28, 2018, http://www.hani.co.kr/arti/opinion/column/851117.html.

17. Choe Sang-hun and David E. Sanger, "Kim Jong-il, North Korean Dictator, Dies," *New York Times*, Dec. 19, 2011, https://www.nytimes.com/2011/12/19/world/asia/kim-jong-il-is-dead.html.

18. *Chosŏnmal taesajŏn*, s.v., "hyŏnji chido," accessed Mar. 20, 2016, http://www.uriminzokkiri.com/uri_foreign/dic/index.php.

19. For DPRK's official definition of the term as of 1992, and further details of its political usage in North Korea, see Yu, "Pukhan-ŭi kwan'gwang chŏngch'aek-kwa ridŏsip," 3–4.

20. *Chosŏnmal taesajŏn*, "hyŏnji chido."

21. Yi Kyo-tŏk, *Kim chŏng-il hyŏnji chido-ŭi t'ŭksŏng*, 1–2.

22. "Yŏngwŏnhan uri-ŭi Kim chŏng-il tongji" (Our Eternal Comrade Kim Jong-il), *Rodong Sinmun*, Dec. 20, 2011.

23. Tŭngdaesa, *Inminhaeng ryŏlch'a-rŭl hamkke t'asigo*, preface.

24. Tŭngdaesa, preface.

25. Tŭngdaesa, pictorial.

26. The song was written by Chŏng Sŏng-hwan, composed by U Chŏng-hŭi, and sung by Hwang Suk-kyŏng and Kim Sŏn-hŭi. The first verse in Romanized Korean is

as follows: "Kijŏk sori chŏngdaun pam ryŏlch'a ch'angga-e / ŭnhyeroun pulbit-i nŏmch'yŏ hŭrŭne / i pam-to changgunnim inmin-ŭl ch'ajasŏ / sarang-ŭi man-ri kil iŏ kasine / inminhaeng ryŏlch'a-ŭi pinnanŭn chŏ pulbit / sarang-ŭl an'gosŏ tallinŭn pulbit."

27. Paek, *Yajŏn ryŏlch'a*, 366.
28. Ahn, "Pukhan'gyot'ong inp'ŭra hyŏnhwang," 12.
29. Railways Act, article 2.
30. Suzy Kim, *Everyday Life*, 45.
31. Virilio, *Speed and Politics*, 30.

Bibliography

Archival Sources

Publications and Manuscripts of the Government of the Republic of Korea

Key National Expressway Planning Inspectorate. 1967. "Kukka kigan kosok toro kŏnsŏl ŭi ŭiŭi—ch'oan" (The Significance of Key National Expressway Construction—Draft).

Key National Expressway Planning Inspectorate. 1968. "Sŏul-pusan kan kosok toro nŭn wae kŏnsŏl hayŏya hanŭn'ga: kosok toro kŏnsŏl ŭi t'adangsŏng—an No. 1" (Why Should We Build the Expressway between Seoul and Pusan: The Feasibility of the Expressway Construction—Draft No. 1).

Ministry of Construction, Republic of Korea, and Korea Expressway Corporation. 1973. *Kosok toro hyogwa chosa pogosŏ* (Investigation Report of the Effect of the Expressway). Sŏngnam: Korea Expressway Corporation.

———. 1974. *Sŏul-pusan kan kosok toro kŏnsŏlji* (The Seoul-Pusan Expressway Construction Project Log Book). Sŏngnam: Korea Expressway Corporation.

———. 1976. *Kosok toro hyogwa chosa pogosŏ* (Survey on the Effectiveness of the Expressway). Sŏngnam: Korea Expressway Corporation.

Ministry of Construction and Transportation, Republic of Korea. 1980–1989. *Ap'at'ŭ chugŏ hwan'gyŏng t'onggye* (Statistics on Apartment Residential Environment). Seoul: Ministry of Construction and Transportation.

Ministry of Home Affairs, Republic of Korea, Public Information Attaché. 1970. "Pugang kwa pŏnyŏng ŭi silk'ŭ rut'ŭ: kosok toro kŏnsŏl saŏp ŭi ch'ujin kyŏngwi" (The Silk Route of Power and Prosperity: Details of the Expressway Construction Project). *Tosi munje* (Urban Affairs) 5 (6): 160–65.

Ministry of Public Information, Republic of Korea. 1968. "Kosok toro: yŏgi minjok chung hŭng ŭi kil i yŏllyŏtta" (Expressway: Here Is the Way to National Restoration).

Ministry of Transportation, Republic of Korea. 1973. *Kyot'ong t'onggye yŏnbo* (Statistics yearbook of transportation). Seoul: Ministry of Transportation.

National Assembly of Korea. 1964a. The Legislation and Judiciary Committee (LJ), Minutes no. 40-6. February 5.

———. 1964b. The Plenary Session (PS), Minutes no. 40-12. February 17.

Park Chung Hee. 1967. "Che 6 tae pak taet'ongnyŏng kakha ch'wiimsa—Choguk kwa minjok ap'e sinmyŏng ŭl pach'irira" (The 6th Inaugural Speech by President Park—I Will Lay Down My Life for My Fatherland and Nation). *Tosi munje* (Urban Affairs) 2 (7): 2–8.

———. 1968. "Chungdan ŏmnŭn choguk kŭndaehwa tojŏnge yŏnggwangi" (Glory Be in the Pauseless Path to the Modernization of the Fatherland). In *Chibang haengjŏng* (Journal of the Public Official Benefit Association) 17 (171): 4–18.

Presidential Secretariat, Republic of Korea. 1966. *Pak chŏng-hŭi taet'ongnyŏng yŏnsŏlmunjip che2chip* (President Park Chung Hee Speeches Collection Vol. 2). Seoul: Presidential Secretariat.

———. 1969. *Pak chŏng-hŭi taet'ongnyŏng yŏnsŏlmunjip che5chip* (President Park Chung Hee Speeches Collection Vol. 5). Seoul: Presidential Secretariat.

———. 1971. *Pak chŏng-hŭi taet'ongnyŏng yŏnsŏlmunjip che7chip* (President Park Chung Hee Speeches Collection Vol. 7). Seoul: Presidential Secretariat.

Publications and Manuscripts of the Government of the Democratic People's Republic of Korea

DPRK Supreme People's Assembly. *Railways Act*. Legislated in the Sixth Decision of the Regular Conference, October 22, 1987. Revised in the Ordinance no. 1825 of the Standing Committee, August 23, 2011.

Sahoegwahagwŏn ŏnŏhagyŏn'guso, ed. 2017. *Chosŏnmal taesajŏn* (Great Dictionary of Korean). http://www.uriminzokkiri.com/uri_foreign/dic/index.php.

Textual Records at the U.S. National Archives and Records Administration

Acheson. 1951. "To Amembassy Pusan, Department's Telegram no. 695, March 5, 1951." April 9. RG59 Records of Department of State, decimal file 1950–1954, box 2540.

Bunce, W. Kenneth. 1966. "Monthly Report: June 1966—USIS-Korea." July 14. RG306 USIA Exhibits Division, Records Concerning Exhibits in Foreign Countries, 1955–67, box 20.

Conners, W. Bradley. 1951. "Report on USIE Korea." December 7. RG59 Records of Department of State, decimal file 1950–1954, box 2539.

Hemsing, Albert E. 1972. "Audit Report—Financial and Management Operations, USIS-Korea." February 28. RG306 USIA, Inspection Staff, Inspection Reports and Related Records, box 8.

Marks. 1966. "A Telegraph sent to Manila." August 3. RG306 USIA, Office of Research, Records of Research Projects, East Asia, 1964–1973, box 8.

Muccio, John J. 1950a. "To Secretary of State, REDEPTEL 92, August 24." September 3. RG59 Department of State, decimal file 1950–1954, box 2539.
———. 1950b. "Transmitting Report on September Operations of USIE in Taegu." October 6. RG59 Department of State, decimal file 1950–1954, box 2539.
Office of Research. 1966. "Communication Fact Book: South Korea, R-17-66." January. RG306 USIA, Office of Research, "R" reports, 1964–1974, box 29.
Stewart, James L. 1947. "Report on the History and Growth of the Office of Civil Information, USAFIK." November 10. RG554 Records of General HQ, Far East Command, Supreme Commander Allied Powers, and United Nations Command, box 42.
U.S. Army Forces in Korea. 1948a. "History: Public Information Dept." August. RG554 Records of General HQ, Far East Command, Supreme Commander Allied Powers, and United Nations Command, box 39.
———. 1948b. "Report of Activities of the Office of Civil Information, USAFIK—10 November 1947 to 15 January 1948." January 15. RG554 Records of General HQ, Far East Command, Supreme Commander Allied Powers, and United Nations Command, box 42.
U.S. Department of the Army. 1950. "Outgoing Classified Message to the Commander in Chief of the Far East (CINCFE), Tokyo, Japan." October 27. RG59 Records of Department of State, decimal file 1950–1954, box 2539.
USIS-Korea. 1964. *USIS Film Catalogue 1964*. Seoul: USIS-Korea.

Films and Television Shows

American Road, The (1953)
American Working Women (n.d.)
Arrival of a Train, The (1895)
Autobiography of a Jeep, The (1943)
Ch'aenŏl siksŭnain (Channel 69) (1996)
Changmiŭi nanal (Days of Roses) (1994)
Chibang sinmun p'yŏnjipcha (Korean Editor) (1958)
Chisang ch'oego-ŭi yŏjŏng: Segye-ro Ppŏnnŭn Han'guk (Reaching the World) (1968)
Chiwŏnbyŏng (Volunteer) (1941)
Ch'ŏngch'un ŭi sipcharo (Crossroads of Youth) (1934)
Ch'ongjabi (Man with a Gun) (1995)
Chŏpsok (The Contact) (1997)
Chosŏn haehyŏp (Straits of Chosŏn) (1943)
Country Editor (1954)
Ghost (1990)
I Am a Truck (1955)
K'amera ch'uldong (Camera Dispatch) (MBC-TV, 1974–present)
Keijō (K. *Kyŏngsŏng*) (1941)
K'idŭ k'ap (Kid Cop) (1993)
Kigwansa-ŭi adŭl (The Locomotive Engineer's Son) (1971)
Kil (The Road) (1967)
Kkotp'inŭn p'aldogangsan (Blooming P'aldogangsan) (KBS-TV, 1974–1975)
Konghae-e tojŏn (Challenges against Pollution) (USIS-TV, 1971)

Kunyong yŏlch'a (Military Train) (1938)
Kwan'tong ŭi kil (Road to the Kangwŏn Province) (1975)
Kyōi no sekai—nonfikshon awā (World Wonders—a Nonfiction Hour) (Nippon TV, 1972–1982)
Manshū no tabi (Journey to Manchuria) (1937)
Miguk ŭi onŭl (Korea-America Today) (USIS-TV, 1965)
Mimong (Sweet Dream) (1936)
Naeil-ŭi p'aldogangsan (P'aldogangsan of Tomorrow) (1971)
Nai-Sen-Man shūyū no tabi (Journey from Mainland to Chosŏn and Manchuria) (1937)
Niksŭn tokt'ŭrin p'ŭrogŭraem ribyu (Nixon Doctrine Program Review) (USIS-TV, 1969)
Ŏhwa (Fisherman's Fire) (1938)
Ŏkchi pongjabi (Birds of a Feather) (1961)
Ŏnŭ taehwa (A Conversation) (1968)
Ŏrin ch'ŏnsadŭl (Little Angels of Korea) (1967)
P'aldogangsan (Six Daughters) (1967)
Pando ŭi pom (Spring of the Peninsula) (1941)
Pịt'ŭ (Beat) (1997)
Pŏnyŏng ŭi kil (The Road to Prosperity) (1974)
Rŏnŏwei (Runaway) (1995)
Sarang kwa maengsŏ (Vow of Love) (1945)
Sen-Man shūyū no tabi (Journey Chosŏn and Manchuria) (1937)
Shina no yoru (China Nights) (1940)
Small Town Editor (1952)
Sok P'aldogangsan: segye-rŭl kanda (The Land of Korea: P'aldogangsan 2) (1968)
Sŏnggong sidae (The Age of Success) (1988)
Story of Lincoln Tunnel, The (c. 1943)
Susa panjang (Chief Inspector) (MBC-TV, 1971–1989)
Taedam ssirijŭ (Inquire Series) (USIS-TV, 1970)
Tōkyō no josei (Woman in Tokyo) (1939)
Tokyo-Peking: Through Tyosen and Manchoukuo (1939)
T'ongil ŭi kil (The Road to Reunification) (1970)
Tongmul-ŭi wangguk (Animal Kingdom) (KBS-TV, 1969–present)
Tonŭl katko t'wiŏra (Millions in My Account) (1995)
Ttosuni: Haengbok ŭi t'ansaeng (Tosuni: The Birth of Happiness) (1963)
Tuesday in November (1945)
T'ŭkp'awŏni pon asia (Korean Reporter in Asia) (USIS-TV, 1970)
Uri-ŭi p'aldogangsan (P'aldogangsan of Our Own) (1972)

Newspapers and Magazines

Chayu Segye (*Free World*)
Chosŏn ilbo
CNN (Cable News Network)
The Globe and Mail

Han'guk ilbo
Han'guk kyŏngje
Han'gyŏre
Ik'onomisŭt'ŭ (*The Economist*)
The Korean Herald
Kyoch'egye (The Monthly of Korean Transportation and Communications Review)
Kyŏnghyang sinmun
Maeil kyŏngje
Maeil sinbo
Newsis
The New York Times
NPR (National Public Radio)
Reuters
Rodong sinmun
Tonga ilbo
The Washington Post
The Washington Times
Wŏlgan nae ch'a (Monthly My Car Magazine)
Wŏlgan pijinesŭ (*Business Monthly*)
Yŏnhap nyusŭ

Oral Histories and Personal Collections

[Anonymous]. 1959. "Personnel Breakdown." April 8. Personal Collection of Theodore Conant.

Heyman, Alan C. 2012. Interviewed by Han Sang Kim, January 12.

Other Sources

Agamben, Giorgio. 1999. *Remnants of Auschwitz: The Witness and the Archive.* Translated by Daniel Heller-Roazen. New York: Zone Books.

———. 2000. *Means without End: Notes on Politics.* Translated by Vincenzo Binetti and Cesare Casarino. Minneapolis: University of Minnesota Press.

———. 2005. *State of Exception.* Chicago: University of Chicago Press.

Ahn, Byung-Min (An Pyŏng-min). 2012. "Pukhan'gyot'ong inp'ŭra hyŏnhwang mit t'ongire taebihan hyanghu taeŭng panghyang" (The Current Conditions of North Korean Transportation Infrastructure and Future Strategy for the Preparation of Reunification). *Taehant'omokhakhoeji* (Journal of the Korean Society of Civil Engineers) 60 (3): 11–16.

Amad, Paula. 2013. "Visual Riposte: Looking Back at the Return of the Gaze as Postcolonial Theory's Gift to Film Studies." *Cinema Journal* 52 (3): 49–74.

An, Jinsoo. 2018. *Parameters of Disavowal: Colonial Representation in South Korean Cinema.* Oakland: University of California Press.

Augé, Marc. 1995. *Non-Places: Introduction to an Anthropology of Supermodernity.* Translated by John Howe. London: Verso.

Baek, Jieun. 2016. *North Korea's Hidden Revolution: How the Information Underground Is Transforming a Closed Society*. New Haven, CT: Yale University Press.

Baek, Moon Im (Paek Mun-im). 2012. "A Study of Travelogue and Film on Seoul by E. Burton Holmes." *Hyŏndae munhak ŭi yŏn'gu* (Journal of Korean Modern Literature) 47:59–96.

Ball, Karyn. 2005. "Paranoia in the Age of the World Picture: The Global 'Limits of Enlightenment.'" *Cultural Critique* 61 (Autumn): 115–47.

Baumbach, Nico. 2019. *Cinema/Politics/Philosophy*. New York: Columbia University Press.

Beckman, Karen. 2010. *Crash: Cinema and the Politics of Speed and Stasis*. Durham, NC: Duke University Press.

Benjamin, Walter. 1991. *Gesammelte Schriften Band II 2*. Frankfurt: Suhrkamp Verlag.

Böhm, Steffen, Campbell Jones, Chris Land, and Matthew Paterson, eds. 2006. *Against Automobility*. Malden, MA: Blackwell.

Bok, Whan Mo (Pok Hwan-mo). 2004. "A Study of the Role of the Movie Unit of the Chosun Government-General during the Early Stage of the 1920s." *Yŏnghwa yŏn'gu* (Film Studies) 24:249–77.

Bruno, Giuliana. 1992. "Bodily Architectures." *Assemblage* 19:106–11.

Chang, Kyung-sup. 2014. "Individualization without Individualism: Compressed Modernity and Obfuscated Family Crisis in East Asia." In *Transformation of the Intimate and the Public in Asian Modernity*, edited by Emiko Ochiai and Leo Aoi Hosoya, 37–62. Leiden, Netherlands: Brill.

Chapin, Henry, and Denis Deneau. 1978. *Citizen Involvement in Public Policy-Making: Access and the Policy-Making Process*. Ottawa: Canada Council on Social Development.

Cheah, Pheng. 2013. "World as Picture and Ruination: On Jia Zhangke's *Still Life* as World Cinema." In *The Oxford Handbook of Chinese Cinemas*, edited by Carlos Rojas and Eileen Chow, 190–206. New York: Oxford University Press.

Chen, Hongwei Thorn. 2018. "Cinemas, Highways, and the Making of Provincial Space: Mobile Screenings in Jiangsu, China, 1933–1937." *Wide Screen* 7 (1): 1–34.

Cho Chun-hyŏng. 2011. "A Study on Korean Films in the Time of a Political Upheaval in the Early 1960s." PhD diss., Chung-Ang University.

Ch'oe Un-sik. 1995. *Han'guk ŭi yuksang kyot'ong* (Land Traffic in Korea). Seoul: Ewha Women's University Press.

Choe, Youngmin. 2016. *Tourist Distractions: Traveling and Feeling in Transnational Hallyu Cinema*. Durham, NC: Duke University Press.

Choi, Byung-Doo. 2012. "Gyeongbu Expressway: Political Economic Geography of Mobility and Demarcation." *Korean Social Sciences Review* 2 (2): 181–218.

Choi, Ellie. 2018. "Memories of Korean Modernity: Yi Kwangsu's *The Heartless* and New Perspectives in Colonial Alterity." *Journal of Asian Studies* 77 (2): 659–91.

Chŏn Yŏng-sŏn. 2010. *Kojong K'aedillak ŭl t'ada: Han'guk chadongch'a 110-yŏn ŭi iyagi* (King Kojong Rides in a Cadillac: A 110-Year Story of Cars in Korea). Seoul: Inmul kwa Sasangsa.

Chŏng Chong-hwa. 2020. *#Chosŏn yŏnghwa ranŭn kŭndae* (#A Modernity Called Chosŏn Cinema). Seoul: Pagijŏng.

Chŏng Kŭn-sik. 2011. "Social Control and Resistance during the Park Chung Hee Period." In *(T'al) naengjŏn kwa Han'guk ŭi minjujuŭi*, edited by Chŏng Kŭn-sik, 83–130. Seoul: Sŏnin.

Chŏngŭmsa, ed. 1975. *Sajin ŭro ponŭn kwangbok 30-yŏnsa* (30-Year History since the Independence, with Photo Illustrations). Seoul: Chŏngŭmsa.

Chow, Rey. 2012. *Entanglements, or Transmedial Thinking about Capture*. Durham, NC: Duke University Press.

Chu Sŏng-ha. 2018. *P'yŏngyang chabonjuŭi paekkwajŏnsŏ* (Pyongyang Capitalism: An Encyclopedia). Seoul: Puktodum.

Chung, Hye Seung, and David Scott Diffrient. 2015. *Movie Migrations: Transnational Genre Flows and South Korean Cinema*. New Brunswick, NJ: Rutgers University Press.

Chung, Steven. 2014. *Split Screen Korea: Shin Sang-ok and Postwar Cinema*. Minneapolis: University of Minnesota Press.

Comolli, Jean-Louis. 1980. "Machines of the Visible." In *The Cinematic Apparatus*, edited by Teresa de Lauretis and Stephen Heath, 121–43. New York: St. Martin's.

Crary, Jonathan. 1992. *Techniques of the Observer: On Vision and Modernity in the Nineteenth Century*. Cambridge, MA: MIT Press.

Davis, Clarence. 1991. "Railway Imperialism in China, 1895–1939." In *Railway Imperialism*, edited by Clarence B. Davis, Kenneth E. Wilburn, and Ronald E. Robinson, 155–73. New York: Greenwood.

Doherty, Brigid. 2000. "Test and Gestus in Brecht and Benjamin." *MLN* 115 (3, German issue): 442–81.

Duara, Prasenjit. 2006. "Nationalism, Imperialism, Federalism, and the Case of Manchukuo: A Response to Anthony Pagden." *Common Knowledge* 12 (1): 47–65.

Dubois, Thomas D. 2008. "Rule of Law in a Brave New Empire: Legal Rhetoric and Practice in Manchukuo." *Law and History Review* 26 (2): 285–318.

Eckert, Carter J. 2016. *Park Chung Hee and Modern Korea*. Cambridge, MA: Harvard University Press.

Eckert, Carter J., Ki-baik Lee, Young Ick Lew, Michael Robinson, and Edward W. Wagner. 1990. *Korea Old and New: A History*. Cambridge, MA: Harvard University Press.

Etem, Aysehan Jülide. 2019. "*The American Marshall Plan Film Campaign and the Europeans: A Captivated Audience?*, by Maria Fritsche, Bloomsbury, 2018, 369 pp." *Alphaville: Journal of Film and Screen Media* 17:229–33.

Foucault, Michel. 1978. *Discipline and Punish: The Birth of the Prison*. New York: Vintage Books.

———. 1982. "The Subject and Power." *Critical Inquiry* 8 (4): 777–95.

———. 1988. "Technologies of the Self." In *Technologies of the Self: A Seminar with Michel Foucault*, edited by Luther H. Martin, Huck Gutman, and Patrick H. Hutton, 16–49. Amherst, MA: University of Massachusetts Press.

———. 2009. *Security, Territory, Population: Lectures at the Collège de France 1977–1978*. New York: Picador.

Friedberg, Anne. 1993. *Window Shopping: Cinema and the Postmodern*. Berkeley: University of California Press.

———. 2002. "Urban Mobility and Cinematic Visuality: The Screens of Los Angeles—Endless Cinema or Private Telematics." *Journal of Visual Culture* 1 (2): 183–204.

Fujitani, Takashi. 1998. *Splendid Monarchy: Power and Pageantry in Modern Japan*. Berkeley: University of California Press.

Garfinkel, Harold. 1967. *Studies in Ethnomethodology*. Englewood Cliffs, NJ: Prentice-Hall.

Gelézeau, Valérie. 2008. "Changing Socio-Economic Environments, Housing Culture and New Urban Segregation in Seoul." *European Journal of East Asian Studies* 7 (2): 295–321.

German, Kathleen. 2009. "Economic Convergence and the Celebration of Mass Production: The World War II Advertising Campaign to Sell Jeeps." In *War and the Media: Essays on News Reporting, Propaganda and Popular Culture*, edited by Paul M. Haridakis, Barbara S. Hugenberg, and Stanley T. Wearden, 92–111. Jefferson, NC: McFarland.

Gharabaghi, Hadi Parandeh. 2018. "*American Mice Grow Big!* The Syracuse Audiovisual Mission in Iran and the Rise of Documentary Diplomacy." PhD diss., New York University.

Giddens, Anthony, Mitchell Duneier, Richard P. Appelbaum, and Deborah Carr. 2016. *Introduction to Sociology*. Seagull 10th ed. New York: W. W. Norton.

Gillespie, Alex. 2006. "Tourist Photography and the Reverse Gaze." *Ethos* 34 (3): 343–66.

Gordon, Colin. 1991. "Governmental Rationality: An Introduction." In *The Foucault Effect: Studies in Governmentality*, edited by G. Burchell, C. Gordon, and P. Miller, 1–52. Chicago: University of Chicago Press.

Gudis, Catherine. 2004. *Buyways: Billboards, Automobiles, and the American Landscape*. New York: Routledge.

Gunning, Tom. 2006. "'The Whole World within Reach': Travel Images without Borders." In *Virtual Voyages: Cinema and Travel*, edited by Jeffrey Ruoff, 25–41. Durham, NC: Duke University Press.

Hall, Stuart. 1997. "The Work of Representation." In *Representation: Cultural Representations and Signifying Practices*, edited by Stuart Hall, 13–74. London: Sage.

Han, Harlan. 1974. "Attitudes toward Federalism and the 'Localism-Cosmopolitanism' Dimension." *Publius: The Journal of Federalism* 4 (3): 65–74.

Han, Min-ju (Han Min-ju). 2007. "Politics of Representation on the War Front Travelogue of the Latter Japanese Imperialism." *Han'guk munhak yŏn'gu* (Studies in Korean Literature) 33:339–66.

Hansen, Miriam Bratu. 2012. *Cinema and Experience: Siegfried Kracauer, Walter Benjamin, and Theodor W. Adorno*. Berkeley: University of California Press.

Harper, Douglas. 2001. "Highway." In *Online Etymology Dictionary*. Accessed March 24, 2017. https://www.etymonline.com/word/highway#etymonline_v_12002.

Harvey, David. 1989. *The Condition of Postmodernity: An Enquiry into the Origins of Cultural Change*. Oxford: Blackwell.

———. 2005. *A Brief History of Neoliberalism*. Oxford: Oxford University Press.

Hayward, Mark. 2013. "ATMs, Teleprompters and Photobooths: A Short History of Neoliberal Optics." *New Formations: A Journal of Culture/Theory/Politics* 80/81:194–208.

Heidegger, Martin. 2002. "The Age of the World Picture." In *Off the Beaten Track*, edited and translated by Julian Young and Kenneth Haynes, 57–85. Cambridge: Cambridge University Press.

Henry, Todd A. 2014. *Assimilating Seoul: Japanese Rule and the Politics of Public Space in Colonial Korea, 1910–1945*. Berkeley: University of California Press.

High, Peter B. 2003. *The Imperial Screen: Japanese Film Culture in the Fifteen Years' War, 1931–1945*. Madison: University of Wisconsin Press.

Holmes, E. Burton. 1920. *Burton Holmes Travelogues—with Illustrations from Photographs by the Author*. Vol. 10. Chicago: Travelogue Bureau.

Horvath, Ronald J. 1974. "Machine Space." *Geographical Review* 64 (2): 167–88.

Hughes, Theodore. 2012. *Literature and Film in Cold War South Korea: Freedom's Frontier*. New York: Columbia University Press.

Japan Highway Public Corporation, General Affairs Division, ed. 1976. *Nihon Dōro Kōdan nijūnenshi* (Twenty-Year History of the Japan Highway Public Corporation). Tokyo: Nihon Dōro Kōdan.

Jay, Martin. 1988. "Scopic Regimes of Modernity." In *Vision and Visuality*, edited by Hal Foster, 3–27. Seattle: Bay Press.

———. 2011. *Essays from the Edge: Parerga and Paralipomena*. Charlottesville: University of Virginia Press.

———. 2014. "A Parting Glance: Empire and Visuality." In *Empires of Vision: A Reader*, edited by Martin Jay and Sumathi Ramaswamy, 609–20. Durham, NC: Duke University Press.

Jeong, Choong-sil (Chŏng Ch'ung-sil). 2015. "The Tongyeong Youth Corps' Film Screening Tour and Its Audiences' Viewing (1921–1923)." *Chŏngsin munhwa yŏn'gu* (Korean Studies Quarterly) 38 (2): 95–120.

Jeong, Kelly Y. 2011. *Crisis of Gender and the Nation in Korean Literature and Cinema: Modernity Arrives Again*. Lanham, MD: Lexington Books.

Jin, Siwon (Chin Si-wŏn). 2004. "East Asian Railway Networks: Origin and History." *Kukche chŏngch'i nonch'ong* (Korean Journal of International Relations) 44 (3): 125–49.

Joo, Eunwoo (Chu Ŭn-u). 2011. "Cinematic Representation of a Colonial City and Its Modernity: Documentary Film *Keijō (Seoul)* and the Self-Representation of Colonial Power." *Sahoe wa yŏksa* (Society and History) 92:39–91.

Jung, Keun-Sik (Chŏng Kŭn-sik). 2009. "Japanese Colonial Information Control and Visual Propaganda." *Sahoe-wa yŏksa* (Society and History) 82:41–82.

Kang Beom Suk (Kang Pŏm-sŏk). 1999. "A Critical Approach to Visualism in Plato and Descartes: Beyond Visualism." *Sidaewa ch'ŏrhak* (Epoch and Philosophy) 10 (2): 89–118.

Kang, Chun-man. 2010. "Han'guk tambae ŭi yŏksa" (The History of Tobacco in Korea). *Inmul kwa sasang*, March, 178–209.

Kang, Jaeho. 2014. *Walter Benjamin and the Media: The Spectacle of Modernity*. Cambridge: Polity.

Kang, Jung In (Kang Chŏng-in). 2011. "An Analysis of Park Chung Hee's Discourses on Democracy: Focusing on his 'Administrative,' 'National' and 'Korean-style' Democracy." *Ch'ŏrhak nonjip* 27:287–321.

Kanneh, Kadiatu. 1995. "Feminism and the Colonial Body." In *The Post-Colonial Studies Reader*, edited by Bill Ashcroft, Careth Griffiths, and Helen Tiffin, 346–48. London: Routledge.

Kavanagh, Donncha. 2004. "Ocularcentrism and Its Others: A Framework for Metatheoretical Analysis." *Organization Studies* 25 (3): 445–64.

Kay, Jane Holtz. 1998. *Asphalt Nation: How the Automobile Took Over America, and How We Can Take It Back.* Berkeley: University of California Press.

Kim Chang-ho. 1991. *Chadonghwa kisul hyŏksingwa koyong* (Technological Innovations in Automation and Employment). Seoul: Korea Labor Institute.

Kim, Christine. 2009. "Politics and Pageantry in Protectorate Korea (1905–10): The Imperial Progresses of Sunjong." *Journal of Asian Studies* 68 (3): 835–59.

Kim, Dong Hoon. 2017. *Eclipsed Cinema: The Film Culture of Colonial Korea.* Edinburgh: Edinburgh University Press.

Kim, Han Sang (Kim Han-sang). 2008. *Choguk kŭndaehwa rŭl yuram hagi: Pak Chŏnghŭi chŏngkwŏn hongbo dŭraibŭ, 'P'aldogangsan' 10-yŏn* (Sightseeing Modernization of the Fatherland: "P'aldogangsan," 10 Years of Propaganda Series for the Pak Chŏnghŭi Regime). Seoul: Korean Film Archive.

———. 2009. "Culture Film Screening in Chosŏn, from the 1930s to 1940s." In *The Past Unearthed, the Fourth Encounter—Moving Images from Gosfilmofond* (DVD box set booklet), 16–19, 36–39. Seoul: Korean Film Archive.

———. 2011. "The U.S. Film Propaganda in South Korea, 1945–48: The Study on Film Materials Discovered in the U.S. National Archives." *Miguksa yŏn'gu* 34:177–212.

———. 2013. "Cold War and the Contested Identity Formation of Korean Filmmakers: On Boxes of Death and Kim Ki-yŏng's USIS Films." *Inter-Asia Cultural Studies* 14 (3): 551–63.

———. 2013. "Uneven Screens, Contested Identities: USIS, Cultural Films, and the National Imaginary in South Korea, 1945–1972." PhD diss., Seoul National University.

———. 2018. "'My' Sweet Home in the Next Decade: The Popular Imagination of Private Homeownership during the Yusin Period." In *Cultures of Yusin: South Korea in the 1970s*, edited by Youngju Ryu, 119–40. Ann Arbor: University of Michigan Press.

Kim Hŭi-kap. 1992. *Ŏnŭ kwangdae-ŭi sarang* (Love of a Clown). Seoul: Samjin kihoek.

Kim Hyŏng-guk. 1989. *Tosi sidae ŭi Han'guk munhwa* (Korean Culture in the Urban Age). Seoul: Nanam.

Kim Hyŏng-ki. 1988. "Han'guk tokchŏmjabonŭi undonggwa nodonggwajŏngŭi pyŏnhyŏng" (The Movement of the Korean Monopolistic Capitals and the Transformation of the Labor Process). *Sahoegyŏngjep'yŏngnon* (Review of Social and Economic Studies) 1:41–90.

Kim, Jihoon (Kim Chi-hun). 2017. "Biopolitics, Montage, and Potentialities of the Image: Giorgio Agamben and Cinema." *Pigyo munhwa yŏn'gu* (Cross-Cultural Studies) 49:59–93.

Kim, Kyung Hyun. 2011. *Virtual Hallyu: Korean Cinema of the Global Era.* Durham, NC: Duke University Press.

Kim Sŏn-ch'ŏl. 2016. "'Sinnyŏnsa-esŏ ch'ŏldo hyŏndae-hwa iryejŏk ŏn'gŭp'—2016nyŏn pukhan kim chŏng-ŭn sinnyŏnsa punsŏk: inp'ŭra punya" ("Unprecedented Mentioning of Modernizing the Railroad"—an Analysis of Kim Jong-un's 2016 New Year's Speech: Infrastructure). *Wŏlgan kyot'ong* (Monthly KOTI Magazine on Transport) 216 (February): 66–71.

Kim, So-young (Kim So-yŏng). 2010. "Imperial Tour of Emperor Sunjong and the Discourse on Loyalty and Patriotism." *Han'guksa hakpo* (Journal for the Study of Korean History) 39:159–93.

Kim, Suzy. 2013. *Everyday Life in the North Korean Revolution, 1945–1950*. Ithaca, NY: Cornell University Press.

Kim Tŏk-hyŏng. 1970. *Kosok toro wa kukka paljŏn* (The Expressway and the Nation's Development). Seoul: Hŭngsinmunhwasa.

Kim, Won (Kim Wŏn). 2012. "The Competition concerning Appropriation of 'Things Korean': Revival of Nation, Theory of Indigenous Development and Trace of Popular Culture." *Sahoe-wa yŏksa* (Society and History) 93:185–235.

Kim Wŏn-ki. 1970. "Kyŏngbu kan kosok toro kaet'ong ŭi ŭiŭi" (The Significance of the Opening of the Kyŏngbu Expressway). *Chibang haengjŏng* (Journal of the Public Official Benefit Association) 19 (201): 34–39.

Kirby, Lynne. 1997. *Parallel Tracks: The Railroad and Silent Cinema*. Durham, NC: Duke University Press.

Kirkpatrick, Bill. 2006. "Localism in American Media, 1920–1934." PhD diss., University of Wisconsin–Madison.

Kittler, Friedrich A. 2012. *Optical Media: Berlin Lectures 1999*. Translated by Anthony Enns. Cambridge: Polity.

Klein, Christina. 2020. *Cold War Cosmopolitanism: Period Style in 1950s Korean Cinema*. Berkeley: University of California Press.

Korea Elevator Safety Institute (KESI). 2013. *Han'guk sŭngganggi palchŏnsa* (History of the Development of the South Korean Elevator Industry). Accessed March 14, 2015. https://www.kesafe.or.kr/kesi2013/sub/elevator/05_03_06.jsp.

Korea Expressway Corporation. 1972. *Yŏngdong kosok toro sin'gal-saemal kan kŏnsŏlji* (Construction Logbook of the Yŏngdong Expressway Line between Sin'gal and Saemal). Sŏngnam: Korea Expressway Corporation.

———. 1979. *Han'guk toro kongsa simnyŏnsa* (Ten-Year History of the Korean Expressway Corporation). Sŏngnam: Korea Expressway Corporation.

———. 1980. *Han'guk kosok toro simnyŏnsa* (Ten-Year History of Korean Expressways). Sŏngnam: Korea Expressway Corporation.

Korea Productivity Center Pusan and Kyŏngnam Regional Headquarters. 1970. *Kyŏngbu kosok toro ŭi kyŏngjejŏk hyokwa* (Economic Effect of the Kyŏngbu Expressway). Pusan: Pusan Ŭnhaeng.

Korean Film Archive, ed. 2009. *Han'guk yŏnghwasa kusul ch'aerok yŏn'gu sirijŭ: Saengaesa Pae Sŏk-in* (Korean Film Oral History Series: Life History of Pae Sŏk-in). Seoul: Korean Film Archive.

Korean Society for Railway. 2005. *Han'guk ch'ŏlto kŏnsŏl paekyŏnsa* (A Hundred-Year History of the Korean Railway Construction). Daejeon: Korea Rail Network Authority.

Kramer, Hanae Kurihara. 2012. "Film Forays of the South Manchuria Railway Company." *Film History* 24 (1): 97–113.

Kushner, Barak. 2006. *The Thought War: Japanese Imperial Propaganda*. Honolulu: University of Hawai'i Press.

Kwag, Seung-Mi (Kwak Sŭng-mi). 2006. "The Enjoyment and Narrative Appropriation to the Travel Culture in the Colonial Period." *Taejung sŏsa yŏn'gu* (Journal of Popular Culture) 12 (1): 229–56.

Kwon, Ki Tae, J.-H. Ko, H. Shin, M. Sung, and J. Y. Kim. 2020. "Drive-Through Screening Center for COVID-19: A Safe and Efficient Screening System against Massive Community Outbreak." *Journal of Korean Medical Science* 35 (11): e123.

Kwon, Nayoung Aimee. 2015. *Intimate Empire: Collaboration and Colonial Modernity in Korea and Japan*. Durham, NC: Duke University Press.

Lamarre, Thomas, 2009. *The Anime Machine: A Media Theory of Animation*. Minneapolis, MN: University of Minnesota Press.

Lasker, Bruno. (1938) 1978. *Propaganda from China and Japan: A Case Study in Propaganda Analysis*. New York: AMS Press.

Lee, Jin-kyung. 2010. *Service Economies: Militarism, Sex Work, and Migrant Labor in South Korea*. Minneapolis: University of Minnesota Press.

Lee, Kyoung Hoon (Yi Kyŏng-hun). 2009. "Colony and Tourist Resort: Manchuria as a Modern Theatre." *SAI* 6:73–112.

Lee, Sangjoon. 2013. "The Emergence of the Asian Film Festival: Cold War Asia and Japan's Re-entrance to the Regional Market in the 1950s." In *Oxford Handbook of Japanese Cinema*, edited by Miyao Daisuke, 232–50. London: Oxford University Press.

———. 2017. "The Asia Foundation's Motion-Picture Project and the Cultural Cold War in Asia." *Film History* 29 (2): 108–37.

Lee, Sang-woo (Yi Sang-u). 2008. "The Greater East Asia as Imaginative Geography—the Occidentalism and Racism in the Colonial Korean Plays in the Early 1940s." *Han'guk kŭgyesul yŏn'gu* (Journal of Korean Drama and Theater) 27:163–201.

Lee, Seok-Won (Yi Sŏk-wŏn). 2015. "The Paradox of Racial Liberation: W. E. B. Du Bois and Pan-Asianism in Wartime Japan, 1931–1945." *Inter-Asia Cultural Studies* 16 (4): 513–30.

Lee, Wang-moo (Yi Wang-mu). 2007. "A Study of the Emperor's Parade: His Majesty of Sunjong in Daehan Empire." *Chŏngsin munhwa yŏn'gu* (Korean Studies Quarterly) 30 (2): 59–88.

———. 2011. "A Study of the Emperor's Parade: His Majesty of Sunjong in Northern Province of Daehan Empire." *Tongbuga yŏksa nonch'ong* (Journal of Northeast Asian History) 31:285–318.

Li, Jie. 2013. "A National Cinema for a Puppet State: The Manchurian Motion Picture Association." In *The Oxford Handbook of Chinese Cinemas*, edited by Carlos Rojas and Eileen Cheng-Yin Chow, 79–97. Oxford: Oxford University Press.

———. 2020. "Cinematic Guerrillas in Mao's China." *Screen* 61 (2): 207–29.

Lim, Jie-hyun (Im Chi-hyŏn). 2020. "Globalization of Memory: How Do the Memories of Holocaust, Colonial Genocide, and Stalinism Cross-Refer and Appropriate One Another?" Special Talk at CGSI Weekly Colloquium, Sogang University, Seoul, September 10.

Lyon, David. 1994. *The Electronic Eye: The Rise of Surveillance Society*. Minneapolis: University of Minnesota Press.

MacCannell, Dean. 1973. "Staged Authenticity: Arrangements of Social Space in Tourist Settings." *American Journal of Sociology* 79 (3): 589–603.

———. 1976. *The Tourist: A New Theory of the Leisure Class.* New York: Schocken Books

Mandel, Ernest. 1998. *Late Capitalism.* London: Verso.

Marx, Karl. 2009. "Theses on Feuerbach." In *Frederick Engels: Feuerbach—the Roots of the Socialist Philosophy; Karl Marx: On Feuerbach.* Translated by Austin Lewis, 94–97. New York: Mondial Books.

McLuhan, Marshall. 1962. *The Gutenberg Galaxy: The Making of Typographic Man.* Toronto: University of Toronto Press.

———. 1964. *Understanding Media: The Extensions of Man.* Cambridge, MA: MIT Press.

Merleau-Ponty, Maurice. 1964. *Sense and Non-Sense.* Translated by Hubert L. Dreyfus and Patricia Allen Dreyfus. Evanston, IL: Northwestern University Press.

———. 1968. *The Visible and the Invisible.* Edited by Claude Lefort. Translated by Alphonso Lingus. Evanston, IL: Northwestern University Press.

Min Pyŏng-u. 1966. *Ssalgapkwa chŏngch'iwa: kwahakkisulgwa kyŏngje* (Rice Price and Politics: Science Technology and Economy). Seoul: Kyomunsa.

Ministry of the Environment, Japan. 2002. *Heisei 14-nenban junkangata shakai hakusho* (White Paper on Cyclic Society, 2002 Edition). Accessed September 22, 2013. http://www.env.go.jp/policy/hakusyo/hakusyo.php3?kid=216.

Mitchell, Timothy. 1991. *Colonising Egypt.* Berkeley: University of California Press.

———, ed. 2000. *Questions of Modernity.* Minneapolis: University of Minnesota Press.

Mitchell, W. J. T. 2007. "World Pictures: Globalization and Visual Culture." *Neohelicon* 34 (2): 49–59.

Moon, Seungsook. 2005. *Militarized Modernity and Gendered Citizenship in South Korea.* Durham, NC: Duke University Press.

Morris-Suzuki, Tessa. 1995. "The Invention and Reinvention of 'Japanese Culture.'" *Journal of Asian Studies* 54 (3): 759–80.

———. 1997. "Robots and Capitalism." In *Cutting Edge: Technology, Information Capitalism and Social Revolution*, edited by J. Davis, T. Hirschl, and M. Stack, 13–27. London: Verso.

Murphy, John. 2009. *The Eisenhower Interstate System.* New York: Chelsea House.

Nakane, Takayuki. 2009. "Cheguk ilbon ŭi mansŏn kwan'gwangji wa kodo kyŏngju ŭi p'yosang" (Manchū-Chōsen Tourist Attractions in the Japanese Empire and the Representation of the Old Capital Kyŏngju). In *Han'guk munhak yŏn'gu* (Studies in Korean Literature) 36:55–78.

National Film Preservation Foundation. 2000. *Treasures from American Film Archives: 50 Preserved Films.* San Francisco: Water Mark.

National Institute of Korean History, ed. 2005. *Kŭnhyŏndae kwahak kisul kwa salmŭi pyŏnhwa* (Modern and Contemporary Science and Technology and the Transformation of Life). Seoul: Tusan tonga.

Nelson, Laura C. 2000. *Measured Excess: Status, Gender, and Consumer Nationalism in South Korea.* New York: Columbia University Press.

Neurnann, Peter G. 1990. "Risks to the Public in Computers and Related Systems." *Newsletter ACM SIGSOFT Software Engineering Notes* 15 (1): 4–23.

Nihon Dōro Kōdan Sōmubu hen. 1976. *Nihon Dōro Kōdan nijūnenshi* (Twenty-Year History of the Japan Highway Public Corporation). Tokyo: Nihon Dōro Kōdan.

Nishizawa, Iwata. 1917. *Japan in the Taisho Era: In Commemoration of the Enthronement.* Tokyo: Japan Gazette.

O Che-myŏng. 1993. *Pürehit'ŭ ŭi kyoyukkŭk* (Brecht's *Lehtstücke*). Seoul: Hanmadang.

Ohtsuka, Yasuo. 1994. *Jeeps Over the Pacific.* Tokyo: Hobby Japan.

Okawa, Hitomi. 2007. "Image of Chosun Reflected in Propaganda Films during Japanese Colonization: In the Case of *Chosun Sketch* (1939)." MA thesis, Ewha University.

Osa, Shizue. 2009. "Senji ka no 'manshi' shisatsu ryokō—senchi to kankō·rekishi no shōhi" (Wartime "Man-Shi" Observation Tour—Battleground and Tourism, Consumption of History). *Jeonbuk Sahak* 34:275–315.

Paek Nam-ryong. 2016. *Yajŏn ryŏlch'a* (The Field Train). Pyongyang: Munhakyesul ch'ulp'ansa.

Pak Chŏng-su. 1984. "My Overseas Studying Years (318)—Pak Chŏng-su, National Assembly Member (7)." *Maeil kyŏngje*, January 14, 9.

Pak Hyŏng-jun. 1991. *Hyŏndaenodonggwajŏngnon: Chadonghwae taehan yŏn'gu* (Modern Labor Process Theory: A Study on Automation). Seoul: Paeksan sŏdang.

Pak Kyŏng-su. 2012. "Kŭndae ch'ŏlto rŭl t'onghae pon singminji Chosŏn mandŭlgi" (Building Colonial Korea through Modern Railroads). *Ilbonŏ munhak* (Japanophone Literature) 53:253–72.

Pak Sŭng-hŭi. 1990. "Kongjang chadonghwae ttarŭn nodonggwajŏngŭi pyŏnhwa: Han'gugŭi kyŏngu" (The Change of Labor Process Caused by Factory Automation: The South Korean Case). *Kyŏngjewa sahoe* (Economy and Society) 8:123–51.

Pak Yŏng-jun. 2006. *Manu Pak Yŏng-jun Chŏnjip 13* (Complete Collection of Pak Yŏng-jun Vol. 13). Seoul: Tong-yŏn.

Palladino, Grace. 1987. "When Militancy Isn't Enough: The Impact of Automation on New York City Building Service Workers, 1934–1970." *Labor History* 28 (2): 196–220.

Pardo-Guerra, J. P. 2012. "Financial Automation, Past, Present, and Future." In *The Oxford Handbook of the Sociology of Finance*, edited by Karin Knorr Cetina and Alex Preda, 567–86. Oxford: Oxford University Press.

Park, Hyun-hee (Pak Hyŏn-hŭi). 2016. "Enlightenment and Disenchantment—*Sweet Dream* (1936) as Traffic Film of Colonial Korea." *SAI* 21:37–79.

Park, Kyung-soo (Pak Kyŏng-su). 2012. "Kŭndae ch'ŏlto rŭl t'onghae pon singminji Chosŏn mandŭlgi" (Creation of Colonial Korea through the Modern Railway System). *Ilbonŏ munhak* (Japanese Language Literature) 53:253–71.

Paton, Stewart. 2008. *A Dictionary of Chinese Characters: Accessed by Phonetics.* London: Routledge.

Prakash, Gyan. 1999. *Another Reason: Science and the Imagination of Modern India.* Princeton, NJ: Princeton University Press.

P'yo Hak-kil. 1993. "Chinjŏnghan kukchehwa e sahwalgŏllin han'gukkyŏngje: kŭmyung silmyŏngjewa yŏn'gyedoen kukchehwa" (True Internationalization as Korean Economy's

Matter of Life and Death: Internationalization Linked to the Real-Name Financial Transaction System). *Han'gungnondan* (Monthly Korea Journal) 51 (1): 51–54.

P'yŏnjippu. 1975. *Sajin ŭro ponŭn kwangbok 30-yŏnsa* (30-Year History since Independence, with Photo Illustrations). Seoul: Chŏngŭmsa.

Ray, Sandeep. 2017. "Two Films and a Coronation: The Containment of Islam in Flores in the 1920s." In *The Colonial Documentary Film in South and South-East Asia*, edited by Ian Aitken and Camille Deprez, 107–27. Edinburgh: Edinburgh University Press.

Rothberg, Michael. 2001. "W. E. B. Du Bois in Warsaw: Holocaust Memory and the Color Line, 1949–1952." *Yale Journal of Criticism* 14 (1): 169–89.

Ryang, Sonia. 2012. *Reading North Korea: An Ethnological Inquiry*. Cambridge, MA: Harvard University Asia Center.

Said, Edward W. 1979. *Orientalism*. New York: Vintage Books.

Sangach'ulp'ansa, ed. 1966. *Chaebŏldŭl 1* (Conglomerateurs Vol. 1). Seoul: Sangach'ulp'ansa.

Schivelbusch, Wolfgang. 1986. *The Railway Journey: The Industrialization of Time and Space in the 19th Century*. Berkeley: University of California Press.

Schwoch, James. 2009. *Global TV: New Media and the Cold War, 1946–69*. Urbana: University of Illinois Press, 2009.

Seiler, Cotten. 2008. *Republic of Drivers: A Cultural History of Automobility in America*. Chicago: University of Chicago Press.

Seo, Dongjin (Sŏ Tong-chin). 2005. "The Will to Self-Empowerment, the Will to Freedom: The Understanding of the Transition of Korean Capitalism and the Transformation of Subjectivity through the Self-Empowerment Discourses." PhD diss., Yonsei University.

Seo, Gi-jae (Sŏ Ki-chae). 2005. "The Modern Japan: A Related Travel Media and a Colony Chosen." *Ilbon munhwa yŏn'gu* (Japanese Cultural Studies) 14:73–91.

Seoul Development Institute. 2010. *Chip'yo-ro pon sŏul pyŏnch'ŏn: chuyo t'onggyewa tonghyang* (Changing Profile of Seoul: Major Statistics and Trends). Seoul: Sŏul sijŏng kaebal yŏn'guwŏn.

Shimokawa, Koichi. 1994. *The Japanese Automobile Industry: A Business History*. London: Athlone.

Sibul, Eric Allan. 2008. "Forging Iron Horses and Iron Men: Rail Transport in the Korean War and the Influence of the US Army Transportation Corps on the Development of the Korean National Railroad." PhD diss., University of York.

Sobchack, Vivian. 1992. *The Address of the Eye: A Phenomenology of Film Experience*. Princeton, NJ: Princeton University Press.

———. 2004. *Carnal Thoughts: Embodiment and Moving Image Culture*. Berkeley: University of California Press.

Son Chŏng-mok. 2003. "Tosi 50nyŏnsa 12—kyŏngbu kosok toro kŏnsŏl kwa tosi ch'egye" (50 Years of Cities no. 12: The Construction of the Kyŏngbu Expressway and Urban System). *Tosi munje* (Urban Affairs) 38 (411): 106–17.

Son, Min Suh. 2008. "Electrifying Seoul and the Culture of Technology in Nineteenth Century Korea." PhD diss., University of California, Los Angeles.

Song, Jesook. 2006. "Family Breakdown and Invisible Homeless Women: Neoliberal Governance during the Asian Debt Crisis in South Korea, 1997–2001." *Positions: East Asia Cultures Critique* 14 (1): 37–65.
Spivak, Gayatri C. 1999. *A Critique of Postcolonial Reason: Toward a History of the Vanishing Present.* Cambridge, MA: Harvard University Press.
Statistics Korea. 2013. Number of Automobiles by Classification. Accessed January 20, 2014. http://kosis.kr/gen_etl/start.jsp?orgId=999&tblId=DT_999S_153062&conn_path=I3.
Sugrue, Thomas J. 2005. *The Origins of the Urban Crisis: Race and Inequality in Postwar Detroit.* Princeton, NJ: Princeton University Press.

Tetsudō-in. 1913. *An Official Guide to Eastern Asia: Trans-Continental Connections between Europe and Asia.* Tokyo: Imperial Japanese Government Railways.
Thomas, Nicholas. 1994. *Colonialism's Culture: Anthropology, Travel, and Government.* Princeton, NJ: Princeton University Press.
Tourism Sciences Society of Korea (TOSOK). 2012. *Han'guk hyŏndae kwan'gwangsa: haebang ihu uri nara kwan'gwang sanŏp ŭi yŏksa* (The History of Modern Tourism in Korea). Seoul: Paeksan Ch'ulp'ansa.
Toyota Motor Corporation. 2012. *75-Year History through Text.* Accessed January 12, 2014. http://www.toyota-global.com/company/history_of_toyota/75years/text/index.html.
Tsuchiya, Yuka. 2014. "The Atoms for Peace USIS Films: Spreading the Gospel of the 'Blessing' of Atomic Energy in the Early Cold War Era." *International Journal of Korean History* 19 (2): 107–35.
Tŭngdaesa, ed. 1997. *Inminhaeng ryŏlch'a-rŭl hamkke t'asigo* (Together Aboard the Train to People). Pyongyang: Tŭngdaesa.

Urry, John. 2002. *The Tourist Gaze.* Los Angeles: Sage.
———. 2004. "The 'System' of Automobility." In *Theory, Culture and Society* 21 (4/5): 25–39.
———. 2007a. *Mobilities.* Cambridge: Polity.
———. 2007b. *The Tourist Gaze.* 2nd ed. London: Sage.

Verhoeff, Nanna. 2012. *Mobile Screens: The Visual Regime of Navigation.* Amsterdam: Amsterdam University Press.
Virilio, Paul. 1986. *Speed and Politics: An Essay on Dromology.* Translated by Mark Polizzotti. New York: Semiotext(e).
———. 1988. "The Third Window (Translation of an Interview in *Cahiers du Cinema*, April 1981)." In *Global Television*, edited by Cynthia Schneider and Brian Wallis, 185–97. Cambridge, MA: MIT Press.
———. 1989a. "The Last Vehicle." In *Looking Back on the End of the World*, edited by Dietmar Kamper and Christoph Wulf, 106–10. Translated by David Antal. New York: Semiotext(e).
———. 1989b. *War and Cinema: The Logistics of Perception.* Translated by Patrick Camiller. London: Verso.

Vukoder, Bret. 2020. "Filmic Aesthetics and Technologies of War, Policy, and 'Truth' in the Motion Pictures of the United States Information Agency." PhD diss., Carnegie Mellon University.

Waller, Gregory A. 2008. "Free Talking Picture—Every Farmer Is Welcome: Non-theatrical Film and Everyday Life in Rural America during the 1930s." In *Going to the Movies: Hollywood and the Social Experience of Cinema*, edited by Richard Maltby, Melvyn Stokes, and Robert C. Allen, 248–72. Exeter, UK: University of Exeter Press.

Wee, Gyoung-Hye (Wi Kyŏng-hye). 2010. "The Film Exhibition Practices and Cinema-Going Experience in the Local from the Mid-1950s to the 1960s." PhD diss., Chung-Ang University.

———. 2013. "Cultural Hybridity in 1920s Colonial Chosen: Mokpo Movie Theater and Dongchoon Circus." *Hanil minjok munje yŏn'gu* (Journal of Korean-Japanese National Studies) 25:37–78.

Williams, Mark. 2018. "Archives of Liveness: Television Newsfilm Reconsidered." In *Rediscovering U.S. Newsfilm: Cinema, Television, and the Archive*, edited by Mark Williams, Mark Garrett Cooper, Sara Beth Levavy, and Ross Melnick, 288–309. New York: Routledge.

Yi Ch'ŏl-hŭi. 1974. *Susabanjang (1)—kosoktoro e nallin chip'ye tabal* (Chief Inspector Vol. 1—the Expressway Drifted with Rolls of Bills). Seoul: Sŏnmyŏng ch'ulp'ansa.

Yi Ch'ŏl-sun. 2004. "The U.S. Policy toward Korea in the Late 1950s." In *1950-yŏndae Han'guksa ŭi chae chomyŏng*, edited by Mun Chŏng-in and Kim Se-jung, 275–342. Seoul: Sŏnin.

Yi Hyo-dŏk. 2002. *P'yosang konggan-ŭi kŭndae* (Modernity as Representation Space). Translated by Pak Sŏng-kwan. Seoul: Somyŏng ch'ulp'an.

Yi Hyŏng-yŏl. 1993. "Kŭmyungsilmyŏngjewa yŏnghwa sarang ŭi yŏnghon" (The Real-Name Financial System and the Film *Ghost*). *Wŏlgan Sahoep'yŏngnon Kil*, October, 190–91.

Yi Kyo-tŏk. 2002. *Kim chŏng-il hyŏnji chido-ŭi t'ŭksŏng* (The Characteristics of Kim Jong-il's On-Site Guidance Tour). Seoul: T'ongil yŏn'guwŏn (Korea Institute for National Unification).

Yi Sang-u. 2012. *Pak chŏng-hŭi sidae: 5.16 ŭn kudet'ada* (The Park Chung Hee Era: May 16 Was a Military Coup). Seoul: Chungwŏn munhwa.

Yi Sang-yŏng. 1988. "Kukkaŭi nodongjŏngch'aekkwa kongjang chadonghwa" (The State Labor Policy and Factory Automation). *Tongyanggwa chŏnmang* (Journal of Korean Social Trends and Perspectives) 1:93–120.

Yi Ŭn-chin. 1990. "Chadonghwaŭi hyŏndan'gye" (Automation at the Present Stage). *Kyŏngjewa sahoe* (Economy and Society) 8:107–22.

Yi Yŏngjae. 2019. *Asiajŏk sinch'e: naengjŏn han'guk, hongk'ong, ilbon ŭi t'ŭraensŭ/naesyŏnŏl aeksyŏn yŏnghwa* (Asiatic Bodies: Trans/National Action Films in Cold War Korea, Hong Kong, and Japan). Seoul: Somyŏng ch'ulp'an.

Yi Yŏng-mi. 2015. "Ttosuninŭn tonŭl moa sajangi toeŏssŭlkka?" (Did Ttosuni Finally Become an Entrepreneur after Saving Money?). *Inmulgwa sasang* (Persons and Thoughts) 206:155–69.

Yu Pyŏng-hŭi. 2015. "Pukhan-ŭi kwan'gwang chŏngch'aek-kwa ridŏsip" (Tourism Policy of North Korea and Its Leadership). *Han'guk haengjŏng hakhoe haksul palp'yo nonmunjip* (Korean Association for Public Administration Conference Proceedings) 12:1–33.

Yu Sŏng-ho. 2001. "Yŏksa wa ilssang e taehan 'yullijŏk' t'usi—Pak yŏng-jun ŭi chŏnhu munhak" (An Ethical Scan of History and Everyday Life: Pak Yŏng-jun's Postwar Literature). *Pip'yŏng munhak* (Literary Criticism) 15:285–99.

Zeller, Thomas. 2007. *Driving Germany: The Landscape of the German Autobahn, 1930–1970.* New York: Berghahn Books.

Index

Page numbers for figures and tables are in italics.

Harvard East Asian Monographs
(most recent titles)

409. Tie Xiao, *Revolutionary Waves: The Crowd in Modern China*
410. Anne Reinhardt, *Navigating Semi-Colonialism: Shipping, Sovereignty, and Nation-Building in China, 1860–1937*
411. Jennifer E. Altehenger, *Legal Lessons: Popularizing Laws in the People's Republic of China, 1949–1989*
412. Halle O'Neal, *Word Embodied: The Jeweled Pagoda Mandalas in Japanese Buddhist Art*
413. Maren A. Ehlers, *Give and Take: Poverty and the Status Order in Early Modern Japan*
414. Chieko Nakajima, *Body, Society, and Nation: The Creation of Public Health and Urban Culture in Shanghai*
415. Pu Wang, *The Translatability of Revolution: Guo Moruo and Twentieth-Century Chinese Culture*
416. Hwansoo Ilmee Kim, *The Korean Buddhist Empire: A Transnational History, 1910–1945*
417. Joshua Hill, *Voting as a Rite: A History of Elections in Modern China*
418. Kirsten L. Ziomek, *Lost Histories: Recovering the Lives of Japan's Colonial Peoples*
419. Claudine Ang, *Poetic Transformations: Eighteenth-Century Cultural Projects on the Mekong Plains*
420. Evan N. Dawley, *Becoming Taiwanese: Ethnogenesis in a Colonial City, 1880s–1950s*
421. James McMullen, *The Worship of Confucius in Japan*
422. Nobuko Toyosawa, *Imaginative Mapping: Landscape and Japanese Identity in the Tokugawa and Meiji Eras*
423. Pierre Fuller, *Famine Relief in Warlord China*
424. Diane Wei Lewis, *Powers of the Real: Cinema, Gender, and Emotion in Interwar Japan*
425. Maram Epstein, *Orthodox Passions: Narrating Filial Love during the High Qing*
426. Margaret Wan, *Regional Literature and the Transmission of Culture: Chinese Drum Ballads, 1800–1937*
427. Takeshi Watanabe, *Flowering Tales: Women Exorcising History in Heian Japan*
428. Jürgen P. Melzer, *Wings for the Rising Sun: A Transnational History of Japanese Aviation*
429. Edith Sarra, *Unreal Houses: Character, Gender, and Genealogy in the* Tale of Genji
430. Yi Gu, *Chinese Ways of Seeing and Open-Air Painting*
431. Robert Cliver, *Red Silk: Class, Gender, and Revolution in China's Yangzi Delta Silk Industry*

432. Kenneth J. Ruoff, *Japan's Imperial House in the Postwar Era, 1945–2019*
433. Erin L. Brightwell, *Reflecting the Past: Place, Language, and Principle in Japan's Medieval Mirror Genre*
434. Janet Borland, *Earthquake Children: Building Resilience from the Ruins of Tokyo*
435. Susan Blakely Klein, *Dancing the Dharma: Religious and Political Allegory in Japanese Noh Theater*
436. Yukyung Yeo, *Varieties of State Regulation: How China Regulates Its Socialist Market Economy*
437. Robert Goree, *Printing Landmarks: Popular Geography and* Meisho zue *in Late Tokugawa Japan*
438. Lawrence C. Reardon, *A Third Way: The Origins of China's Current Economic Development Strategy*
439. Eyck Freymann, *One Belt One Road: Chinese Power Meets the World*
440. Yung Chul Park, Joon Kyung Kim, and Hail Park, *Financial Liberalization and Economic Development in Korea, 1980-2020*
441. Steven B. Miles, *Opportunity in Crisis: Cantonese Migrants and the State in Late Qing China*
442. Grace Huang, *Chiang Kai-shek's Politics of Shame: Leadership, Legacy, and National Identity*
443. Adam Lyons, *Karma and Punishment: Prison Chaplaincy in Japan*
444. Craig A. Smith, *Chinese Asianism, 1894–1945*
445. Sachiko Kawai, *Uncertain Powers: Sen'yōmon and Landownership by Royal Women in Early Medieval Japan*
446. Juliane Noth, *Transmedial Landscapes and Modern Chinese Painting*
447. Susan Westhafer Furukawa, *The Afterlife of Toyotomi Hideyoshi: Historical Fiction and Popular Culture in Japan*
448. Nongji Zhang, *Legal Scholars and Scholarship in the People's Republic of China: The First Generation (1949–1992)*
449. Han Sang Kim, *Cine-Mobility: Twentieth-Century Transformations in Korea's Film and Transportation*
450. Brian Hurley, *Confluence and Conflict: Reading Transwar Japanese Literature and Thought*
451. Simon Avenell, *Asia and Postwar Japan: Deimperialization, Civic Activism, and National Identity*
452. Maura Dykstra, *Empire of Routine: The Administrative Revolution of the Eighteenth-Century Qing State*
453. Marnie S. Anderson, *In Close Association: Local Activist Networks in the Making of Japanese Modernity, 1868–1920*
454. John D. Wong, *Hong Kong Takes Flight: Commercial Aviation and the Making of a Global Hub, 1930s–1998*
455. Martin K. Whyte and Mary C. Brinton, compilers, *Remembering Ezra Vogel*
456. Lawrence Zhang, *Power for a Price The Purchase of Appointments in Qing China*
457. J. Megan Greene, *Building a Nation at War: Transnational Knowledge Networks and the Development of China during and after World War II*